**COUNSELLING HEROIN
AND OTHER DRUG USERS**

COUNSELLING HEROIN AND OTHER DRUG USERS

PAUL LOCKLEY

FREE ASSOCIATION BOOKS / LONDON / NEW YORK

Published in 1995 by
Free Association Books Ltd
Omnibus Business Centre
39–41 North Road
London N7 9DP
and 70 Washington Square South
New York, NY 10012–1091, USA

99 98 97 96 95
7 6 5 4 3 2 1

ISBN 1 85343 312 8 hbk

A CIP catalogue record for this book is available from
the British Library

Produced for Free Association Books Ltd by
Chase Production Services, Chipping Norton, OX7 5QR
Typeset from the author's disk in Iowan Old Style
Printed in the EC by T J Press, Padstow, England

IN MEMORY OF

TINA
MAGGIE
JOSIE
CHRIS
DICK
HALE
YVONNE
RICHARD
DOT
MARY
HUGH

and all others.
Peace.

CONTENTS

PREFACE

This book is intended to assist and support all those who are working with or counselling injecting heroin and other drug users. The approach taken is person-centred. The assumption made is that readers have familiarity with counselling. It is not recommended that those without such experience should start their counselling with these particular clients.

The emphasis has been on linking theory with practice, and attending to the reality of drug use. To assist in this aim, the book contains many quotes from drug users, taken from over fifteen years of working with them. Almost all of these quotes are spontaneous and those used have, wherever possible, been checked out with other drug user sources. Such quotes will, I hope, give something of the flavour of different drug user thoughts, feelings and life-styles. Additionally, it is intended that clients should come across as persons in their own right, in accordance with basic counselling tenets.

The counselling is applicable to individual drug users, but my own experience and involvement in counselling couples, working with families, running groups and facilitating support groups, has shown the necessity of working on various levels. Individual counselling is not the only answer nor the total answer to helping drug using clients. However, it is a major part of the assistance that can be given.

The book starts with an introduction to drug use and an explanation of drug related behaviour, from starting to use drugs, right through to coming off and staying off drugs. Also examined is the sometimes difficult counselling relationship with drug users, practical aspects of counselling and three specific topics. These topics cover heroin use and children, from pregnancy to teenage years; death, whether from overdose or HIV infection; and support for drug counsellors. Clearly, not everything can be covered, but the content should be sufficient to make new drug counsellors aware of some of the principal problems that may affect the counselling and the counsellor. Accordingly, various ideas to lessen, manage or avoid such problems are suggested.

Apart from assisting individual counsellors, this book is intended not only to give some idea of the nature of the counselling, but to increase drug service openness and accountability and to allow for consumer input and choice.

All of this work would not have been possible without the help and support of many different persons and organizations. My appreciation goes to past employers: Lothian Social Work Department, Tayside Social Work Department, Dundee Drug Problem Centre, and Scottish AIDS Monitor.

Also my thanks go to Charles Anderson, Lecturer, Edinburgh University; Martin Williams, Senior Lecturer, Dundee College of Education; Martin Plant, Alcohol and Drug Research Group, University of Edinburgh.

A separate appreciation to Dr J Strachan, Psychiatrist, Royal Edinburgh Hospital.

My appreciation is also extended to Danzig and Co., Chartered Accountants, Edinburgh for computer and laser printer facilities.

Gill Davies, of Free Association Books, has shown helpfulness and great patience at all times, and has been a source of encouragement, for which I am grateful.

But most of my gratitude goes to the families and partners of drug users, and all drug users who have helped in the compilation of this book, both directly and indirectly.

1 INTRODUCTION TO DRUG USE

DRUG USE IN CONTEXT

Introduction

This book aims to help those counselling or who intend to counsel heroin and other drug users. Such work can be challenging at times, frustrating on occasions. Yet we should also appreciate that it can be undertaken by any counsellor, applying the usual person-centred qualities and skills, combined with an understanding of drug using clients. There is often a temptation to claim that work with such clients is extremely difficult and is highly specialized. Counselling is thus restricted to a small number of self-designated experts, rather than being normalized and being seen as work that any counsellor can do.

To work most effectively with heroin users, it is necessary to look at the basic requirements for counsellors, to ensure that they have relevant knowledge, attitudes and understanding. The skills of counselling are assumed to be applicable to all clients and so can be carried over to working with drug using clients. However, before counsellors can apply any skills, knowledge or understanding, they have to have the confidence to be able to apply them. The initial task is to instil confidence into potential counsellors and dispel the idea that the work is the province of experts.

Counselling and drug effects

The process of building confidence starts with learning something about drugs. The major inhibiting factor regarding work with drug users is a perceived ignorance of drugs and their effects. For this reason, we need to review the subject of drug effects at the very beginning. Descriptions of drug related behaviour then become easier to understand.

Heroin

Heroin is a drug obtained from a simple chemical processing of morphine, a constituent of opium, the resin of the oriental poppy. Like all drugs of interest to illegal drug users, heroin acts by affecting the transmission of messages in the brain nerves, so altering the mood of the user. Illegal drugs are almost always psychoactive: they can change moods and perceptions.

Heroin belongs to a class of drugs, the opioids, which all produce fairly similar effects. They do so by entering the bloodstream, reaching the brain and occupying certain sites, called receptors, on nerves in the brain. The principal outcome is an interference in the sensation of pain. For this reason, heroin is a very effective painkiller and is used medically in terminal cancer.

The action of opioid drugs such as heroin, morphine, methadone, buprenorphine and codeine mimics the processes that occur naturally. The human body contains proteins in the brain called endorphins which normally act in the same way to control pain by occupying receptors sites. When heroin is taken, it replaces endorphins at the receptor sites and acts even more efficiently in pain-control. If the drug user suddenly stops taking heroin then, in the absence of both heroin and endorphins, pain results.

The effects of heroin, besides that of analgesia, are constipation, depression of breathing, suppression of coughing, feelings of nausea, and possible vomiting. Sedation occurs and is usually a characteristic light nodding sleep known as 'gouching'. One strong sign of opioid use is a large decrease in eye pupil size, whatever the light intensity, which is known as the eyes being 'pinned'. There are also other, more attractive, aspects to heroin use, such as feelings of euphoria and an elimination of anxiety.

For most people, the known effects of drugs are those which are medically useful; any others are merely side-effects. Thus for many counsellors, expecially those with medical knowledge, a change of perspective is required. Illegal drugs are rarely used for their medical effects: experiencing the side-effects is the objective. For example, heroin is a strong analgesic, but heroin users do not take it to lessen physical pain but to experience its anxiety-relieving and euphoric effects.

Perceived differences in effects

Counsellors need to be aware that the same drug may be experienced differently by drug users. This is important to bear in mind. Counsellors are not so much interested in drugs as in drug users and their situations. The situations are not always easy to understand, as drug using clients can be very defensive and not tell the truth. As a result, when clients describe how they are feeling, they may be disbelieved. Clearly, if clients are in fact telling the truth, this can lead to

confrontation. Part of the reason for confrontation comes from counsellors believing they know how drug users actually feel: if clients
have taken a drug then they must feel and behave in set ways. Counsellors have to understand that drug effects do vary to some extent
from person to person, and what their clients report can indeed be
the truth.

When considering the effects of different drugs, we have to take
account of medical and pharmacological perspectives, but we should
never ignore the descriptions of drug using clients. There is no essential way that clients will be affected by drugs, so counsellors have to
take into account a number of factors.

Drug effect factors – dosage

A change in dosage of a drug alters the experienced effects. The
greater the dosage, the greater and more intense the effects. At a very
low level there are unlikely to be any perceived effects at all. Obvious
though this may be, it is of importance to drug users. Street heroin is
bought either in small paper envelopes or 'packets', or in larger
amounts by weight. In neither case can drug users be sure what
exactly they are buying. Street heroin is adulterated, usually with
glucose, and can be of variable strength. Bought from a street dealer,
the strength may be between 5–20 per cent pure heroin, while the
dealer's uncut heroin strength can be 20–40 per cent, and that of
suppliers can be upwards of 40 per cent pure.

From a drug user's point of view, knowing the strength, and
thus the dosage, of the drug bought is important, because of the
risk of overdosing. Equally, the user does not want to pay money
for what is little more than glucose. Normally, street drugs are of
fairly consistent strength. This can change with the appearance of a
supplier marketing aggressively, whose dealers may provide heroin
of markedly higher potency on the street. Apart from the amount,
the type of adulterants used is relevant as they are often potentially
harmful. Adulterants known to me in street heroin have included
chalk, aspirin, bleach and Warfarin.

Dosage is not a simple matter of how much drug is taken, but
how much is taken as a ratio over body weight. The greater the body
weight, the less effects any particular drug will have. Less heavy
persons tolerate drugs less well. This is of relevance to female drug
users. Women can also experience differences if the drug taken is
fat-soluble, as is heroin. Women tend to have a greater proportion of
body fat and so absorb such drugs for longer periods.

Tolerance

The effects depend not just on the drug taken but the interaction of drug user and drug. One aspect is the person's tolerance to a drug. Tolerance happens when a person's body becomes accustomed to the drug and requires more of the drug to obtain the same effects. There are two basic types of tolerance. One is linked to the liver and kidneys: taking a drug can increase the amounts of enzymes which metabolize that drug. For example, tolerance to alcohol can increase, so that over time a person can gain the ability to drink much more alcohol before becoming intoxicated. However the tolerance to heroin comes from a second form of tolerance, cellular tolerance. Taking heroin rapidly decreases the number of receptor sites on nerves in the brain, so more heroin is needed to produce the same drug effects. Over a few months of regular heroin use, the amount of the drug that can be taken without the risk of overdose can increase over a hundred times. In fact, there appears to be no limit to how much heroin can be ultimately taken.

Tolerance can mean that the drug user tends to want more and more drugs to achieve the desired euphoria. This can be gained by bingeing from time to time. Drug takers will often vary their drug intake to obtain what they see as being their correct level.

Varying the drug level requires some awareness of personal tolerance, and an appreciation of the decline of tolerance that comes through a lack of drug use. For example, drug users who come out of prison and have not been using drugs, imagine they can handle the large amounts they were formerly taking before going into prison. They forget that their tolerance will have become so low that they are likely to overdose.

If drug users are tolerant to a particular drug such as heroin, then they will also be tolerant to similar drugs, other opioids such as methadone or morphine. This is the basis of prescribed medical assistence given to drug users. Street heroin is replaced by a prescribed opioid substitute, usually methadone. To avoid discomfort, the equivalent amount of substitute drug has to be given. Thus prescribing does not change the amount of drug taken and does not end physical addiction.

Addiction

Addiction can be categorized into two types. There is psychological addiction, the formation of a habit which is difficult or uncomfortable to break. Any constant behaviour pattern can become a habit and the person finds comfort in its continuance and discomfort in its ending. The habit can include the use of drugs but the habit lies in the person, not the drug.

Physical addiction applies to certain drugs, including opioids such as heroin. The user's body has been so altered by the drug that it needs the drug. Its lack produces a bodily reaction, the withdrawal syndrome. The syndrome is a pattern of physical symptoms such as sweating, running nose, diarrhoea, enlarged pupils, sleeplessness, muscular pains and anxiety. As may be noted, these tend to be the opposite of those produced by drug the itself. These withdrawal signs decrease in severity after seventy-two hours and are minimal after two weeks, though broken sleep can last longer.

The effects of a drug clearly depend on whether the person is physically addicted to it, or not. Heroin to the non-dependent tends to induce sedation, whereas to the addicted it either produces euphoria and activity or brings normality to the withdrawing drug user.

Expectations

Regular drug users have certain expectations of the drug they take and the effects they will produce. At times the expectations can be so strong that they can be misleading. This can occur, for example, when the drug user is withdrawing and expects the bought drug to relieve the symptoms. Even if the user is given pure glucose, some users will react as if they have actually been given heroin and their discomfort eases. What makes the situation even more complicated is that drug users can also expect their withdrawals to start if they have not had heroin for some time. This expectation can be so strong that they may believe they are withdrawing, when this is not the case.

Although, when discussing addiction, a division was made between the physical and the psychological, this is in part an arbitrary separation. In reality there is no clear distinction between mind and body. Thus there can be psychological effects after stopping drug use but these can be expressed in physical terms. In one extreme example, a client stopped using heroin and declared she did not feel any withdrawal pains, whilst her non-using lover was doubled up with pain.

Multi-drug use

Most drug users take more than one drug, though they might not really be aware of this fact. This usually happens because the second drug is socially acceptable, and so drug users do not classify it as a drug. For example, one client complained of sleeplessness weeks after ending her heroin use. The solution lay in a reduction in her usual coffee consumption which was at least twelve cups a day.

The role of alcohol is equally overlooked at times and can be even more significant. Its depressant effects can operate synergetically with drugs which have a depressant effect, such as heroin. The separate drug effects are combined to produce more than a mere addition of effects, as each drug potentiates the other. Alcohol with heroin thus increases the chance of extreme respiratory depression, of overdose, and difficulty in coming out of coma.

Other forms of multi-drug use may be devised to obtain particular desired effects. Sometimes drugs may be taken sequentially, as when heroin is taken after strong stimulants such as amphetamine to 'bring the user down', to end the intense stimulation. However, more common is the synergetic use of depressants such as tranquillizers or barbiturates purposely to increase heroin's depressive effects and so become quickly intoxicated. Alternatively, heroin can be mixed with other drugs, such as a 'snowball', a mixture of cocaine and heroin. Cocaine provides the short-term euphoria and heroin gives a longer lasting and smoother effect. A more recent mixture is 'lazy dog', the drug Ecstasy being mixed with heroin. Mixing drugs can provide different effects. Equally, the effect of heroin depends to some degree on what other drugs may have been taken.

Interpretation of effects

Drugs produce various altered states of mind, and users have to learn to interpret those effects. For example, if a person is drunk then the experience of losing co-ordination, mental alertness, and being disinhibited might be experienced as frightening or unpleasant. Yet in time most young persons come to learn to enjoy the experience, to reinterpret the effects as pleasurable. Similarly, the effects of heroin come to be reinterpreted as enjoyable, even if initially the drug is experienced as being unpleasant.

Mode of use

Taking drugs by injection can be qualitatively different from taking them orally or smoking them. The usual method of injection is straight into a vein, as it takes only a matter of seconds for the drug to reach the brain. Not only does this mean the drug effects are quickly felt but the effect of injecting into the vein produces the 'rush', the almost orgasmic sensation as the drug affects the receptor sites. Heroin is a very popular illegal drug partly because, being fat-soluble, it is absorbed quickly by brain tissues and produces a large rush.

Other factors

Drugs can be experienced differently according to how well they are metabolized. There may be genetic reasons why some persons can deal with certain drugs better than others. The very young and the elderly also require special consideration.

Heroin is the preferred drug for many drug users, but when street heroin is not available, other drugs, usually opioids, will be used, the effects will differ. Some opioids such as Diconal (dipipanone) produce effects which last a short time, whereas others such as Temgesic (buprenorphine) and methadone have longer lasting effects. Morphine tends to cause the body to release histamine, so the user feels very itchy. Fortral, (pentazocine) along with the usual opioid effects, can produce hallucinations. However, if heroin users cannot obtain any opioid, then they will take almost any drug: barbiturates, tranquillizers (benzodiazepines), or amphetamine.

Knowledge of drugs

Drug knowledge is helpful, but that knowledge has to be properly applied. Counsellors should not pretend to be experts, but the ability to talk intelligently about drugs does create a common language and bond with clients. Some drug users, who have been using drugs for a long time, find talking about anything but drug related matters difficult.

Information also allows counsellors to take more reasoned and reasonable attitudes, and so react in more helpful ways. By having some grasp of the clients' actual state, they can help clients stay reality-based. Also counsellors who have some knowledge of drugs and drug use can show that by being able to talk about drug matters, they have interest in the subject and in drug users. The self-esteem of many such clients is so low that counsellor interest in them is perceived very positively.

Working towards an understanding

Drug use also needs to be understood in a wider context. There are numerous explanations, theories and views about illegal drug use and the difficulty is knowing which to choose. What is advanced here is only a personal view, arrived at through reading and work with drug using clients.

The first need to decide is what illegal heroin use really is. It can be described as an individual's pattern of behaviour, as illegal behaviour, as the taking of a possibly harmful substance, as a way of producing physical and mental changes, as sharing with others a certain life-style. All these different aspects have to be part of any overall understanding. Because there are so many different aspects of drug use, there is not likely to be a simple explanation.

History

Drug use may appear to be a modern phenomenon, a condition associated with poverty, unemployment or urban deprivation. In fact, drug use goes back into history. For instance, the hallucinatory tops of the peyote cacti have been found in sites in Texas and Mexico dating back to 10,000 BC. Alcohol, in the form of wine was produced in Colchis, an country approximating to modern Georgia, from about 5,000 BC. The use of opium also probably occurred around this time in the Middle East.

The evidence comes from archaeological excavations and such evidence is always open to various interpretations, but both alcohol and opium were mentioned in the Ebers papyrus dated about 1,500 BC. This Ancient Egyptian work also mentions the use of the hallucinatory plant henbane. Cannabis was mentioned in the Indian writings of the Artharve Veda which dated back to at least 1,400 BC. More recently, the chewing of the betel nut has been recorded from AD 800, and pottery chards from Tiahuanaco from about the same date point to the use of coca leaves in what is now Mexico. As can be seen, the taking of drug substances is not a recent phenomenon so it is not one that is necessarily caused by modern conditions or needs.

Geography

Drug use is not confined to a few specific locations or countries. It occurs worldwide.

The main drug of Europe has been alcohol, mainly as wine or beer. However in the Middle East, cannabis is widely used, as it is in India. In India and in countries to the east, the betel nut is chewed with lime. In north eastern Africa and the Yemen, khat, the stimulant leaves of the bush Catha edulis are chewed. In other parts of Africa the kola nut is used, as it contains caffeine. A better source of caffeine, though, is the coffee bean from Kenya, South America and Java. Africa also has plants such as the shrub Tabernanthe iboga and niando, a variety of spurge, which contain the hallucinatory drugs ibogaine and yohimbine respectively.

In the Far East, opium has long been produced from the oriental poppy, and in Thailand they also use the native kratom bush. Pacific islanders drink kava-kava, an intoxicating drug made from an indigenous shrub. In Australia the aborigines smoke a local plant known as pituri. North American Cree Indians used to smoke the plant rat-root. Mexico and countries to the south produce a variety of hallucinatory substances; 'magic mushrooms', the peyote cactus and seeds of the Morning Glory flowers, containing the drugs psilocybin, mescaline and a substance aligned to LSD. The Amazonian forest contains the lliana Bannisteriopsis caapi, Cuba produces cohoba snuff, both hallucinogenic. South America also produces on the slopes of the Andes the Erithoxylon bush, from which cocaine is ultimately produced. Other drug substances widely growing throughout the globe are the tobacco plant and many hallucinogenic fungi.

Use of drugs

By combining the historical and geographical criteria, we note that drug use covers both space and time. It is universal. It can be argued that drug use of some form has always occurred and human society has always been a drug using society. However this is not an entirely satisfactory view. Some drugs are illegal, which is an essential part of the difficulty of being a drug user. So an understanding of drug use requires knowledge of why drug laws were enacted.

In fact, there are two aspects to illegal drug use: that of rule breaking behaviour, of taking the substance, and that of making the rules, of passing the relevant drug laws. Emphasis tends to be given to drug taking behaviour, but why drug laws were enacted is in itself not unimportant.

Making the laws

Sometimes it is assumed that drug laws are enacted for the benefit of potential drug takers. Drugs are dangerous and harmful, taking drugs is dangerous, and the public has to be protected. The reality is rather different. Laws often represent differing interests in society.

Early English drug laws related to alcohol. Laws were brought under the English Acts of 1495 and 1504 which gave the Justices of the Peace the power to suppress alehouses in their neighbourhood, should they divert people from archery, a vital means of defence in those days. Apart from external defence, there was also the threat from within. The first tax on beer, brought in 1642, was to pay for the Parliamentarian Army. In 1652, after the English Civil War, legislation was enacted which saw the enforced licensing of alehouses to prevent possible political gatherings and dissent, alehouses being the favourite meeting places of the radical Ranters sect.

Apart from considerations about defence of the realm, Governments have brought in drug laws for economic reasons. When drunkenness was made a criminal offence in 1606, it was done so partly on the grounds that excessive drinking caused 'the overthrow of many good Arts and manual Trades, and the disabling of divers workmen'. The first half of the seventeenth century saw 'The Great Gin Epidemic', when the Government encouraged the production of gin to dispose of the surplus grain harvests. Eventually there was a tax on gin. Ever since that time, the rate of drunkenness has been under the control on the Government, and this rate is closely aligned to the cost of alcohol, and the extent to which it is taxed.

Emerging legislation

Legislation relating to alcohol is of interest because the drug is harmful to the body, unlike heroin, and accounts indirectly for thousands of deaths annually. The dangers were not known initially, whereas they are today. However, this has not resulted in any great change in legislation. Once the Law is in place, precedents are set and it is difficult to change the thinking around it.

The point to be made is that drug legislation is not a simple process; it is a human process, a process which reflects competing interests, reflecting different ideas of the time. As laws about opioid drugs emerged later than those relating to alcohol, we might expect differences. Opioid drugs are of recent interest, they represent new drugs and Governments have often always reacted idiosyncratically to new drugs.

When coffee was first used as a drink, the reaction of the Egyptian authorities in the fifteenth century was to ban its sale, burn all coffee stocks, convict persons for having drunk it, and to circulate warnings against its use. Similarly, in 1675, Charles II of England issued a proclamation for the Suppression of Coffee Houses, an enactment that proved totally unenforceable and so consequently was soon forgotten. The smoking of tobacco led to a counterblast from King James I of England in 1604, a remonstrance that was to be equally unavailing.

Moral panics can lead to poorly considered legislation, such as the wartime Defence of the Realm Act 40B in 1916 when it was found that cocaine was being sold to the troops, though as later discovered, on only a minute scale. Sometimes the panic can be manufactured, as in the United States, when the Commissioner of the Narcotics Bureau, Harry Anslinger, orchestrated a campaign against marijuana in the late 1930s, partly to ensure the continuance of the Bureau.

Role of the United States

Drug legislation and drug use is often seen in nationalistic terms, and what happens in other countries is seen as irrelevant. However in the Western World the leading role has been taken by the United States.

Historically, the role of the United States has evolved for two main reasons. The country has tended to have a puritanical outlook, culminating in the Volstead Act, that heralded in total prohibition. This attitude towards drugs is more understandable when we remember that the United States has experienced considerable difficulties with drug taking. There was a sudden increase in the use of painkilling opium between 1840 and 1850, partly as a result of cholera and dysentery epidemics. Its use surged again as a result of the Civil War and the accompanying 470,000 wounded and disabled survivors. Cocaine use began in the 1880s, and by the turn of the century there was a very high incidence of Americans taking morphine, opium or cocaine. Because of this, the United States moved towards not merely drug legislation but international control. British legislation against opium in 1908 was largely a result of American pressure at the International Conference at Shanghai, despite the fact that by 1908 opium was no longer a drug problem in Britain.

Cannabis, though not viewed as a dangerous drug by the 1894 Indian Hemp Commission, was termed a 'hard' drug following lobbying at the International Conference on the Opium Trade. So just as national drug legislation reflected sectional interests, so international legislation has tended to reflect national interests. The final outcome is legislation that has not always been totally rational from a disinterested perspective. Thus in 1923 South Africa insisted to the League of Nations that cannabis be treated as a habit forming drug, despite there being no supporting evidence. After intensive lobbying the next year by Egypt and Turkey at the Second Opium Conference, international control was put on the export and import of cannabis. This in turn was to lead to the drug being included in the British 1924 Dangerous Drugs Act.

Drug legislation

The first opioid drug law enacted, the Pharmacy Act of 1868, related to the sale of opium. This law was not intended to control opium, only to decide whether apothecaries or physicians should be allowed to sell it. Subsequent legislation demonstrated the increasing power of the British medical profession, which dominated drug legislation until the 1960s. Up to that date, illegal drug use in Britain was an insignificant problem, and much of the addiction was a result of initial therapeutic use or of easy access, a sizeable proportion of addicts being in the medical profession.

The rising number of young recreational drug users in the 1960s was to cause official concern. Interestingly, this differentiation between recreational and medical use of drugs was made in King James's opposition to the smoking of tobacco. The distinction was that of 'Persons of good calling and quality, who took the drug as a physick to preserve health', and 'a number of riotous and disordered persons, of mean and base condition, who spent their time and money on tobacco.' Attention was given to the increasing recreational drug use, though similar concern was not shown over the equally large rise in the use of prescribed and over-the-counter drugs.

Summary

Part of the difficulties associated with drug use arise from illegality. But it is equally possible to see that drug legislation itself might contribute to the drug problem. Such legislation is not neutral, but has always represented some sectional or national interest. This in turn has not always produced very logical results. Strict legislation against cannabis was introduced in Britain and this has continued. Despite the drug being viewed as not dangerous by the Wootton Report of 1968, it was classified as a dangerous Class B drug under the 1973 Misuse of Drugs Act. The non-dangerous nature of the drug was again upheld by the Advisory Commission of the Misuse of Drug's Technical Subcommittee and the 1982 Commission's Expert Committee, but this did not change Government thinking. Thus we should not think that drug laws are necessarily particularly logical or that they will contribute to a lessening of the drugs problem.

The object here is not to advocate any changes in drug legislation, but to point out that counsellors usually believe that all they have to contend with are drug users and their problems. Indeed, drug users can be seen as being problem persons. However, this is just one part of a much greater picture. The counsellor's remit does not include suggesting new drug legislation and enforcement. This does not mean such topics do not affect the counsellor's attitudes and beliefs. These attitudes and beliefs remain with the counsellor, they are not to be given to clients. Nevertheless, interactions with clients are likely to a reflect underlying beliefs about drug use. Drug users have been demonized to the extent that balanced attitudes are not always easy, yet part of the demonizing comes through legislation.

If we return to the example of cannabis, in the form of marijuana, penalties in the United States increased in 1951 and again in 1956 under the Narcotic Control Act, so that possession of any amount brought a minimum penalty of three years imprisonment for a first time offence. Thereafter penalties decreased to the extent that marijuana was decriminalized by the State of Oregon in 1973.

Not only do laws change over time, but some laws are effective and others ineffective. Prohibition in the United States eventually proved not merely largely ineffective but was a major contributor to the increase in organized crime in that country. However, laws passed in India after independence against the use of cocaine have proved to be very successful. Sometimes legislation can have unforeseen consequences, such as the banning of the smoking of opium in Hong Kong after the Second World War which led to an increase in other opioids, including heroin, and to drugs being used intravenously.

Seeing the difficulties with drugs as being confined to a few persons who are 'problem' people, has resulted in theories of drug use which label drug users as problematic and made it more difficult for them to take up an accepted role in society. Only by having a broad view of drug use can counsellors develop more helpful attitudes and be more effective.

Bridge to illegal drugs

Illegal drug use consists of two aspects; drug legislation and the behaviour that goes against those rules. We have noted that drug taking has always occurred in virtually all societies and some drugs are socially acceptable. By not legislating against some drugs, society sends out a message about them, that they are acceptable, not harmful, and part of normal behaviour.

These drugs also act as a bridge to illegal drug use. Part of this bridging arises from the perception of these drugs as being acceptable for adults, but not for children. The fact that drug use is seen as something that only mature persons are allowed to do sends further messages to those young persons who want to be seen as mature.

Apart from these perceptions about drug use, drugs such as caffeine, nicotine and alcohol serve as a means by which users can negotiate their entry into illegal drug use. The drug user takes the acceptable drug and feels better. So even before any illegal drug is taken, people know that taking substances can make them feel better.

This fundamental factor, obvious though it may appear, is a key to the manipulation of mood by substances. If people want to feel better then they simply take something.

Ongoing learning from acceptable drugs

Furthermore, the novice drug user discovers that the initial effects of drugs are not necessarily pleasant. Coffee is horribly bitter, alcohol tastes unpleasant and smoking makes your head spin when first tried. It is quite possible that if using these drugs was merely an individual act, then they would never be taken a second time. However others who take drugs say how good they really are, how good they can make people feel, and it is just a matter of getting used to them. For novice users, it is often easier to take them again, rather than to refuse and upset people.

So the young person does have another cup of coffee or accepts a second cigarette, and the effects are not so bad this time, as has been promised. So one's friends are right and the warnings about drugs put out by health authorities do not seem quite so believable. What is more, the effects are interpreted increasingly through social learning, through friends. Feeling a bit drunk, staggering about the place, feeling sick, beginning to slur words, is seen as amusing, as desirable, as good. The fact that such learning usually happens when everyone is in the same state lessens the feeling of strangeness; on the contrary it can signify being part of the group.

Apart from interpretation of effects, the user might have to learn how to take the drug properly. Thus the novice cigarette smoker learns to inhale the smoke, draw it down into the lungs. The alcohol user learns that drinking on an empty stomach courts possible severe intoxication. The coffee drinker learns that the taste can be adjusted with the use of sugar and milk, just as alcohol may taste better with mixers such as fruit juices or lemonade. Learning to adjust drugs so they become more palatable is another useful lesson.

The role of alcohol in early drug use is especially important as young people can experience what it is to be intoxicated, what it is to be somewhat out of control, what it is like to feel different. Also the person experiences acceptance by others of being intoxicated, of behaving in an uncontrolled manner.

Legal and illegal drugs

Socially acceptable and illegal drugs are viewed officially as being in completely different categories. The Law itself depends on clear distinctions. However, the result is that the accompanying personal behaviour tends to be seen in black and white terms, people are either innocent or guilty. One aspect of exaggerating illegal drug use harm may be seen in the myths that surround it: myths such as crack cocaine is instantly addictive, heroin is a drug harmful to the body, PCP users possess superhuman strength, that there have been many deaths from people under the influence of LSD jumping from windows in the belief they could fly. Such instant myths serve the purpose of frightening people, further demonizing illegal drug use.

Injecting drug use

Though we all tend to involve ourselves in some sort of drug use, it is the whole idea of injecting drug use which seems most foreign to most of us. For this reason it may be of help to see how injecting use fits into drug use and to remind ourselves that what seems a modern phenomenon has roots in the past, that similar behaviour has occurred previously.

History

Counsellors have to try to understand how it is that people came voluntarily to stick needles into themselves. If we want to know how the present situation has come about, then we have to look to the past.

An interest in injecting started in England shortly after the publication of Harvey's book, *De Circulatione Sanguinis*, concerning the circulation of the blood. Francis Potter started experimenting on animals in 1649 and Christopher Wren used a small bladder attached to a quill to carry out the first injection on a markedly unenthusiastic servant in 1655. Doctors carried on treating patients by injection for the next twenty years or so, but the method eventually died out.

Renewed interest in intravenous injecting began again in France under the leadership of the physician Magendie at the opening of the nineteenth century. This probably arose as a result of Jenner's successful work on vaccination from 1798 onwards. Intravenous treatment was still not very successful, though the isolation of the drug morphine from opium in 1804 did continue interest in the technique, though interest switched to the best way of giving morphine to patients.

At a time when there were virtually no medicinal drugs of any effectiveness, a drug like morphine that stopped pain was a boon. The big breakthrough in treatment with morphine came with Dr Alexander Wood of Edinburgh who started to treat patients by subcutaneous injections from 1853 onwards. This method of injection, just under the skin, was to become very common, and was strongly advocated by Dr Anstie in the pages of *The Practitioner*. However two years later it became apparent that patients were becoming addicted to the morphine. Nevertheless, hypodermic morphine injections continued to be used increasingly by doctors, who saw them almost as a panacea. Indeed, doctors would often leave morphine and syringes with patients for their own personal use.

While we tend to see the 1960s as a very drug orientated decade, it fails to compare with drug use in the 1880s. The *Lancet* complained of a 'plague of morphine, opium, chloral and bromides'. In Paris, the number of regular morphine users was estimated at 40,000 in 1883 and 100,000 ten years later. Surprisingly, injecting drug use declined markedly at the beginning of the present century. The most important reasons for this decline were more responsible medical practices, the discovery of the painkiller aspirin and, above all, medical progress which advocated treating causes rather than symptoms. The use of diphtheria antitoxin, vaccination for typhoid and the discovery of Salvarsan for the treatment of syphilis, reinforced this more scientific perspective.

Modern use

Injecting drug use was restricted to medical treatment by members of the medical professions and was not a problem in Britain in the early twentieth century. By the 1920s there was another surge in worldwide drug use and in Egypt around 1925 there arose the practice of taking drugs intravenously. This was almost certainly modelled on the successful treatment of the endemic parasitic injection schistosomiasis by intravenous injection of tartar emetic. By 1929 there were outbreaks of malaria caused by the sharing of syringes, so over the next three years there was a switch to snorting drugs such as heroin. However it seems the technique and custom of intravenous use was taken from Egypt by seamen to the United States in the early 1930s.

Evidence of this comes from an outbreak of malaria among intravenous drug users in New Orleans in 1932–3 and the increase in cases of falciparum malaria in New York City from 1933 to 1943. The percentage of intravenous users increased rapidly in the United States, partly as a result of a decrease in the strength of street heroin following the Mafia takeover of heroin supplying from the Jews and Chinese.

Changes in use

The Second World War disrupted opium supplies in the United States and made heroin virtually unobtainable. Its supplying only began to grow by 1950 and grow quickly by the end of the decade. New users tended to be younger and used intravenously straight away, rather than first snorting and then using subcutaneously.

It was noted by the British Home Office in 1955 that heroin use was spreading in London, the result of gross over-prescribing by a few doctors. In fairness it should be said that there were changes in society which produced a slow spread of illegal recreational drugs among the young, and the over-prescribing doctors were doing their best in an unpopular and little known area of medical work.

The 1970s and '80s

Heroin use continued at a very low level, with prescribing being a major source of the drug. A change came in the late 1970s, when there was the sudden increase in the availability and use of street heroin, rising to a peak in 1982 and 1983. Many English users of heroin in the 1980s took up the technique of chasing the dragon, snorting the fumes of the heated drug but intravenous use remained popular in Scotland. Disposable syringes, which were cheap, were used for injecting but they tended to melt when sterilizing in boiling water was attempted. This led to syringe sharing and infections being transmitted by, firstly, hepatitis B and later by HIV.

Summary

The emphasis in drug counselling, till quite recently, has tended to reflect the medical perspective, with attention being on the drugs used and little interest shown in the mode of use. The advent of HIV infection has changed the situation, though many injecting drug users interpret this as the authorities being more concerned with possible transmission into the general public, rather than wanting to help drug users. Counsellors do not take sides, but should be aware of the various agendas that drug use creates.

2 STARTING DRUG USE

SETTING THE SCENE

Introduction

Counsellors, though working with only part of the total drugs problem, can still make a contribution by helping individual drug users to help themselves. To be able to do so, counsellors require an understanding of personal drug use. This comes mainly from the users themselves: we should not assume that users have no insight into their own situation. However asking users why they take drugs is likely to provide only a superficial answer. The best course is to get user clients to talk in general about their drug use. However any understanding of drug use depends not merely on what is said by users but our interpretation of what has been said; we are not neutral. For this reason it is necessary to go back to first principles.

First steps

To understand illegal drug use we have to understand that it is a rational form of behaviour. Drug users are not irrational. Of course, from the perspective of most of society, their behaviour may at times seem inexplicable, it may reflect anti-social attitudes, beliefs and actions, it may include behaviours of which we do not approve. Yet the behaviour is still rational. As such, drug use is capable of being explained.

It is essential to grasp this, as there may be times when drug users are described as persons with disordered personalities, persons with psychopathic inclinations, persons out of control. Young injecting drug users are seen almost as a separate class of humanity, a frightening tribe of people. The drawback of seeing drug users as essentially strange, bizarre and irrational in their behaviour, is that there is little need even to try to understand them. Furthermore, they become cases, they are no longer persons. What is required is that we suspend judgement and examine drug use behaviour. Our role is neither to condone nor condemn.

Rationality in use

Illegal drug users take drugs for their effects, for the changes in mood and perception, for the experiences they produce. Drugs differ in their effects, and users take specific drugs for the particular effects associated with them. Indeed, drug users usually will not pay money on the streets for anything less than the drugs that they want. Prescribing doctors will also be well aware that giving drug users other than what they want can lead to argument and confrontation.

One argument against rationality is that drug use behaviour is self-destructive. Indeed the psychoanalyst, Menninger, actually described drug use as a form of slow suicide, though this fails to explain why more users do not kill themselves; nothing would be easier. Yet, on the contrary, drug users take precautions not to overdose or put themselves at very high risk.

A further notion is that drug users who inject themselves are not normal in some way. After all, few of us would willingly stick a needle into ourselves and then force a solution of dissolved substance into our body. However this is a matter of perceptions. We would allow doctors or nurses to do the same. If we were told we needed an injection, then it would seem strange to refuse it. Yet drug users may be equally experienced in performing injections and they might also feel they need to have such injections.

Perceptions

Drug use is not simply a question of taking drugs. For instance, users might not be physically addicted to the drugs they use, due to the very adulterated drugs sold on the street. However this does not stop users from behaving as if they were so addicted. Their behaviour is explicable not through the drugs taken, but the drugs they think they have taken, which act as a hook for various personal and social behaviour patterns. Some users may want to be part of the drug user life-style and the excitement associated with that life-style, rather than wanting drugs simply for their chemical effects.

Pointers to an understanding

Personal experience of working with drug users can be illuminating, especially if it highlights the unusual or even the bizarre. It can provide pointers to the meaning of the drug use experience.

The first example arose on separate occasions, when two drug users came off heroin. It seemed that the chances of success were very slim, as both lived with dealers. In fact both clients split with their boyfriends and came off heroin completely. When coming off, they told me how they had been sexually abused when younger. None of this is particularly relevant, except my work with them was almost exclusively around the sexual abuse. Once these former drug users were able to talk about their past, they felt that heroin was no longer needed. In fact one user was amazed that after two months she had not used drugs; they were irrelevant to her life. These episodes did strike me as indicating that drug use was not simply about drugs, but about people and their lives.

The second example came from an investigation I did into the past lives of forty chronic heroin users. What seemed striking was the presence of common factors such as the high rate of heavy parental alcohol use, of unresolved physical and sexual abuse, ongoing difficulties with sexuality, and the high rate of parental conflict. Such factors are not causal in any way, but merely indicate possible factors that should enter into any explanation of illegal drug use.

Need for a working understanding

Some understanding of client drug use is required to be able to help and to know when to help. There are times when clients do want to come off drugs and yet they fail to get help, and sometimes this failure lies with the helpers. Mistakes are likely to be made from time to time, but their number can be reduced if there is understanding. The following two quotes come from clients who did come off heroin, despite the lack of help.

Chris: 'The people from the hostel were up to see me. One of them asked why I wanted to come off and I said I had been a junkie for five years. He said that was no answer, so why did I want to come off. I didn't know what he wanted me to say. Finally, he said it was pointless carrying on with the interview, and I just walked away.'

And if this impasse seems to have come about by the interviewers possibly being inexperienced, we should not assume the expert is going to do better. The next example shows a failing of two persons, helper and drug user, to come together in a common understanding.

Lisa: 'The psychiatrist asked me about my primary school and all that kind of stuff. That was no use. He didn't ask me why I wanted to come off.'

All of us will have made miscalculations, so these examples should not make us feel superior. Rather, we should see the task being to turn mistakes into successes, turn misunderstandings into part of a greater understanding which can lead to better practice.

Setting the stage

In order to arrive at an understanding, I composed a list of quite basic questions relevant to illegal drug use. If these are answered, then it is possible to construct one account of drug use.

Directional questions. The following questions are quite basic, but they will help to form an explanation, provided they can be satisfactorily answered.

1. Why do some people start illegal drug use and others do not?

2. Why do some drug users inject?

3. Why do some people continue to use drugs and others stop?

4. Why do people continue to use drugs when they are getting into medical, personal, relational, familial and social difficulties?

5. Why do users say they want to stop using, yet continue to do so?

6. Why do users stop using?

7. Why do ex-users restart using?

8. When is a drug user no longer a drug user and when is an ex-user no longer an ex-user?

These questions will be taken in turn and related to actual observed drug user behaviour.

Attitudes

When trying to understand drug use, we have to get away from judgements and moral causes. All we can work with is reality. Those who moralize are on shaky ground, going against the basic principles of counselling by being judgemental.

Gerry: 'People say that smoking hash is dangerous but it is no more dangerous than cigarettes, and you don't smoke as much with hash. I mean, you don't get many twenty joints a day men, do you? And, provided you take proper precautions, heroin will not harm your body like alcohol does. I take the occasional shot of smack and have a smoke at the weekends. I certainly don't get blootered like others do on booze. I don't bother anybody.'

My interest is not in discussing Gerry's opinions, but discovering how he arrives at his perceptions, beliefs and why he behaves as he does.

STARTING DRUG USE

Availability

Illegal drug use is likely to take place if there are illegal drugs available and obtainable locally. We have seen that the societal use of drugs is normal, so we would expect such use. Whether they are legal or illegal, drugs will be tried if they are to hand. Though distinctions are made between legal and illegal drugs, yet to drug users the distinction may be unimportant.

Lance: 'At the time it was cheaper to get stoned on a fiver packet of heroin than to drink all night to get drunk. It was quick and you didn't have to spend time like you would on booze. But the main thing was it was there; it was everywhere, so you were going to try it.'

Of course, this does not tell us the whole story, as availability is also the product of real or potential demand. So the supply of drugs has to be seen as being like the supply of any commodity; it depends on the market-place. The supply of illegal drugs is a business, and the drug dealer is a person in business. For those with limited employment prospects or little chance of making much money, then being a drug dealer, with its low overheads and ready market, has its attractions.

So there are people who, for the right price, are perfectly willing to become part of the supply chain that makes illegal drugs available. However this does not explain the situation from the buying end.

Curiosity and experimentation

Most illegal drug taking starts in adolescence, a time when people are changing in body and mind, and tend to question received opinions. Adolescents are open to new ideas and experiences, and are likely to be curious about substances such as drugs. Curiosity is a very necessary human quality and human progress, science and culture is partly founded on such curiosity.

As noted, behaviour is partly dependent on perceptions, and teenagers might to some extent see the world differently. The possible dangers in drug use may not be seen as dangers. Even if the dangers are appreciated, they can act as an incentive rather than a disincentive to experimenting with drugs, just as their illegality can make their use seem even more attractive.

Curiosity is an ongoing characteristic and can result in experimentation with a variety of drugs. However it would be incorrect to imagine that this means there is an escalating sequence of drugs tried and used, that starting on one drug will necessarily lead to other more dangerous substances being tried. People might use hard drugs after trying other drugs, but we still should not think this represents a predetermined course.

Josie: 'I got into glue-sniffing first when I was twelve. My mates were trying it so I tried it, and liked it. After that I tried smoking hash and drinking, but I didn't really like the drink. Then I took heroin as I had heard about it, and it was something new. At first I was sick all the time but I kept on until I wasn't.'

There are several factors which explain why Josie ended up as she did, but these were factors which related to her and to her life.

Drug use usually occurs when drug users are in their late teens, though it can start as early as thirteen or fourteen. At this stage of the young person's life, curiosity is a quality often expressed in the company of others. It is worth bearing in mind that drug use factors are not simple personal qualities, but can be a result of the interaction with other people.

Risk-taking

One factor often associated with curiosity is that of risk-taking, risking the unknown, getting a thrill from the danger involved. Risk-taking may be individual but it can also relate to the group situation, and teenage groups may well be attractive to young people because of their risk-taking, including the use of drugs.

Alistair: 'I started taking drugs when I was sixteen. I was reckless then and thought I knew everything. I knew nothing. It has taken me years to mature, to take things calmly.'

For most users, drug taking provides an element of risk but not total recklessness. The feeling of being high, the increase in adrenalin, can become an integral part of drug use but this is still done in safety. The need for this high, this feel-good factor, exists for all of us and is quite normal. Many sports and activities involve a degree of risks. Counsellors sometimes imagine that by stressing the risky nature of drug use, they will dissuade young people from using drugs, whereas they may be providing indirect encouragement. The desire for an adrenalin high is common with drug users. Perhaps it was not so surprising that when I asked a group of heroin users, men and women, who were coming off drugs what they wanted to do, the only activity they could all agree upon was to go parachute jumping!

Rebellion

Associated with risk-taking may be rebellion. For young people, rebellion against their parents and other adults can be part of their life. And one aspect of such rebellion may be drug use.

Gloria: 'I ran away to London and ended up on Probation for stealing a pair of earrings. It was just an act of rebellion against my parents. Later I got pregnant and got married but didn't tell my parents at the time. The marriage didn't work, he was just mucking around. I got into drugs but most of that time was rebellion against my parents.'

Rebellion can be against many things: against the Government, against society, against authority, against uniformity, against perceived puritanism, as well as against parents. Drug use may directly or indirectly involve all of these factors.

Peer pressure

Perhaps the most important factor in starting illegal drug taking is that of peer interaction, the fact that friends and acquaintances are taking drugs. It has to be borne in mind that most of those who start using illegal drugs are likely to be adolescents, the age when the influence of one's peers is very important. Thus taking drugs is not merely a personal decision but also reflects the person's peer relationships. If somebody in the person's neighbourhood group is using illegal drugs, then it is not merely a matter of how the person feels about it, but how the group as a whole regard it. They may reject this person because of the drug use or, more likely, the user will drop out of the group and move to one where using is the norm or is acceptable. However, it can happen that if the user is the acknowledged leader of the group then there is a greater likelihood of the group as a whole accepting the user and even, in time, of using drugs.

If the majority of a group is taking drugs, then it becomes harder for the non-users to prevent drug using becoming or continuing to be the group norm. No pressure has to be put on the non-users to use. However they will feel left out of a group activity and isolated. This can be hard to take for those unsure of themselves or those who have feelings of past rejection in their lives. And these feelings characterize many adolescents.

Drugs in the group

The non-user in the group might be offered illegal drugs. This offer can be made in a perfectly friendly social manner, with no question of pressure being exerted on the group member to take them. It would appear that the non-user merely has to refuse the offer and all should be well. However the non-user in the group might find it easier to accept than to refuse, as a refusal might affect relationships in the group. The refusal also formalizes the fact that there are both drug users and non-users in the group, and recognition of this can lead to strains or even crisis in the group.

Drug use can be seen as a product of peer pressure, but this conveys an image of a group member being forced into taking drugs. The reality is that no direct pressure is required. The pressure comes from the single member himself or herself.

Tina: 'I was placed in Muirhouse and it was four years before I got into it, though the only persons I knew were using. I would sit and they would talk about dope and I didn't know what they were talking about. They would sit there gouching and later say how good it was. I felt right out of it. Then one day Bob Marley died and he was my hero; well he was everyone's hero as his was the only music we listened to. No-one seemed to care, no-one seemed bothered. I was the only one upset. So finally, I thought I must try that stuff.'

Actually, it may be easier to take drugs than refuse. Drug taking, like smoking cigarettes or having a drink, has social implications and not being a participant can cause a person to feel awkward. For those persons with little self-esteem, what may seem a slight awkwardness can seem like a major embarrassment.

Teenage groups and change

Members of teenage groups are open to mutual influence, and find it difficult to say precisely what they want, as they are often both unsure of others and unsure of themselves. The uncertainty about oneself is a natural product of an evolving identity, and identity can change rapidly through teenage years. One medium for such changes is the group situation. Indeed, for those with real identity problems, the group situation can seem the answer, a place where problems can be resolved.

Bev: 'The lassie had been in care. I think she had no real identity, didn't know who she was. In the drug community she must have thought, this is where she belonged and they will look after me. Of course, no-one does. But all she wanted was to get a habit, go down the Shore and be part of a group. I don't think she had anybody.'

Clearly, to feel so badly about oneself indicates the relevance of the person's past life. But drug use is not simply a product of the past but part of a person's overall life-situation.

Images of self

For younger people, teenage groups can project a mature and exciting image, an image that group members might know to be incomplete or even false. However the image can be what the group wants to project and the image can attract others.

Josie: 'Cally is only fifteen and wants to be like us, or like we were. Bill wants her to come off but keeps giving her his Valium and draws her into the drugs scene. She's still at school and fights with her teachers because she wants her Valium.'

Young people chase after images, and the teenage group can be a place where such images and associated feelings are discussed. And there are parts of the media and business that act to create those images and fulfil those hopes and dreams.

Cherie: 'It was a matter of the times. The messages of the media seemed to show a world of peace and I wanted to be part of it. When I was eleven I told my grandfather I wanted to take drugs when I was older. I wanted to be like those people on the telly. But when I took them I did not like them and didn't continue.

Later I got into hash and liked it. When I was fourteen I had my first shot. It was morphine. At that time the bands I was into, they all sang about drugs and some of them took them. I was fascinated by it. We never seemed to get a habit as we were trying one new drug after another.'

For young people, it may not be so much the effects of the drugs as what those drugs represent, and the imagined life they can impart.

Family influence

However we must not ignore an equally important group, the family. Adolescence is a time when children are beginning the process of leaving the family, in emotional terms. For some young people, this can be difficult if family life has not prepared them for any such move. The peer group can provide a welcome half-way house, a bridge out of the family. For some adolescents living in unhappy families, the peer group can even be a welcome refuge. Accordingly, the peer group may exert a strong influence over its members, but we should not discount the family, part of the reason for members making peer groups important.

The family can exert its influence in various ways, but there are two aspects which are quite common. Firstly, there is the structural aspect, as when the youngest child in the family is treated as the 'baby' of the family. This can lead to disciplinary boundaries being relaxed and the youngest child's behaviour not being checked. Even the rest of the family might treat him or her differently. For mothers especially, the youngest is not merely the youngest but the last of her children, and this can be significant. A lack of consistency in family behaviour increases the likelihood of risky behaviour and this might include starting illegal drug use.

The second aspect arises from family behaviour itself. Parental drug use, and this includes prescribed drugs and alcohol, can also play a significant part in family functioning. Most common is heavy alcohol use by one or both parents, which occurs in a high percentage of the families containing chronic heroin users. Such alcohol use, seen from an early age, makes the children accustomed to seeing people under the influence. In time, they come to accept such behaviour, or at least become hardened to it. Alcohol may produce a model of how to solve everyday problems; somehow the heavy use of alcohol aids in finding answers to life's difficulties. However heavy drinking in the family may itself cause poor family functioning, which can include drug use by the children. Finally, parental heavy alcohol use may make parents unable to support and help their children in times of difficulties, with consequent effects in child behaviour.

Less common as a relevant factor for illegal drug use is addicted parental drug use. This does happen, however, and is often a result of therapeutic drug use.

Lisa: 'My mother was addicted to DFs, she's been using them for twelve years. And my Gran takes pills. She started it all off, as she used to take barbiturates. She was the first junkie in the family!'

The fact that someone in the family takes tablets regularly does not force anyone to do the same, but it does show a lack of rules and laxity in relation to such behaviour. Also we see that drug use can be intergenerational, pointing to the role of the family as being related to the drug use.

Jane: 'My Gran used to take drugs – black bombers – and she used to give some to my Mum to keeping her going working shifts. My Dad ended up drinking and then there is me on junk.'

Poor family functioning

It is important to remember that parents or families do not cause illegal drug use. Poor family functioning can produce a range of family behavioural symptoms and these might include drug use. Thus drug use is not caused by poor functioning but is a symptom of poor functioning.

Gloria: 'My parents expected too much from me. I didn't sit my 'O' levels as I thought I would fail them. Later I ran away from home and by the time I was seventeen I was pregnant. I got into smack two years later, partly because I didn't drink – I didn't like the taste – but I needed something.'

What constitutes poor family functioning is itself debatable. What does seem undeniable is that part of illegal drug use can only be understood in the context of family functioning.

Melanie: 'I was seven years in and out of hospital. Mainly it was asthma, though at one time they suspected cystic fibrosis. I was spoiled rotten and never smacked. I used to play up on my asthma and my brother and sister used to get on to me, sometimes hit me as they were both quite a bit older. I started glue-sniffing because everybody was doing it. They were also doing lighter fuel. I did it to be part of the gang. I was always worried that no-one would like me. I was never very popular but wanted to be liked.'

As may be seen, drugs are merely a means to an end, a way of helping users achieving some desired state. And this can go far beyond mere chemical effects. Drug use might be one of several quite different symptoms of difficulties in family functioning, and a relatively late arrival in a line of symptoms.

Andretta: 'My Mum and Dad didn't get on, and my Mum didn't talk to Dad for a few years. She would come home from work and go upstairs to drink her wine. She only spoke bad of my Dad and would speak of other men who fancied her. I hated this 'cos I loved my Dad and he adored her. One night she stayed out all night and my Dad went crackers and hit her. That turned me against him, and I left the home and went to stay with my Mum. I left school, got a job, but hated it. I fell for Johnny when I was fifteen as he paid attention to me. I think he was sorry for me, but I thought he fancied me. I fell pregnant, but he didn't want to know and neither did my Mum. To this day I resent my Mum for not loving me. Later on I realized I didn't like Johnny ... I met this pure git. First I got into hash and then speed. He was popping pills and paranoid, accusing me of going out with other guys. He broke my jaw in three places. I learned to inject Tunial and Nembies, then fixed morphine and Diconal.'

As can be seen, a lot happened to Andretta before she started to fix heroin. Her drug use was just one of many difficulties in her life, and not necessarily the most significant one. Counsellors have to be careful not be get caught up and see drug use as being the most important client issue, at least not before helping clients to assess the situation.

Attributing causes

When we consider initial drug use, then emphasis has to be placed on the entire situation. Counsellors should be wary of simple answers, that the cause of such use is to be found in the user or the user's family. We must always remember that drug users are active people who can determine their own behaviour.

Josie: 'They said my taking drugs was because of my parents, but I told them not to give me any of that stuff. It was my choice. I was a wee radge and it was up to me.'

It should be recognized that most family members are likely to be against drug use, and they will almost certainly try to stop others from getting involved. Drug use is not therefore caused directly by poor family functioning but is symptomatic of it.

Jane: 'When I was on drugs, my Mother tried everything in her power, physically hitting me, as she thought this might bring me to my senses. I think in a lot of ways she blamed herself but she had absolutely nothing to do with it. When I was taking drugs she would sit and cry and say, "I lost your Dad. God, I don't want to lose you." Things like that, they were tearing me apart. But they didn't penetrate deep enough, though it would hurt at the time.'

This situation applies even if there is a drug user in the family. Other family members may also get into drug use, but they are not usually encouraged to do so by users. Heroin use is not likely to be advocated even by those who take it.

Jane: 'I told my brother it was a mug's game. But he got someone to give him a shot by conning them he had had smack before. He came up the next day boasting about it. Of course I was not amused at all. He said, "I'm truly sorry about yesterday. I will not do it again." The same afternoon he asked me to score for him. I refused, so he got the same guy to score for him and he carried on using from that day since.'

There is no simple explanation of illegal drug use, but there may be a search for causes, though this might amount to no more than a search for someone to blame. However a concentration on causes may ignore the fact that drug users have choices.

Drug use as part of the whole

Illegal drug use has to be seen in the total context of a person's life. Part of any work with drug users is allowing them to convey what drugs mean to them in this total context. To some young people, drug use may seem a very rational option when seen in this context.

Sapphire: 'My parents split up when I was only three years old.

My Mum was a drinker and she could be violent towards me. I used to run away from home and was put in a Children's Home. None of the family visited and I started to use hash when I was thirteen. A year later I got into barbs. After that I attempted suicide as I thought there was no point in living. I left the Home when I was eighteen and went to live with a heroin user. Heroin was good as it stopped me from feeling depressed.'

It is easy to equate family with parental behaviour but the family can be, and usually is, more extensive than parents. We have to look to who is close to whom, both physically and emotionally.

Role of partners

Starting drug use may occur when a person begins a long-term relationship with someone who takes illegal drugs. It may not be known at the beginning of the relationship, and if this is the case then the non-user is placed in a difficult position.

Sarah: 'My husband was on drugs when I married him but I didn't find that out till two weeks after the wedding. I threw him out of the house. Then I felt sorry for him and took him back. At that time I did not take drugs or even drink. Three years later I too was on smack.'

We should not fall back on direct determinism, seeing such people as unable to stop themelves from using drugs. Usually there is a fair time before the non-user starts to use.

Sharon: 'David was into dope before I met him but I didn't use for years.'

Sometimes the non-user stays a non-user, despite all the drug use that is going on around and the life partner being a user. Mere availability of drugs is not enough to ensure personal use. However these cases are not common, the continual influence of others is not easy to ignore.

Janice: 'I've lived with junkies for twelve years; the stuff has been around all the time and people get stuff offered to them. But no-one has offered me a shot. I would like to be offered just for once.'

Nor should we think that some people are immune to the influences of others.

Skip: 'My wife was using, for seven years she was using. I never used during that time. It was only after I had left her that I began to use smack.'

And for some people, having a partner using drugs is not totally a bad thing, giving one partner someone to care for and giving a point to the relationship.

Problems

A small number of young people get into drugs as their life is difficult and drugs provide some sort of solution. This idea will feature later, but at this stage it has to be said that only a few people start their drug use as a result of personal difficulties. Such persons feel they need something to help them, and drugs is the particular form of support they chose.

Bev: 'When I was staying with Robbie, he wouldn't let me go out anywhere. He would lock me in the house and even then he would accuse me when he came back in of having had men in. Once he ripped all my clothes up so I couldn't go out. When I left him, I went with Dougie as I thought he would protect me from Robbie. Some mistake! He was the same, except he stabbed me. Actually that's not as bad as being beaten up as it does not hurt as much, just stings afterwards. I think it was after this that I started to take drugs.'

The use of drugs is thus a quite rational attempt to deal with the troubles, just as drugs might be used as a result of medical intervention to deal with medical difficulties. For users, the important fact is the efficiency of the drugs, not whether they are legal or have been prescribed.

Martha: 'About five years ago my Mum died. I was very close to her: I don't think I have ever got over her death. I was put on tranquillizers by my G.P. but these were stopped after I overdosed on them. I then found that cannabis helped me and have taken it ever since.'

Personal difficulties may involve only the person or they may involve those close to that person. The difficulties do not have to be those of drug users, merely they become their problems.

Annette: 'My parents' marriage was breaking up so they packed me off to private school. While I was there I started to get into drugs. Then I got pregnant and was married. My husband came from a similar unhappy family, and was into drugs.'

Thus the taking of drugs may not be related directly to the drug taker but to others. It is a way of dealing with what is happening to part of the drug user's life.

Enjoyment

Another relevant factor is that of enjoyment or the hope of enjoyment. Much drug use starts as a road to personal and shared enjoyment, especially the use of drugs such as cannabis, alcohol or LSD. Such drugs may be associated with parties, discos or raves.

Sometimes it is difficult for us to realize that drugs effects *are* enjoyable. We can be affected by the messages that depict drug use as a sad and unhappy form of behaviour, as the resource of the desperate. Yet we have to realize that drug use would not be a problem if it was experienced as being completely negative. The denial of the good aspects of drug use is not helpful, as it is seen by drug users as being either unrealistic or simply dishonest.

Jasmine: 'I take amphetamine, smoke hash, sometimes drop a tab of acid, and lately was using heroin.'

Me: 'And why do you take them, these drugs? Do they make you feel less anxious or do they make you feel better, make you feel easier when talking to people?'

Jasmine: 'No, I just like being stoned. I like the feeling.'

Sometimes the feeling of enjoyment is understated. It is seen as wrong to say that drugs are enjoyable. After all, society wants users to be punished for using them, to feel guilty, to stop taking drugs. Thus, personal agendas and needs can get in the way of seeing the situation as it is, how things really are.

Chris: 'You don't know what it's like, you have to experience it, the pleasure it gives. When people say they can't give up, don't believe it. It's bullshit! They don't want to give up, they like it too much.'

The public messages about drug use do not give a balanced view, they fail to mention how enjoyable drug use can be. By ignoring this aspect, we cannot hope to take a realistic view of the situation.

Giselle: 'I like smack, there's no getting away from it. It's the best thing there is. It can do more for you than any man can.'

Socially acceptable drugs are used for enjoyment, and illegal drugs can be used in much the same way. What may seem strange to some is no more than the result of the imposition of the label of illegality on drug use.

Beth: 'I have a snort of smack when I feel like it, like people take a drink.'

Taking alcohol would be seen as normal, the use of heroin abnormal. However as Beth did not like the taste of alcohol, for her it would be abnormal to take alcohol. As counsellors, we have to be careful not to let our own perceptions interfere in the task of trying to understand the client's perspective.

Getting into illegal drug use

What has to be observed is that although there might be reasons for starting illegal drug use, yet there is rarely one dramatic decision to use drugs. Instead there is usually a drift into use, sometimes so imperceptible that the drug user can give no reason for it.

Jane: 'I tried drugs as a matter of curiosity and drifted along, taking shots when I could score. Finally I ended up hooked. Most of those who I have talked to say the same thing. They did not start for any reason they could remember. They drifted along until they got hooked. You do not decide to be an addict but one morning you wake up and you are addicted.'

It should also be remembered that though there might be reasons for drug use, yet these are not contingent reasons. There are people who live in the same neighbourhood, who belong to the family, people who have reasons for using, but who do not. However there is never any necessity. The person enters into a relationship with the drug using behaviour and has to allow that behaviour to take place. In the following example, which admittedly is about restarting drug use, we see some of the mechanisms whereby the user gives himself permission to use. The process is described by his wife.

Layna: 'Sam doesn't think. He has a hit and that's it. After he came out of prison last time, he was making excuses to have a shot.

He had a few hits and then said he had to have another in case he had withdrawals. Then he got a habit and was happy, as he had a reason for using.'

Drug users are people and they have an active role in life. Even when taking drugs, they are doing largely what they want to do, including dealing with the forces and pressures that arise in their lives. This constant action is the counsellor's source of hope; what a person can do, that person can undo.

No real cause?

It had been assumed that there are particular factors involved in illegal drug use, and some have been forwarded to account for such use. However these factors, whether they be teenage peer group influence, rebellion, personal problems or pleasure, are all fairly normal kinds of experiences that anyone might expect young people to encounter.

If this is the case, then are there really any causes, or do we say that illegal drug use emerges from life itself? What is apparent is that there is no simple cause and we should not fall in with the medical paradigm that suggests that what is required is some form of treatment. Despite the language that is used, 'drug epidemic', 'drug treatment', 'relapse' and 'cure', drug use is a form of behaviour and not a medical problem. The behaviour has more in common with compulsive eating and compulsive gambling; the fact that the behaviour is centred around drugs, rather than food or betting, does not make it a medical concern at heart.

TAKING DRUGS BY INJECTION

Introduction

For persons like myself, whose reaction to having an injection is at best one of abject cowardice, there remains the question as to why anyone should voluntarily take drugs by injection. For many people, the syringe and needle represent the symbol of drug using, a symbol that sets them apart from the rest of humanity. As counsellors, we might think we understand drug users until the moment we see them desperately trying to hit a vein, and then we realize there is a gulf between us. However this gulf can be spanned if we try to approach in stages the whole subject of injection use.

Forms of injections

The first stage is to see how acceptable injecting use began. The hypodermic syringe was first used medically as it allowed a precise amount of a drug to be given to a patient. It did away with having to calculate the dosage in relation to whether the stomach was full or empty, a calculation that is especially difficult with opioid drugs, which slow down the digestive process. Injection produces effects more efficiently, as less drug is required, and effects are produced more quickly.

There are three main methods of injection. The first is that of injecting just under the skin, subcutaneous injections. This is done by injecting almost horizontally so that the needle lies under the skin and above the muscles. This method has been used medically for the injecting of insoluble suspensions. Irritating drugs should not be injected this way as they can cause severe pain and possible tissue damage. Only small volumes should be injected this way.

The second method is intramuscular injecting, where the needle is held closer to the vertical and pushed into a muscle. This method is not suitable for drugs in suspension, such as crushed tablets, nor for the injection of large volumes of solution.

The third form of injection is when the point of the needle is pushed into a vein. The almost immediate onset of the drug effects makes overdosing much more likely and also allergic shock reactions, which can result in overdosing. Also any contaminants, including bacteria and viruses, in the drug solution go straight into the bloodstream without the body having any time to counteract them.

Intramuscular injecting may be used by novice users but they soon move on to intravenous use. The reason for this is that intramuscular use is slower to produce effects. Heroin taken orally takes about twenty minutes to have effect, intramuscular use takes about two minutes but intravenous use produces almost instantaneous effects.

Mechanics of injecting

The mechanics of injecting are fairly simple. A tourniquet or 'tie-up' is tied round the upper arm to raise a vein in the crook of the elbow. The street drug, sold for five or ten pounds, is contained in what used to be an old apothecary's folded paper envelope, about one inch by half an inch. This is known as a 'packet', though locally it is also known as a 'bag'. The small amount of adulterated heroin is dissolved in a minimum of water to produce the maximum rush, and gently warmed to dissolve all of the drug. Heroin heating is usually done in a dessert spoon using two matches, so black bottomed spoons may be a sign of heroin use. Often the solution is acidified by adding vinegar or lemon juice to dissolve any chalk, though usually street heroin is now sold already mixed with citric acid crystals. The solution should not be too hot or blisters might be produced. The warm solution is often drawn through a filter of cottonwool or cigarette filter to prevent particles of adulterant in the street drug being injected. The syringe is checked to ensure that there are no air bubbles in it by squirting out a little liquid. Then the needle is put into a vein and the drug solution is injected. The plunger is withdrawn and if blood is drawn up then the user knows the vein has been correctly hit. The plunger is again pushed down and the tie-up immediately released to get the maximum effect of the rush.

Illegal injecting use

Medical use of injections differs from illegal injecting in two main ways. Firstly, medical use is socially sanctioned and this obviates anxiety about its legality and others knowing what is taking place. Secondly, medical use is merely a method of putting medication into a patient's body, whereas illegal injecting can be taken as an experience in itself, where the ritual of injecting, the chasing after the rush and all the attendant risks are part of the whole experience. Medical and illegal injecting use differ, but they are both understandable and acceptable, though in their separate contexts.

Starting to inject

Firstly, it should be said that injecting drug use is very much a matter of local custom. Users inject themselves because that is how everyone else takes heroin. For inexperienced users, what other drug users tell them is hardly thought of as being strange, but is taken as the norm.

Lynne: 'I didn't know anything about drugs when I started. I used to snort and then Layna said, "Why don't you fix it?".'

Usually there are few reasons for injecting apart from peer pressure at the start. For most people sticking needles into themselves is not the usual way of behaving. Heroin users or any other kind of drug user are no different.

Tina: 'When I started I was so scared of the needle that they had to give me the shot.'

Intravenous injecting is easiest done in the crook of the elbow. We might expect only one arm to be used as for most people injecting with the 'wrong' hand is difficult, so right handed users will find it difficult to inject into their right arms. The fact that this is so often not the case, points to the injecting having been done by another user.

So users start with someone else injecting them. They have to trust the person, who is not a doctor, to inject them. This in itself is not necessarily a neutral act.

Josie: 'Dick and me had been arguing but I thought it was over. He stuck the needle in but not cleanly, and he was waggling it about. He wanted it to hurt. There was nothing I could do, and then he pulled out the needle and tore the skin.'

Medical injections have none of these personal complications: they are neutral actions. But there is a meaning to illegal injections, as they enter into the relationships between users in a way that is almost impossible in professional medical use.

The person who starts to use by injection will almost certainly not have his own syringe and needle. As a result not only may someone else inject him, but someone else's set of works is likely to be used, with the consequent risk of infection. It is not unusual for users to be unable or unwilling to fix themselves and so have to always rely on other users. Even users who have been injecting for years may still dislike the actual act itself.

Tina: 'I still have never got used to injecting, even after all these years. When I have the hit, I still worry if it's the last one I'll ever have, if I won't overdose or something.'

For drug users who have to rely on others to inject them, there is another form of dependency. This reliance on another occurs quite often in drug using couples, and it has a definite effect on their relationship. There can even be couples, neither of whom inject themselves, though this is uncommon.

Ken: 'I can't give myself a fix, nor Vivien either. We have to get someone else to do it for us.'

One aspect of injecting another user is that for the person who is injecting, there can be a heavy legal penalty if the person injected has an overdose. This fact can also enter into the relationship between injecting couples.

There might be some advantage in not being able to self-inject. It might make the person rely on others, who may not be reliable. This puts a measure of control on a person's use as there is not always someone handy who will oblige.

Lisa: 'My problem would have been worse if I had learnt to hit myself.'

Some drug users will not inject themselves as they are scared of the needle. Paradoxically, even injecting users can be scared and will worry when they are to be given an injection by a doctor. On the other hand, users can be relieved when they manage to inject themselves.

Layna: 'After my first fix of speed I went into the pub and when ordering a drink I held out my arms so the barman could see where I had injected. I felt proud of what I had done.'

Some users will use intramuscularly as this is easier than using intra-venously, but this method of use is not likely to last for long. It does not produce satisfying results for drug users, and once users have tried intravenously they are not likely to return to intramuscular use. However a few long-time users may return to intramuscular use if their veins have been very damaged.

Sandra: 'I've been into junk for eight years now and all my veins have gone. I just skin-pop it now.'

Injecting and relationships

Injecting does involve relationships with other drug users, especially at first when the user will be injected by other users. In a way this is no different from medical injections, when we allow nurses and doctors to inject us because of the relationship they have with us.

Thus injecting use is not peculiar but a practice that has its own set of meanings. As counsellors, we have to discover those meanings.

3 CONTINUING DRUG USE

CONTINUING OR NOT

Once a person has taken an illegal drug, the question arises as to what happens next. Is there a descending road once a person has taken illegal drugs, a downward spiral into addiction and enforced drug use? Once more we have to refer back to the factors that influenced the start of drug use.

Peer pressure can influence someone to try drugs, and rather than upset the group, that person goes along with it and takes the drug. This confirms the person as being part of the group and this may be enough for the group. It may be quite admissable for the drug user then to say that the drug 'does nothing for me' and not take any more. This shows the group that he or she is not against the group as such, not against drug taking, but is not interested in continuing to take drugs. Sometimes people enter drug use merely wanting to experiment, wanting to try drugs or a certain drug. What happens next is very much dependent on how that experience is judged. If it is not liked then the drug might not be taken again.

There are further reasons for not continuing to take drugs. Perhaps the drug failed to live up to personal expectations. It seemed not to be a very enjoyable or significant experience. After all the build up to daring to take the drug, the experience may be judged a let-down. Drug use can simply lack any great significance to the person. Just as people can drift into illegal drug use, so they can just as easily drift out again. Continuing is not due to the drug itself; no drug is addictive after just one try.

Vera: 'I've taken heroin once. After I took it I was sick for forty-eight hours and there was blood coming up. I have never tried it since.'

In fact many drugs are unpleasant when experienced initially, and it is not surprising that some experimenters do not wish to repeat the experience. However this may not be the end of the story. The life situation of the person may be such that another trial of the drug may be taken at a later date, when the memory of its unpleasantness has faded.

Sam: 'The first time I took heroin I was sick. In fact I was so sick I never touched it for a year.'

And to complicate the situation, sometimes the fact that drugs are so pleasant can put off users, as they fear that they will not be able to control or stop any future drug use.

Digger: 'I tried smack once. I stopped because it was so good.'

So clearly there can be a variety of possible consumer reactions. We have to get away from the idea that people are going to all behave the same.

Why people continue to use

So some users will stop and others will continue. Sometimes they will try one drug and then another. It would be simple to see this as no more than experimentation, a continuing search for different sensations.

Ray: 'I started drinking and then I went into hash. Later on I used Valium and then I was into speed and LSD. Finally I got into smack.'

On the other hand, the testing of various drugs might point to possible underlying needs. The person may be looking for something that suits in some way.

Jane: 'I used barbs and then tried cocaine and thought that it was more what I was looking for. Finally I tried smack and that was it. I knew I had found what I had been looking for.'

So the question again is why do users continue to use and continue to try different drugs? Firstly, having overcome the rules and inhibitions about illegal drug use, it might appear to the user that there was no going back: there might be the feeling of 'in for a penny, in for a pound'. Once the barrier to using has been broken then there seems no reason to stop.

But there can also be other reasons. For most users, taking drugs is a matter of enjoyment. Users get over the initial possibly unpleasant drug effects as tolerance to any associated nausea develops. The effects may well be reinterpreted so that they are perceived as enjoyable. Such enjoyment is assimilated into the user's total range of attitudes, beliefs and behaviour.

So what occurs is a normalization of the drug activity, it becomes an ordinary part of the person's behaviour. This can happen with any drug, even though an outsider might not see the behaviour as quite so ordinary.

Tina: 'Carrie and I were splitting a packet of smack at the weekend and that was all. Then I used a packet myself but only once a week. This way we don't land up with a habit.'

All the time we have to vary our own frame of reference, to observe that what is ordinary to some, may be viewed differently by others.

Hidden advantages

As the drug use continues, even at a low rate, the user finds that there can be hidden advantages in such behaviour. For instance, the user may have drifted into taking opioid drugs, but then finds that this helps to dispel feelings of boredom, though this was not the reason initially for using them.

Max: 'Sometimes Sharon would sit for hours looking at the wall, really getting into it. Time doesn't seem to mean that much and you never seem to get bored when you are using smack.'

Boredom is one of the scourges of teenage years, so drug use may have special attractions to young persons. Because teenage years are years of personal change, a lack of change or stimulation can be unwanted. The teenager's cry of 'I'm bored!' can be irritating to parents but it can also be misunderstood. Rather than teenagers being difficult, it can be an honest reflection of where teenagers are at.

Tina: 'I used to take barbs as they used to make me yappy. Russell used to say that I was a pert wee thing, right quick with the answers.'

Again, feeling self-confident is a concern of these years and drugs can give the users a lift. But drug use can also bring relief from anxiety. When going through a difficult time, as adolescence sometimes is, the relief from worry that opioids or depressants can bring may be welcome. But these drugs, if taken continuously, keep away anxiety and become a way of dealing with life. Or, to be more accurate, if the person has difficulty in dealing with life then the drugs help to deal with the emotional hurt caused by life. If problems cannot be solved, then the next best plan is to ease the emotional pain those problems cause.

> *Bruce*: 'I think I have always been scared of missing something. To me, my unemployment tied in with my boredom. Even when I was working in the pub, I looked around and saw other people smoking dope and the like. Also there was this feeling of not being good enough, not having the correct qualifications to cope with a job. So to escape reality I used drugs.'

In understanding the significance of opioid use, the fact that it is the supreme drug to deal with emotional pain, far better than any tranquillizer, is of paramount importance. There are both good and bad aspects of continued opioid use, but for youngsters whose life seems meaningless and without any real hope, then a drug like heroin, the strongest obtainable street opioid, has many attractions.

Underlying problems

Usually young people do not set out to use drugs with the intention of coping with life, but they discover, often having tried several different kinds of drugs, that drugs such as heroin appear to help them. The idea of escaping reality is one used by many opioid users, but what is not so clear is the nature of the reality they are trying to escape.

> *Hale*: 'I took smack to escape reality.'
> *Me*: 'What does that mean?'
> *Hale*: 'To escape from life.'
> *Me*: 'But what exactly are you escaping from?'
> *Hale*: 'I don't know ... I don't know.'

As counsellors, we might see life in a fairly structured and organized manner. We might identify problems and then propose that work should be done on those problems. However, for the young drug user, life is not that simple and not so clear. This does not make them wrong and counsellors right. To young people, life can seem a mess, but that is life for them. Drugs seem to help at the time but users can forward no reason as to why they help. Indeed, there may be no conscious reflection about drugs making life easier. Drug use is subsumed into the general way of life and its forbidden nature makes it another part of youth counterculture.

Opioids are the best drugs at defusing anxiety, at surmounting many of the difficulties that arise for young people, but depressants such as alcohol or benzodiazepines can also do the job. However depressants, because of their lesser efficiency in anxiety suppression, have to be taken in large amounts.

Georgina: 'Today's Tuesday and I began drinking last Thursday. I don't remember much. I ended up in Perth and don't remember how I got there.'

Josie: 'For two weeks we would wake up, take downers, crash out, wake up for lunch, take more downers and crash out, and then the same for tea.'

In fact all illegal drugs are psychoactive; they affect how the user feels. Any psychoactive drug can be used to try to make the user feel better, though some are more efficient than others. The effects of opioids are particularly effective as in the right amounts they allow the drug user to operate as normal, free of anxiety but also free of intoxication.

Ending the path with heroin

It is likely that a range of drugs will be tried. Many people will try what they see as safe or soft drugs, but leave what they see as dangerous or hard drugs. Availability may also be a factor. Opioid drugs are likely to be available, at least in large town and cities, but knowing where to get them may be difficult to find out and there is no assurance that young people would be sold the drug. So many people do not bother with opioid drugs.

However there are others who drift into opioid use, especially in areas where such use in endemic. Rundown housing estates may have an opioid drug culture and taking drugs such as heroin or buprenorphine (Temgesic) by local groups of young people has become more acceptable. Young people find there are advantages in the use of such drugs, both through being part of a subculture and also in dealing with their life situations, so they stay with the drug. Instead of experimenting and trying other drugs, users continue to use opioids.

The nature of underlying problems

The underlying problems which drug use can help are those which the user cannot solve or situations that the user cannot improve.

Normally we have to deal with problems or difficulties in life all the time, and we manage to do so with a fair degree of success. Thus we are able to deal with and cope with whatever life presents us. We are survivors and get through life somehow.

However there are some difficulties that are by their very nature difficult to manage – difficulties such as parental loss, personal sexuality, physical and sexual trauma, and severe family dysfunctioning. These problems are not necessarily incapable of being coped with or even solved, but some people are not able to resolve them and not able to consign them to the past. These problems affect the present, they bring continuing pain to those concerned.

If the person is unable to make the problems disappear, then the next best action is to make the associated emotional pain disappear. Thus the answer to uncopable personal problems is to deal with the pain they cause; this at least can be altered.

Continuing heroin use

It has been said that drugs continue to be taken as they are experienced as being enjoyable. Perhaps we should look at such statements closely. The truth is that the euphoric effects of an opioid drug like heroin last only a few times, and the effect of the rush for the intravenous user also dies away quite quickly. So the question is, why should users experience enjoyment in their drug use? The answer could be that the relief of anxiety comes to be interpreted as pleasure.

Jane: 'I always used to say that I took smack for the enjoyment. Looking back, I think it was a crutch for me at the time.'

If we think about why people continue to take mood altering drugs, then we know that some are taken for the experience of the effects, for example LSD. Other drugs such as alcohol or cannabis might be taken for social interaction. However opioids such as heroin have the effect of allaying anxiety and this in itself can be pleasurable.

Maggie: 'It's like being an invalid, as if you have lost four of your five senses and you cannot get in touch with the outside world. Gradually the world comes back to you but it's so far away. You see the world but it's like you were in a coccoon.'

Another advantage of opioid use is that the risks associated with taking drugs no longer seem important. The anxiety which would be caused by the worst scenario is kept in check.

– 45 –

Chris: 'Funny, you do not care about dying when you are on drugs. You do not know how to care, your mind shuts off. It says, "Leave it, that's not a good thing to think about," so you do not think about it.'

So opioid users continue to use and find that their life seems easier as the difficulties of life do not affect them. Clearly, in these circumstances, there is less incentive to stop taking the drugs.

Chris: 'I never used to care, floating like a lily on the stream of life.'

What should also be appreciated is that blanking out troubles is more than a series of individual acts of avoidance, it becomes a way of life. What is happening, though it may not be understood at the time, is that a way of life is being determined by the user, and a way of life that includes drug use.

Effects of continuing opioid use

It might be imagined that once a person has started to use opioids then physical addiction will lock that person into continuing use. The user has to have it in order to avoid going through the pains of withdrawals. However as long as users continue to use, they will not only fail to experience withdrawals, they may not even know they are physically addicted.

Lynne: 'There was a girl who for a year didn't know she had a habit. Someone said she was using heroin and she said no, she only used smack. She was that ignorant.'

Indeed, withdrawals can be a shock when they do come. Most users start in a casual fashion with little knowledge of what is to come. There can be real ignorance of what is happening, as opposed to not wanting to know what might happen.

Lisa: 'I woke up one morning and had pains in my back and stomach. Craig said that I had a habit. If I had known about a habit, I would never had started in the first place.'

For users to have so little knowledge might seem unlikely, but no-one offering heroin will point out the drawbacks, and any drawbacks the would-be user hears may well be discounted. The fact that warnings come from adults and persons in authority might be further reason to ignore the down side of drug use. Yet the fact is that the good effects of drug use diminish quite rapidly.

John: 'The first shot is great, the second and the third are not so good, and after that it is all downhill. You are using to support your habit.'

Though enjoyment diminishes, anxiety reduction will still continue. What is helped by heroin may be quite minor worries. If this was the sum total of advantages then heroin use would quickly be seen as of little advantage. However once a person has become accustomed to being anxiety-free, then being faced with worries again might not seem very inviting, even if those worries are insignificant.

Richard: 'If I was faced with a bill I would panic. If on heroin, I would not bother. I would do nothing. Barbara would be worried but not me.'

Drug users who have been taking drugs for some time will find it difficult to adjust to reality, to being without chemical effects. In time, what may be seen as an abnormal drug induced state becomes the norm for the user. Thus the user, when considering stopping drug use, is considering moving to what for him or her is an abnormal state.

Conrad: 'For nearly seven years, since I was fourteen, up until several months ago, I've been addicted to various drugs ranging from glue-sniffing to heroin. Until I was 15 I was mainly involved in glue-sniffing to release the boredom of going to school. Then for the next two years I preferred the feeling of being stoned or the rush so I switched to cannabis, speed and tranquillizers. Then until I was over 18 I was into dope, speed, acid and magic mushrooms nearly every day, just for the sake of feeling stoned or high.'

It is not the particular drugs that might be important but merely the fact of being high, of being able to feel in a certain way. However there might come a time when a certain drug particularly suits the taker, when the person finds the drug that produces those effects which seem to hit the spot.

Jane: 'I used barbs and then tried cocaine and thought that was more like what I was looking for. Finally I tried smack and that was it. I knew I had found what I had been looking for.'

The heroin user might not have intended to use the drug to manage anxiety but discovers that this is one of the benefits of its use. Most heroin users will have unresolved underlying problems. But a great number of young persons have problems which could also be described as unresolved but they do not use drugs. However there is additional evidence that the resolution by non-drug means of underlying problems facilitates the process of coming off drugs, as drugs become redundant.

ROLE OF THE SUBCULTURE

Subculture

Once the user has begun to use drugs then there appear a variety of different benefits. One principal benefit is that the user may well be dependent on other drug users to obtain drugs and to help in the raising of money, quite likely through illegal means, to pay for the drugs. The user is drawn into the local drug subculture and this has advantages in that the subculture can provide a second family, a group of persons to whom the user can relate. Admittedly, the subculture might not eventually prove so friendly a place, but if the user's family is unsupportive and problematic, then the drugs world can be appealing.

Maggie: 'When I started using I met a lot of people. For the first time, I had friends which I never had before.'

Apart from just meeting others, the user can become part of the subculture, part of a local group of young people. There is the comforting feeling of belonging.

They can also obtain status through being a member of the local drug grouping. In this drug subculture there can be a hierarchy and consequent status. Status might depend on the substances used. Glue-sniffing is bottom of the pile, pill popping is higher in status, opioids higher than depressants, cocaine higher than amphetamine, heroin higher than prescribed opioids, and intravenous use higher than oral use. New drugs or drugs difficult to obtain locally give high status to the user. Whatever the different criteria, belonging totally to the subculture, being highly involved in it and subscribing to its norms will ensure the high regard of others. Failure to do so will result in users not being seen as part of the group.

Marion: 'Some young kids don't know what it's about. They have never had a habit. They are plastic junkies.'

Of course, the nature of the drug subculture means that members have to subscribe to the subcultural beliefs, norms and behaviour.

The user's identity is affected by being part of the subculture. Belonging to any group is likely to have an affect on its members and a person's identity is largely determined through personal interaction, through the reactions of others. One aspect of identity concerns whether the person becomes known as a drug user and, in particular, whether the user accepts the label of being a junkie. At one level it is a simple question of whether the label is outwardly accepted.

Jolene: 'I would never have called myself a junkie. I would have been too embarrassed.'

On the other hand it may be a matter of how those persons involved feel about themselves. Some may not view the label as being prejudicial and accept the label inwardly so they feel they are junkies. Some drug users, some heroin users, do not see themselves as junkies even if they have been using for several years. Sometimes the user may be quite unsure where the line is to be drawn.

Jenny: 'I don't class myself as a junkie ... No, I am a junkie. That's me kidding myself.'
Me: 'Do you feel yourself to be a junkie?'
Jenny: 'Everyone says I am.'
Me: 'And what do you say?'
Jenny: 'I don't know. I don't really think I am a junkie.'

It may seem surprising that anyone would want to be called a junkie but this term is only of low status to those who are not illegal drug users. To heroin users, the identity as a junkie might be a positive term, and this might well be the case for those who are either trying to find some identity or have a very low opinion of themelves anyway.

There are further advantages in that illegal drug use and the accompanying life-style brings excitement. Sometimes, indeed, it is the life-style that is the source of excitement and drugs and the need for money are a hook on which to hang that life-style.

Jane: 'To begin with it was good tricking the system, going into a shop with pupils like flying saucers, and no-one stops you. You wonder how no-one knows you are a junkie, why they don't throw you out of the shop.'

Entry into the criminal subculture may seem a step downwards, as most heroin or illegal drug users are not born into criminal families. Having to commit offences to get money for drugs means having to change moral standards. The consequence of this change is that the user's self-esteem is likely to be lowered, and this can create barriers, making it harder to get out of the drug subculture.

Jane: 'I was never born a criminal. I was never brought up to it. But when you've got a habit you don't think of the consequences.'

For many drug users, being a drug user is to take on another way of life. It is not simply a matter of using heroin but everything that is entailed.

Subculture and crime

It is very difficult not to become involved in committing offences when on drugs. The artificially high price of illicit drugs means that most users cannot afford to use such drugs without having a regular high income. Trying to keep to a low drug use can be difficult for many users, as there can be a slow spiral into greater drug use. The net result is that the user depends either on misusing prescribed drugs or on forging prescriptions on stolen prescription pads. I still wonder if doctors like to prescribe dihydrocodeine as so many drug users have trouble spelling it. But the usual method consists of getting together sufficient money to buy drugs, and large amounts of money are easiest obtained by illegal means.

Maggie: 'Say I was on a fiver a day, then that would be easy to borrow. I could go to a dealer and ask for a lay on (drugs on credit). But someone might say the easiest way is to do a couple of cheques. The first is always dead easy and you would end up stoned out of your skull all day. Then you would be doing cheque books and using it, not for you, but for your arm.'

The user at the time is likely to ignore the negative side of such illegal activities, and find that the new behaviour allows for the discovery of new skills. For users who have never seen themselves as having any or many skills, the illegal activities bring a positive sense of worth.

Josie: 'If there is one thing I am good at, it is doing cheques. I can forge anyone's signature. I could do yours, I've done so many! David now, he's into credit cards. He is the best at altering them and does a good job. Everyone takes them to him.'

Many drug users are likely to have dealt in drugs at some time and this itself can be a source of new skills and accompanying status.

Chris: 'I have dealt over three periods and have never been caught. I was always careful. You can flush the packets away if you put them right round the bend and flush them. I used to practise every day with a matchbox. Nobody was going to catch me. Some dealers are too greedy, they don't want to get rid of the gear, yet they are likely to get years if caught.'

Furthermore the subcultural life-style is such that there is plenty to do and thus boredom is less likely. So the image of the drug life-style being one of indolence can be wide of the mark.

When looking at the reasons for drug use we have to be careful not to let our own opinions impinge. Rather we should see things from the user's point of view. For instance, because the cost of illegal drugs is very high, it is assumed that drug users will always be desperate for money, never having enough. This need not be the case.

Dean: 'I was never so well off as when I was using. Then I had to make money, I had no option. Now that I'm off, haven't got the bottle to do the things I used to. I'm much worse off now when it comes to money.'

Thus one of the difficulties of having come off drugs is that life can seem very boring and the expected saving of money and dreams of suddenly being well-off simply do not transpire.

INJECTING USE

The rush

One good effect that comes with injecting is the rush. At first, the sensation of the rush is that of warmth quickly going along the arm or wherever the user has injected. Then the warmth seems to invade the whole body, there can be a tickling sensation in the stomach and for some users the feeling can also be orgasmic as the drug reaches the brain. The effect is greatest when the user has just started to use intravenously. The effect can be like a bolt being shot from the base of the spine through to the top of the user's skull. This very intense sensation only occurs for the first two or three times and some users seem to spend their time chasing that initial rush, that intense feeling that they are unlikely to experience fully again. The rush is only to be experienced by injection into the vein.

Bev: 'I wanted the rush. The feeling you get goes up to your brain and every nerve there seems to tingle. And with coke the feeling is even better.'

Dean: 'It's the rush that interests me. If I don't get it then I have another packet or have a hit of barbs.'

There are other advantages that become apparent in time. Injecting is a skill and status is given in the subculture to those who learn to inject themselves with a degree of expertise.

Josie: 'I didn't know how to use the groin till someone explained where the veins were, and I still wasn't sure. Then one night I got out of the bath and the veins were standing out so I straightway marked them with a biro, so then I knew where to find them. Now I can inject in the groin.'

In time, the expertise is not confined to injecting but to a whole range of different activities related to the drug injecting.

Lisa: 'Diconal is terrible for sticking in the syringe, and if you have drugs there, the police can use it as evidence.'

The status of the user comes not just from having the relevant knowledge but from the fact that this knowledge may be based on practical experience.

Bev: 'I've hit an artery. It's easy to do, in your groin, as the colour of the blood is almost the same as in the vein. The sensation is really painful; it's like a red-hot poker being pushed down the middle of your leg. Now I am more careful and use an empty syringe first when using my groin to check it is not arterial blood, then I unscrew the syringe and put the shot in.'

It should be added that some of the expertise can only be obtained through drug use, and not through medical practice. For example, one variation of injecting is the taking back of a shot. If the user 'blows a vein', pushing the needle goes right through vein walls and the drug is injected into the muscle. If the shot remains close to the vein, if it stays in a small pocket and is visible as a red blotch, then the user can insert the needle again and take up most of the shot into the syringe. This technique can also be used if the shot congeals after a fix. The shot is not re-injected but simply squirted down the back of the throat.

Some of the expertise is more general, a knowledge about the whole injecting way of life.

Maggie: 'Nine out of ten junkies keep their works clean. You use the works until they're no good, until the barrel sticks. You use the grease off your nose, margarine, cooking oil, anything to get the barrel moving again.Once the needle is blocked then you try to clear it with water from the tap, or you can use a fine copper wire, or keep moving the barrel up and down. If the needle is barbed, it will rip open your skin when you take the needle out. You get the matchbox out and file down the needle and then use glass or a mirror to rub it down. You always clean works in cold water. Hot water congeals the blood and there is verdigris in the hot water. You wrap the works in tissue paper and wrap it round with your tie-up, usually a lace. You hide your works in the zip of a bag, down the front of your trousers, in the hem of your coat. I used to carry my set here in my left armpit.'

Apart from the expertise, there is status for users who demonstrate their nerve, such as when they balance a mirror on their knees, bend the needle and inject themselves in the neck, into the jugular vein. Such behaviour may seem remarkable, but jugular injections may be used medically, and the user becomes accustomed to the method.

Also there is the status that can come from the sophistication that can accompany injecting or matters pertaining to injecting.

Jane: 'Roy has a hit of smack if it's weak but he prefers to smoke it, as he is afraid of the needle and how it can affect his health.'

Injecting and fast effects

With injecting, the effects are very fast. This plainly is an advantage when withdrawing, as the user wants to stop the pains as quickly as possible. Often this means not just the pains of withdrawals but the user's total anxiety about the expected pains.

Lisa: 'The pain of withdrawal is worse than labour pains. If given the choice, I would have a bairn rather than withdraw.'

Apart from quickly stopping any withdrawal pains, managing to inject does give a feeling of achievement and a sense of relief. The act of injecting becomes a task in itself.

Dean: 'It feels good if you hit a vein first time.'

Injecting and life-style

What is an advantage to the user may be just a matter of injection mechanics, but injecting can be more than a matter of mechanics. It can be an indication of a way of life; it can even be part of a way of life.

Maggie: 'A set of works is part of your life. You have a packet but without a set of works it's a waste. Snorting does nothing for you when you are using. You need the two, the set of works and the packet. If you haven't got a set then you use anybody's – you accept the risk of getting hep. You ask if the person had hep but you are not really interested.'

This quote was made several years ago, before the advent of HIV infection. It might be thought that HIV would have radically changed things, but nothing should be taken for granted.

Austin: 'If you haven't fixed then you don't know what it is like. If someone has the virus (HIV) and you are withdrawing then you would use it even if you were negative. You wouldn't think about it at the time or you would kid yourself on that you wouldn't get it. But you would have that fix.'

Injecting drugs, like drug use itself, may be seen merely as something that users end up having to do, as opposed to something users want to do. Using represents more than a method of taking drugs. For instance, having a shot can be a happening in itself, behaviour imbued with ritualism.

Mary: 'Making up the shot is important, as well as the rush.'

Sometimes injecting is important, not because of the action in itself, but its relation to the local subculture, and to the user's identity.

Judy: 'I went up to Dylan's and was sitting in his flat. He said, "Do you use?" and I said yes. He said, "Let's see your arms" and I showed them. Then he threw his arms round me and said, "Welcome, you're one of us".'

THE EQUATION OF CONTINUING HEROIN USE

Advantages and disadvantages

With all the advantages of drug use, we might wonder why users should ever want to come off. Non-users might want them to come off but from the point of view of the drug user, there does seem little reason to do so. Everything seems to be going well, the person is enjoying life more, and there is no reason to stop.

Lynne: 'Coming off? We never even thought about it. It never entered our heads.'

Yet the reality is that for most users there is likely to be a desire to stop at some time. And none, to my knowledge, have seen themselves as being heroin users for the rest of their lives. Illegal drug use is seen as a temporary phase.

Layna: 'I don't know anyone who enjoys using unless they are newly started. If you have been using for a few months you get something out of it. But everyone who has been using for some time wants to get out.'

After a time, users may want to stop. Although there are advantages in taking drugs there are also disadvantages. Most drug users know of the drawbacks, or at least some of them.

Barry: 'When I started fixing smack, everyone knew what they were into. We knew the score. Using the needle was always a risk.

Two of my friends who got into heroin in the early days died from overdoses. In those days it was the risk of hepatitis that was the worry, as there was a bad strain going around. Several people died from it. No-one bothers about hep nowadays though it is far more infectious than HIV.'

Apart from the drawbacks of heroin use, users will also be aware of what it was like before starting heroin use. The image might or might not be accurate and any underlying problems may be overlooked, but the time before involvement will be seen as a preferable time.

Layna: 'I would really like to be straight. It must be nice to go through life without a worry. I used to have a great time before I got into it. I would go out for a drink and have a laugh. You don't really have a laugh when you're using.'

At first it seemed nice to live a life with no worries. The drawback is that to achieve such a state, the drug user has not only to take opioids but live with frozen feelings. Not only is there protection from bad feelings but, equally, barriers to good feelings.

Not stopping earlier

If times were so good before the person had begun to use, then the question arises as to why users do not stop their drug use sooner. Part of the difficulty is that users are involved in illegal activity and the reaction to cover up is very great. This in time verges into the habit of denial. This denial can extend not merely to others but to themselves, so drug users will hide from them-selves or deny what really is happening to them. Furthermore, the desire to continue to use and eliminate underlying anxiety is helped by denial and a burying of the known dangers of continued use. Clients will put out lies which they know the counsellor is not likely to believe, simply because denial has become a habit.

Siouxie (under the influence, three syringes in the ashtray): 'You'll be wondering about me. I was up late last night and was having a sleep when you came in.'

It might be thought that drug users are not likely to be bothered about the inherent risks of drug use. Certainly, a drug such as heroin with its strong anxiety relieving power will lessen the appreciation of risks but this happens only after the drug has been taken, not when the user needs to take it. However it must be said that there are users who seem blind to the risks they take.

Dean: 'Bry was always reckless. He would be off drugs for a week, then bang up thirty quids worth. It was like playing Russian roulette with five bullets in the chamber. We always used to say he had death in his eyes.'

The reckless user is regarded as such, even by other users. However the user does not stop using merely because there are risks involved. The user will continue to use as long as the advantages to the user exceed the disadvantages. The disadvantages are those known to the user and which the user judges to be disadvantageous.

Specific disadvantages of heroin use
The disadvantages that come to the user are physical, psychological, familial and social. The physical risks are those of infection spread of HIV or hepatitis B through needle-sharing, the risks of endo- carditis, septicaemia and overdosing. Veins collapse and become blocked, resulting in new sites having to be found. However this has to be acceptable to the user. Some users will draw the line at injecting into their feet or injecting in the groin or neck.

Tina (after a hepatitis test in the dental hospital): 'They couldn't get a vein anywhere, so one of them started to look at my feet. I said, "No way! Give me the needle and I'll get a vein. I've never used my feet!" And so they let me get the vein.'

In fact the main apparent advantage of injecting, being able to experience the drug effects very quickly, turns to be the very oppo- site in time. For long-term users, injecting can be the slowest way of taking a drug.

Layna: 'I cannot get a hit anywhere except in the bathroom. It has to be the bathroom as I raise the veins by putting my hands into boiling water. I must have hot water. Usually it takes me about half an hour to get a hit.'

Generally using by injection presents greater troubles for women as they tend to have smaller veins than men.

Bev: 'My veins go dry or blow after a couple of days using.'

Other disadvantages of continuing to use include addiction, which brings the risk of painful withdrawals. Depression is often a feature of long-term heroin drug use and attempted suicides are very much greater than in the normal population. Generally, users' health tends to be poor through an indequate diet.

Hale: 'It's fucking my body up. My veins are solid. In the last year I have lost a stone in weight.'

There are psychological drawbacks of low self-esteem, poor self-image and dependency. Problems in the family can be those of rejection, over-involvement and isolation. Social losses include unemployment, loss of liberty through imprisonment and diminished future prospects. These are some of the possible drawbacks of being a drug user which might be appreciated by the user.

Initially users see no reason to stop. The medical drawbacks are of little concern, and users might not be addicted or realize they are addicted. The Law will not have caught up with their illegal behaviour and the family might not realize the user is taking drugs. However this situation is likely to change in time.

Conrad: 'To subsidize my drug taking, I was shoplifting nearly every day for about seven months until I realized shop staff knew my face. Sooner or later I would be caught. As my habit grew larger, more money was needed. So I drifted into house-breaking to get larger lump sums of money. As always the police got to know, either from neighbours from adjoining houses giving descriptions or from police informers.'

The drug taking style of life might seem attractive at first with very few real worries attached. However, it soon begins to lose its attractions for the drug user.

The balance

So at first the equation of using is tilted towards continuing use, but over time the drawbacks increase and the advantages, such as the enjoyment from using, decrease. This means that the balance of the using equation moves towards the user seeing and feeling that there is little to be gained from continuing to use heroin. Thus the heroin equation alters according to the changes in the user's life-situation. Sometimes the changes have nothing to do directly with drug use.

Beth: 'I came off the second time I got pregnant. Angie kept on using when she was pregnant and the baby went through withdrawals when it was born.'

Sometimes it seems that there are events or situations that alone cause the user to decide to stop drug use. The sudden shock, of whatever form, in some cases can have an effect.

Tommy: 'I don't know why I decided to stop. Well, I was walking down the road and passed out. Next I woke up in the Royal Infirmary with doctors looking down at me. I didn't know where I was. It gave me a shock.'

And the shock can be indirectly connected to the drug use itself, caused by other factors. Such factors bring reality back to the user in undeniable form.

Avril: 'Going inside, it gave me a shock. Never again, I thought, I'm not doing it again. And I've been off ever since.'

Being sent to prison rarely figures as a major factor in coming off drugs. Drug users can go into prison and either their drug use continues or they stop such use, only to continue it directly after liberation.

Janice: 'Ralph was right into it after he came out of prison. I thought he would be round to see Peter as they are old friends but Ralph never bothered. He knew Peter wasn't interested in drugs any more.'

Heroin user ambivalence

If deciding to stop is a matter of balancing advantages and disadvantages, then it might be the case that these are evenly balanced. The user does not know whether to use or not, whether to stop or not.

Bev: 'My head is going round. I don't know whether I want to use or not. I just wanted to make up a shot to spite my Dad. Then I banged it up my arm, but even then I wanted to take it out and squirt the syringe on the floor.'

Being in a state of ambivalence is made more difficult because it is not merely a case of not knowing what to do, but knowing how the drug user feels when not knowing what to do. The user is pulled in opposite directions and feels unable to control the situation.

Judy: 'I knew I was doing wrong. I actually stopped and thought about it but still did it. I could not get a vein first time and was hunting about for one. I felt about three inches high. Afterwards I was greeting, I felt so bad about it. It was as if there was a power stronger than me, and for the first time I was frightened.'

So this feeling of ambivalence may be unpleasant. Users can live more easily with being a user or coming off, rather than being caught in the intermediate ambivalent position.

Jenny: 'Last night I put the needle in and wondered what I was doing it for. I sat there greeting. What was I doing it for?'

Sometimes users do not reach a dramatic crisis but drift along without getting anything out of their drug taking. It really has become a habit, reflecting no desire to continue but, equally, no desire to stop.

Samantha: 'I don't even like smack but I just keep taking it.'

It may seem that these ambivalent users are controlled by drugs, and 'You don't control drugs: drugs control you' is a common remark by users. However drugs control users only if users allow this to happen. Indeed, much of drug counselling is helping clients to appreciate this fact.

Further work

We have to distinguish between what drug users say and what they actually do. Often they will talk about stopping but fail to do so. It would be tempting to see this as them being dishonest but the reality is far more complex. In their ambivalence, users can change their mind because they have two contradictory thoughts at almost the same time.

Layna: 'I would really like to be straight.'
Layna (same day): 'I must have something. I can't go without something so I can get stoned from time to time.'

We may see this as contradictory and a sign of confusion or even dishonesty. However contradiction is merely a logical construct, and it is quite possible for people to have very different or seemingly opposed feelings. Indeed, this is the very essence of ambivalence.

Further ambivalence

Talking about coming off drugs can be at times misleading. Such talk can be a substitute for coming off, a defence against actually doing it. It makes the user feel better in the short term and can lessen any feelings about guilt that the drug use is continuing.

> *Beth*: 'You have to come off at once. It's no good talking about it. The more you talk about it, the less likely you are to do it.'

There is a variation on this theme, when the user seems serious about coming off and makes plans about doing so. But the plans become the main interest. Counsellors suddenly have the feeling that the words are there but not the action. And if the question arises as to who are these users trying to convince, then the answer must be themselves.

> *Craig*: 'On the first two days I'll take two DFs, three Mogadon and two Valium. On the next two days one DF, two Mogadon and two Valium, then two Mogadon and three Valium, then one Mogadon and two Valium, and finally just two Valium. I'll go and ask the doctor if this is OK, whether I need more or less.'

Users themselves in this situation may indeed be intentionally dishonest, they may be unsure of what they want or they may be truthful, only to change their mind later. However usually they are merely ambivalent, unsure of what they want and torn between different and often opposing desires.

> *Josie*: 'Often I was kidding when I said I wanted to come off. Then I changed and I wanted to come off but wanted to use at the same time. I could not understand it; it went for my head.'

Sometimes this stage is called the contemplative stage, when the user thinks about coming off. Certainly the users are more likely to think about it. However it is also a matter of degree. After the initial excitement, thoughts about stopping will come to the user.

> *Layna*: 'There is a change – you might not believe it – but at

one time I would not bother. But now I think about it, what taking drugs is doing to me.'

However we should be aware that drug users can think about coming off drugs for years. At times it is as if thinking about it is the same as doing it. None of this is significant unless thinking about it is followed up by action.

Control of drug use

The fable of heroin use tells of people out of control, unable to do anything about their drug use. This is a convenient tale for the person who wants to continue to use: it denies all personal responsibility. The view that the power of drugs is such that they force a person to use and use as much as possible is not reality. The determining factor as to how much heroin a person will use is more likely to revolve around how much drugs the user wants, how much money can be raised for drugs or how much drugs can be obtained. Even then the user can control the amount.

Josie: 'I let myself go, I know I did, but was able to get it together. That's what happens. You use heavily, go downhill and then you recognize it. You cut down, get better, and then start using heavier again.'

Even normal heroin use involves a degree of control. Counsellors might see or listen to client drug use behaviour but be unaware of the preceding slow build-up to that behaviour, be ignorant of the degree of control that normal heroin use requires to prevent overdosing. Even normal daily use is subject to a measure of control.

Bev: 'During the day you take enough to keep yourself straight. It is at night, for your last hit, that you can really get stoned and then it doesn't matter as you will finally fall asleep.'

The idea of chaotic drug use is one that is convenient as far as some users are concerned because it legitimizes erratic behaviour. The image of the chaotic user is also used at times by the helping services as it legitimizes their own actions with regards to drug users.

Ray: ' When you are on smack you think it controls you, that it makes you do things. You forget that you can do things.'

Even if immersed in the heroin using life-style, the user still has a measure of control over personal use. The user does not have to go for any help or chemical substitutes. The user can control personal drug intake, whatever the circumstances – if he or she wants.

Hale: 'I was acting as a doorman for a dealer and my habit went right up. I was up to two grams a day and then I said to myself, "What's happening? What's this all about?", and then I gave myself a shake. I cut right down. You can see I'm looking healthy now.'

Control is a matter of degree and how much the user wants to be in or out of control. What is also true is that the outward behaviour of heroin users is variable and erratic, it can appear to be out of control or at least not in full control. Yet this is what the user wants. The user can take the decision whether or not to be in control. This reflects how drug users want their life to be; a life in control or out of control, or somewhere in-between.

Maggie: 'Any time a junkie has no money, he wants to come off. But the moment someone puts a fiver in his hand then he is off to score. He doesn't think of what to do with the fiver. He doesn't think at all. He's just off!'

The difficulty for the drugs worker is that such behaviour gives the impression both of lack of control and that the worker *has* to take control for the user. The worker wants to help, wants to get the user off drugs. This is not possible. The user has to want it.

Josie: 'The school staff were upset when they knew I was on drugs. They told me to stop it. They threatened me but they couldn't do anything. They did not understand they could not make me come off. Only I could help myself.'

So the reality is that no counsellor can get clients off drugs. Clients have to want to come off for themselves and by themselves. However counsellors can assist, ease and support the process, provided they realize that control has to rest with the drug using clients.

Moving towards coming off

In time the advantages of drug use continue to decrease. It is no longer exciting. In fact the hassle and the constant need to get drugs becomes boring. So we see drug use becoming a burden and the user really does want to stop.

Layna: 'I just want relief. I can't go on like this. I don't even know what the matter is. I've never felt like this before; I don't know what to do. This morning I felt like grabbing hold of that electric fire and ending it all.'

The picture of the ambivalent drug user leads to difficulties in that those close to the user and helpers see themselves manipulated, misled or let down by the user's attitudes and behaviour. They want different things from the user and there is a consequent difference in expectations. Moreover the gap is one that gets wider and wider. The lack of understanding leads to helpers misinterpreting what is actually happening.

Chris: 'You can't keep on using, your body can't take it. I was using, going wild, but I've stopped now. I don't know when I'll start again. You do that; keep using and then stop and then you start again. I can't say how long it will be before I start again. Perhaps I won't.'

All these effects, the negative effects of drug use, tend to increase in time and time itself can become a factor, or at least the consciousness of personal time can.

Jenny: 'I'm thirty-two now. I'm not young. I can't keep going on like this. I can't keep doing it.'

Again, we should not see this as merely an obsession with years or age. Its essence lie with what it means; and what it means to be a certain age, and what it means in relation to a total lifetime. There can also be intimations of mortality.

Review of the equation of use
If we look again at drug use then the heroin equation is a balance of advantages against disadvantages of using heroin. If the balance moves towards an excess of disadvantages over advantages, then the user will want to stop drug use. If the balance gives an excess of advantages over disadvantages then the user will want to continue to use drugs. This simple idea is rather more complicated than might at first seem. Firstly, the user has to know of the

advantages and disadvantages or be aware of them in some way. Some advantages and disadvantages are not easily described or they are appreciated only indirectly. Some of the good feelings about being part of a subculture may be hard to put into words but they are still very real to the user. We also have to remember that advantages and disadvantages relate to the person, not merely to the drug taking. A concentration on mere drug use alone not only diminishes the person but is potentially misleading.

If there is a balance of advantages and disadvantages, then there is going to be no clear desire to stop or continue. User ambivalence is demonstrated not just in words but in actions as well. However, even if the user wants to come off drugs, there may not be a sudden end to the drug use, because of the difficulties involved in stopping and the even greater difficulty in staying off drugs.

Objections against the idea of the heroin equation

One of the many possible objections is that it is too rational a concept. It presumes that heroin users are going to make rational decisions, weigh up the pros and cons, be very aware of their actions and the attendant consequences. Yet their behaviour and actions would not lead anyone to think that they are capable of this.

My belief is that heroin users are people still capable of rational behaviour: they merely have a different frame of reference. Also it should be added that they do not often seriously consider their situation and future, and this avoidance can be deliberate. It does not mean they are incapable of self-examination.

Chris: 'I just tried it for fun at first. Then the fun ended. Then I treated it as a way of life. I wanted a shot but did not need it. Finally I needed it. I was desperate, stabbing people or attacking them for money for dope. Now I want it but do not need it. I think that's a good sign.'

Users are capable of doing work on themselves, of planning for what they know will happen, and they are able to talk about it. But coming off drugs is a major change in the life of users.They have become accustomed to a different way of life and almost a different form of consciousness.

Josie: 'I'm used to being stoned. It's difficult to stop. Well, I'm not stoned all the time but I'm used to being that way.'

For some users this form of consciousness is closer to a lack of consciousness. Such users want to blot out life and heroin, or any other drug, is one way of doing this.

Julie: 'Now that I am not using, I was drinking and was really drunk. I'm an everything-oholic. I cannot just drink but have to get really drunk; I want to get out of my mind.'

But heroin has the advantage of being able to chemically turn off anxiety and blunt all feelings, yet the user is still conscious.

Preparing for change

The idea of getting 'the head together', planning to come off is important. To be able to talk such plans over with someone, preferably someone who is straight, can be useful.

Layna: 'I'm going to stay in hospital longer this time, not go at the end of my withdrawals but stay there while I'm still normal. I'm so used to being stoned; I don't know what it's like to be normal.'

Apart from planning, the user has to have the right, positive attitude. It is difficult to feel positive about coming off, especially for those who have used heroin for many years. To give themselves the best chance of achieving what they want, users have to see themselves as actually coming off. They have to believe in themselves.

4 STOPPING DRUG USE

ABILITY TO COME OFF

If users want to stop their heroin use, then we might well ask why does it appear that they so often fail, why do they have so much difficulty in ending it. To begin with, we must question the assumption that drug users, and heroin users in particular, have such difficulties. Although it often appears to helpers that coming off heroin is very difficult, we often do not know about the occasions or we forget the times when drug users have been successful. This is usually because they have come off without any outside help. Drug users can come off without any help, and even taking a high amount of heroin does not prevent a person from stopping their drug use.

Maggie: 'I came down from £150's worth a day and finally got down to two pounds' worth. That's the hardest bit, to do without that two pounds' worth. I met Hugh and he said, "You're the last person I thought would ever come off, you were in so heavy". It was hard. It nearly broke me. When people asked me, I said it was easy, but it wasn't. I lay on the floor and saw pink elephants going in front of my eyes. I got down to two pounds' worth every three days – I had to have that. Then it went up again. Two pounds every two days, two pounds every day. Then I twigged it wasn't helping me to come off. But it was hard to come off completely, though that two pounds' worth would do nothing for me.'

Here we see that the mental aspect is important. Very often it is the very last lap in coming off which is the most difficult. Also there might be an increase in use towards the end, a blip when there is a temporary increase. This is not uncommon.

Although this chapter looks at the difficulties in coming off, yet it should also be remembered that it is possible to come off. Drug users will frequently say that they cannot come off without medication, cannot come off large amounts of drugs, cannot come off for a host of reasons. They can come off: they merely do not want to come off or do not want to come off sufficiently. This is quite acceptable: it is their choice. The point is that it is important to distinguish between what is possible and what is desired.

Still wanting to use

If users are ambivalent about their drug use, then it is understandable that they will be unsure about stopping. However if they want to stop, and this can be after a matter of months or a year or so, then they should be able to stop.

There seem to be two principal reasons why users are likely to continue to use, even though they might want to stop. Firstly, we have to be sure we understand what it means for users to say they want to stop. This is a difficult area as it would be tempting to say that users do not really mean what they say or they do not really know what they want. If this is correct then the question arises, who really does know? Do counsellors know better than users what they really want?

Part of the difficulty is working out what it means to come off heroin. For many users this means being placed on a substitute drug such as methadone. It means continuing to take opioid drugs, though this is also likely to mean ending intravenous use. Sometimes the user will want to stop heroin use but does not want to live without heroin. This may be more than ambivalence; it may reflect difficulties with the idea of loss.

Loss of something is implicit in change. Whenever we move to a new state, the old state is left behind. Moreover the greater the change, the greater is likely to be the sense of loss. If we take drug use, then coming off heroin is a major life change. The loss may be loss of the chemical effects of the drug. The good effects might have long disappeared but there is still difficulty with not taking the drug.

> *Layna*: 'I really wanted to come off but I've been into smack for so long, I don't know if I can. Yes, you were right. I'm scared to live without drugs. I've forgotten what normality is like.'

What adds to the difficulties is that when contemplating such an action, one knows it involves not merely an end to drug use but often a total change in life-style.

> *Martin*: 'It takes a time to change. For a year I've been scoring and thieving. You cannot stop just like that when it's your life.'

Sometimes the user will want to stop heroin use on a conscious level but there are aspects that are not fully in the conscious mind which act against the desire. In particular, underlying problems, such as unmanageable family situations, although not uppermost in the user's mind, may in the long term incline the user to continue to use.

There are also other difficulties concerning the discomfort of withdrawals. To the heroin users withdrawals figure highly in their lives. They are seen as an important factor in determining future actions and behaviour. Yet the whole subject seems to be part of a drug mythology, and the topic is rarely adequately discussed.

Withdrawals reviewed

Firstly, withdrawals only occur when there is a lack of drugs. If someone is using regularly then not only will that person not experience withdrawals, he or she might not even know they are physically addicted. This is quite common with people who have been prescribed sleeping tablets, benzodiazepines, over many years. Even irregular heroin users might not know if they are addicted or not. Moreover if the users do not realize that they are addicted then they might not realize when they are withdrawing.

Layna: 'For two years we used and did not have a big habit. We used to withdraw and thought we had a cold. We've sat in a pub having a drink because we thought we had a cold, but really we were withdrawing.'

The common image of withdrawals, especially from heroin, has been demonized to the extent that most people imagine that they must be incredibly painful. In fact this is not necessarily the case at all. On the other hand, it is wrong to perceive withdrawal pains in too simple a fashion. Often the pains are likened to a bad bout of flu. This may seem an insignificant experience – unless you happen to be going through it.

Me: 'You'll have to excuse me, I've got the flu and didn't sleep last night.'
Layna: 'Feeling a bit rough?'
Me: 'Pretty awful.'
Layna: 'Well now you fucking well know a bit of what it feels like. I haven't been able to sleep properly in five nights!'

Estimating the pain of others can be inaccurate, as it assumes that the pain experienced will be the same for all users. In practice, the pain is likely to a small extent to be dose dependent. Thus very large doses do result in more painful withdrawals. It should be added that large amounts of heroin are not often used nowadays, as pure or pharmaceutical heroin is rarely obtainable and the usual street heroin is comparatively weak.

Peter: 'I had terrible withdrawal pains, I nearly died. I was on pure gear, stolen from chemists and was using a gram a day. I had to come off in hospital.'

Such accounts are now very much a thing of the past. The only exception may be dealers who are themselves using large amounts of dealer's heroin.

Sarah: 'Zero was using up to seven grams of smack a day. Each hit would be a gram at a time. When he was withdrawing he was bleeding from his ears and his mouth.'

When heroin becomes unobtainable locally, withdrawals likely to be unpleasant but not too painful. In fact, sometimes users have hardly noticed their withdrawals, and have been surprised to discover that they might not have been addicted.

Pain threshold

More importantly, the pain threshold is decreased by anxiety, so those who are in a state of anxiety will feel more pain, and likewise those not worried will experience less pain. For example, users who experience withdrawals for the first time, because they may not be expecting the pains and because they will not have experienced the pains previously, are likely to have low anxiety and so the resultant pain is not so intense. Those who have experienced withdrawals previously will probably be anxious about coming off again, and the apprehension can be enough to ensure it will be an unpleasant experience.

This link between what a person thinks and feels and the pain or discomfort of withdrawals, points to the experience tending to differ to some extent for every user. Even each attempt to come off can differ.

Layna: 'I've been through withdrawals many times and it's been different each time.'

Whereas the measure of that pain varies according to the degree of anxiety, so can anxiety vary according to the stage at which the user is at. The user who has come off will see things differently to the user who is coming off, and still in an anxious state. How a person feels is how he or she feels, no matter our view of the situation.

Kate: 'Junkies make too much of withdrawal pains. It is not as bad as everyone makes out. For seventy-two hours you have stomach cramps and the like, but it's not so bad after that.'

But this comment comes from a ex-user who had to come off drugs. This does not make her account incorrect; merely, it is the account of someone off drugs. Users may feel differently about withdrawals when they are yet to go through them. This is a crucial time. Furthermore, we cannot lightly dismiss the difficulties and the pain involved.

Glen: 'It's not the psychological withdrawals that bother me but the physical ones. The longer you have been using, the worse it gets. You worry about the pain and don't have time to bother about the psychological withdrawals.'

The division into the physical and the psychological, between body and mind, may be convenient. However we should not forget that the two are closely related. Assessments of the pain that clients may be experiencing is never a precise process, and is often done in a very simplistic manner.

Depersonalization when withdrawing

The symptoms of withdrawal can vary from person to person, as may those symptoms the user judges the most troublesome. What is most troublesome may depend on a raft of variables. For instance, a person might be able to withstand suffering alone but find the distress greater when there are others around and the situation has to be hidden.

Skip: 'See, it's my legs when I withdraw; I can't stop them shaking. I lie awake in bed and my legs keep shaking. My old man gets up early for his work and he would see me awake, so I would pretend I had just woken up.'

Coming off large amounts of heroin can also lead to feelings of depersonalization, which can be frightening for the user. Concentrating on pain alone may make the user unprepared for a whole range of sensations.

Maggie: 'Although I was dozing, I didn't get to sleep. It was on the third day though that I felt I was really going mad. I can't explain everything I felt at that time but I will try. I felt tired, weak. I was sweating from head to toe. Every time I spoke I felt I was just miming the words and my voice was coming from somewhere else in the room, and every part of my body ached.'

Feelings of depersonalization are not uncommon and the user will benefit from being given reassurance. Getting off drugs may then be seen as a return to normality, even if what happens seems abnormal.

Jane: 'You feel funny. You go into a state of shock at first when you withdraw.'
Marion: 'I can't explain how I feel. It's as if I'm on a bad trip.'

In this state, users sometimes have to hold onto themselves, combat the feelings they are experiencing. As these feelings are rarely mentioned, they are often overlooked. In the following quote one user describes his reaction to withdrawing in prison.

Chris: 'I thought I was going mad, thinking about it when I was inside. Then I thought, "No, you can't go mad. You are Chris."'

Maybe, the experience of looking at reality closely for the first time in ages is itself strange. Being without drugs can be an abnormal condition for the drug user.

Lynne: 'Everything seems unreal and I can't remember things, or things that happened yesterday seem a long time ago. I took the bairn to the bus stop this morning, but it seems ages ago.'

For those who have been using drugs for several years, the loss of not just the drugs but the whole accompanying life-style does come as a shock and can give feelings of unreality. Unfortunately, it is all too easy to dismiss the feelings or lack of feelings as drug user exaggeration or calls for sympathy, rather than accepting that users may experience many different sensations.

Withdrawals and interrupted sleep

We should be aware that it is not necessarily pain that presents the major difficulty for the drug user who wants to come off drugs. Even worse can be the interrupted sleep that can continue over a few weeks. This lack of sleep can be harder to take than the pain, which is over relatively quickly.

Maggie: 'It's the nights that are the hardest. You can take withdrawals during the day but night-time, it's a long time. That's when you want some help.'

Just as there is likely to be anxiety about possible pain, there can also be anxiety about lack of sleep. Here we have to distinguish between the effects of lack of sleep and the anxiety about lack of sleep. The two are not easily differentiated in that those coming off heroin may be unable to say if they have slept or not, whether their sleep was interrupted or not. Anxiety can lead to panic and then there will be little possibility of sleep.

Withdrawing and anxiety

General anxiety about withdrawals may seem incidental but it is a constant factor. It an confuse users as to what is really happening and how they really feel.

Martin: 'I thought I had withdrawals until Christmas, and then it was really bad. I thought it had never been like this before, and then I realized that it was withdrawals and I had never really had them before. When I had been running around thinking I was strung out, it was all in my head. I never had withdrawals before Christmas.'

Ironically, how a person feels when withdrawing is in part dependent on what that person knows or has been told about withdrawing. This in turn can depend on knowledge that is current locally, on the views of the local drug subculture.

Dean: 'The habit is in the head. You become aware of having a healthy habit and it is hard to come off. Everyone round here is like that; thinks that you are going to have bad withdrawal pains. It never used to be like that in London. No-one thought it was that bad.'

This reveals how careful counsellors have to be about giving information about drug use or in simply agreeing with drug using client statements. What is said or silently agreed to can affect the drug user and the subsequent course of coming off drugs.

Knowledge of user's addiction

The whole question of having a habit or not, being physically addicted or psycholgically addicted, is of great importance to heroin users. There is a constant interest in whether someone is physically addicted, whether 'so-and-so is habited up or not'. The reason is that it is often perceived that the user who does not have a habit is in full control, unlike the addicted user. The user has control and, if not physically addicted, can avoid becoming so.

> *Dick*: 'I can feel I'm getting into it. I'm not habited up but I'm beginning to have sweats at night and soon I'll be right in.'

However symptoms can be mimicked through anxiety to some extent, and many casual users have been surprised to discover that coming off drugs was so easy.

Needle addiction

One often overlooked aspect is the nature of the person's dependency. It is usually assumed the dependency of heroin users is a physical one on drugs. In fact the user is often psychologically addicted to the needle, to the process of intravenous use. The pleasure of putting heroin into the vein, easing withdrawal pains and lessening anxiety can be displaced onto the needle. Thus needle use can be pleasurable or at least lessen discomfort. This in turn can lead to needle-buzz, addiction to the needle.

> *Bev*: 'Almost everyone I know at some time has had needle-buzz at some time. Some junkies are happy enough with water, as long as they think there is something in it. One lassie was screaming her head off but was OK after someone gave her a shot of water.'

For some users the mere act of putting the needle into themselves can be pleasurable, or at least it can relieve their anxiety.

> *Lisa*: 'I've seen me without a shot, it's just the needle I wanted. I've banged up water and I've banged up DFs into my arm to get the needle. There's a lot of junkies like that; needle freaks.'

Gary: 'Inside prison I was so desperate that I spent afternoons jagging a safety pin into my arm.'

This addiction is not merely a matter of putting a needle into the user's body. The whole process of drug use can be fascinating and pleasurable for the user.

Lisa: 'What's the point of injecting water? I like to see the blood come into the syringe and then go out again.'

But taking drugs is not just a personal action, it is often done in a group. To complicate matters, this does not mean drug taking has to be a group action.

Gareth: 'Taking is not social, you don't care if others are around or not, and you don't communicate. Sometimes taking is done in a group but this is only for a needle-buzz.'

The importance of needle-buzz is that it often characterizes long-term users who are using little amounts of drugs. Users may not know for sure what the nature of the pleasure they get from such drug taking is.

Beth (said to husband Dean): 'You're kidding yourself, you don't get a decent rush! It's just needle-buzz with you.'

Other users might be more aware of their needle addictive state and see that the real difficulty is to come off the needle rather than the drug.

Craig: 'The real test is to get the user to realize that the needle is the main problem, or at least, as much a problem as the drug itself. I know of a guy who was withdrawing in prison, stuck the needle into a vein, withdrew blood and just kept saying to himself that he had just had his usual shot. It was like a self-induced hypnotic state which worked for him as he felt the pain and saw the blood. His withdrawals abated for a while. Both Lisa and I are hooked on the needle. The first shot in the morning is 90 per cent for the drug but shot after that the shots are 90 per cent for the needle.'

Like drug use, needle use and addiction is open to individual interpretation. Counsellors have to work with these interpretations and not presume there is one generalized explanation.

Jane: 'I would argue that when a drug is going straight into your vein, along with all the shit it is cut with, you not only get addicted to the heroin but to the citric acid which is needed to break down the heroin. When you get the cramps, it's not only due to the heroin, as if you use pure heroin and use the right amount they are not nearly as bad. Some of the chemicals used to cut it make the withdrawals worse. When you are making up the shot it is like anticipation. When you put the needle into your vein and draw the blood into the barrel and push the plunger in, it's like a feeling of achievement. I was addicted to the needle. If I did not have a set, my brother would say, "Snort it!" but I wouldn't. Snorting it or smoking it would do absolutely nothing for me, as it wasn't only the heroin but the needle-buzz I needed.'

Thus some casual users will inject water when they are unable to get any suitable drugs, and this can be sufficient to satisfy them. The exact nature of needle addiction can vary in that for some users, it is the pushing of the needle into the body that is important. Other users can have different perceptions.

Lisa: 'What makes me feel better is when I hit a vein and then pull the plunger back. I see the blood comes into the syringe, like a wee red flower. I like to see that.'

These thoughts and behaviours may seem rather peculiar until we realize how they are associated with the relief in having a shot, and the total pleasure of drug use for Lisa was bound up in both the needle and the drug. Counsellors must be aware of needle addiction, because it is one aspect of drug use that may well not be raised by drug using clients.

Coming off and self-esteem

If users have low self-esteem, then they are also likely to have low self-confidence. If this is the case then attempts to change behaviour and end drug taking will be very difficult. The lack of confidence can be general, and not specifically to do with drugs or drug-centred life. Nevertheless, a lack of confidence and the feeling that what is aimed for cannot really be achieved, will make stopping drug use problematic.

Tina: 'I've been a disappointment to lots of people. I've let them down.'

Low self-esteem makes decisions harder to take and harder to keep. Users may know what they should do, they may want to do it, but with low self-esteem they still might not do it. When people are feeling bad about themselves, they feel they cannot do anything. Users say they cannot come off, believe they cannot come off and fail to come off. For this reason, the user's reservations about coming off are to be heeded.

Dean: 'The trouble is that I feel so negative. I'll wait till I go into hospital and when I come out, hopefully, I will get out of this place.'

Lacking the will-power to come off drugs may reflect a desire to continue to use or it may reflect the user's low self-esteem.

Planning and positives

Part of the process of coming off is mental preparation. The user has to be positive in outlook and this needs planning. It is insufficient to expect a user to look positively at the drug situation: that is equivalent to telling a clinically depressed person to look on the bright side of things. Instead, the user has to be drawn into the process of personal planning and the emphasis placed on doing things and not reacting to perceived difficulties.

Phil (two weeks before stopping heroin use): 'You cannot come off, you cannot do it, if your head's not together, I know, I've given you a load of crap in the past, a bit of a runabout but I'm serious this time.'

Users have become accustomed to confidence coming in chemical form. It is hard to find similar confidence in themselves and in their approach to life. They still believe in magic solutions, enchantment through the syringe, rather than accepting they have to work towards their objectives and that this might take time.

Joyce: 'I really do want to stop but I haven't got the will-power. I wish there was something to give me will-power. I wish I could give up.'

The truth is that users are the only people who can ensure they come off. Coming off is basically something that users have do for themselves.

> *Josie*: 'The school staff were upset when they knew I was on drugs. They told me to stop it, they threatened me but they couldn't do anything. They did not understand they could not make me come off. Only I could help myself.'

In fairness, it has to be said that it can be equally difficult for *helpers* to accept that only users can really help themselves. Somehow we feel that we should be able to give direct assistance and fail to recognize our limitations.

Cravings

Even if a drug is not present, the memory of it is. It is trying to get rid of the memory of it that can prove so troublesome.

> *Martin*: 'I never thought it would be so difficult. In the past when people have started up again, I thought they weren't serious or they did not try hard enough. But now it's me, I realize how difficult it is. I think of getting a shot all the time. The craving is still there.'

These cravings are likely to last a considerable time. The concentration on the drug life-style, when using, results in its continuation in the user's mind. However it should be emphasized that the cravings are merely one part of the problem. The thought of cravings is enough to pose difficulties for the person who wants to come off. After all, ending drug taking is easier than ending the memories of it.

> *Josie*: 'Once you're a junkie you're never away from it. You can never get it out of your head as you like getting stoned; you like it too much. When I come out of hospital I will not use that day, but I will have a shot the next day. I hope I can use once a week.'

Some drug users may have been using drugs for most of their life. To stop memories of drug taking is to try to forget over half a lifetime.

STOPPING HEROIN USE

No fireworks

The actual process of coming off often reflects the ambivalence that the user feels. There is no dramatic renunciation of heroin use but a slow movement to stopping. It might appear that the person wants to come off but this may reflect a desire at a certain time. There is rarely a wholesale conversion to being a non-user. Equally, behaviour can reflect this gradual approach to non-use.

Me: 'Susan came to see me and said that she was keen to get treatment, she wants to get to a hostel.'
Chris: 'Oh, no! Mind, that's what I would have tried. I would have sprung it on you in her place.'
Me: 'I know it's a bit of a con.'
Chris: 'Yes, a wind-up. But she's probably serious. She'll be at the end of her money, her friends, and she has no resources left. She will be honest in a small way. I suppose that's the way it starts.'

At this time of possible stopping, the drug user is tired of using. There need not be any great feeling that drug taking is dangerous or that it is wrong. The main feeling might be that it is all too much of a hassle to continue to carry on, too much bother having to score. Just as young people can drift into drug use, so they can drift out of it. And this drifting out is connected with how they feel.

Ray: 'Another spring and I'm just in the same position as last year. I'm tired, both physically and mentally, my head's nipping and I can't think straight. I'm fed up and sick. I'm doing the same things every day. I'm a robot. I have decided to stop.'

The surprising thing is that one of the advantages of drug use, that it cuts out boredom, is slowly turning into a disadvantage. The drug using life itself becomes boring. This boredom points to not only what a person does but how a person feels. And repeated behaviour, in time, is likely to be seen as being merely more of the same.

Maggie: 'I was really fed up going out to get money to keep my habit going, and then I was fed up going from house to house looking for some smack. When you eventually found somebody who had some gear you had to wait ages for everyone in the house to buy their dope before you. After you bought your dope, if you didn't have a set of works of your own you had to wait on someone finishing with theirs so you could borrow it. All you really cared about was getting your own fix. I was really fed up going through the same things every day, just to stay sane for that day.'

As we have seen, users have to get their 'heads together' and this is not always easy. Usually users have many thoughts and feelings to straighten out and they are not always in the best state to do so.

Chris: 'You have to clear the table for good. Some people clear the table, only to set it again. And it's you who have to clear the table. No-one else can do it for you.'

What also has to be borne in mind is that coming off a drug like heroin is being done by someone who is not straight, but by someone who has gone through the experience of being a drug user. What is possible for the non-user is so much more difficult for the user.

Sandra: 'The doctor said he knew my history, that I had lived with a junkie for three years and brought him off. But I had the will-power then. I had the will-power before I got into smack.'

Many of us, when thinking about drug use, like to hold on to the physical, to the material, rather than perceptions, expectations and past experiences. However to fully understand drug use, we have to see it as a human rather than a chemical process.

Old problems
Another difficulty can be that the user may be taking drugs to cope with an uncopable situation. When the user comes off then the original problem has to be faced and managed. This is likely to be difficult for someone who is not accustomed to dealing with such problems. The user may have to learn how to work on personal problems.

Jason: 'I managed to come off with the help of friends. We talked a lot and I got really close to people. I was able to talk about things I had never talked about before. I was able to get things off my chest, things that had been there a long time. I was able to go out and say things, everything I had always wanted to say. It was also important to learn how you came over to other people.'

Work on underlying problems, identifying if individual drug users have such difficulties and their precise nature, should be carried out from the very beginning. The client might want to work on them at a later time, but they should not be left. The client has to know they will be tackled.

Coming off or stopping?

Again, we have to distinguish between stopping and coming off. Stopping can be easier than coming off as the latter implies a more permanent state. The mental challenge of stopping is much less, in that the user has it in mind to start again at a later date. There is little ideological or identity change if a person merely stops.

Martin: 'Con seemed to be doing well. He wasn't using and I thought he was serious. Then he got a grant and spent it on smack. Every day he was buying it and he spent the lot: there was good stuff from out of town. He wasn't using before because he hadn't got the money and the smack had been weak previously.'

Part of the difficulty in getting a clear head to come off heroin is simply that if the drug is used to ease underlying problems, then stopping the use will resurrect them. sometimes heroin can be used to deal with underlying problems and is in itself not a problem; it is the answer to a problem. Thus heroin use is not a sign that the person is not coping with life, it is a sign that the person is coping in his or her own way. Removing the heroin use is equivalent to taking away a man's crutch. We should not be surprised if he falls down.

Old problems again

So after coming off heroin the user has the difficulty of not merely dealing with the effects of withdrawals but also the re-emergence of longstanding problems. This is being experienced by a person who has perhaps become unskilled in resolving personal problems.

Tina: 'I didn't get to sleep till two or three in the morning. I lie there and think about all my problems. I try to clear my mind and not think about them. When I have a hit I can get to sleep straightaway.'

Unfortunately, the net result of being on heroin for a long time and being accustomed to escaping into anxiety-free states is to make drug users increasingly more unskilled in problem solving.

Maturity

Emotionally we mature partly by having to deal with difficulties, face up to troubles and work through painful experiences. With chronic drug use all this might be avoided. As a result, heroin users may be emotionally immature, not having gone through those situations in life which help us grow. This emotional immaturity may be expressed in various ways, as it affects the person as a whole.

Josie: 'I feel as if I have not grown up yet. I feel as if I'm only fifteen.'

Maggie: 'I feel strange at times, as if I'm not myself. Sometimes I feel as if I am a wee bairn.'

This immaturity is familiar to chronic users, who well might want to stay at this stage. It is a form of regression, hiding from difficulties by a retreat to an earlier age. There is also the advantage that by this regression, users will not merely behave in a juvenile manner but will be treated as if they really are young. This in turn reinforces their juvenile state and allows them to operate with reduced feelings of responsibility.

Tina: 'The thing about junkies is that they have never grown up. Once you start taking dope, you do not age in your mind – though your body ages, of course.'

A degree of justification for this view of user immaturity is endorsed by the views of those users who have stopped their heroin or opioid use. There is now less need for this regression, and ex-using behaviour may well reflect this fact.

Tina: 'I used to act young for my age but I don't now.'

This chemically induced regression may also link up with the user's early life, or lack of time being properly spent as a child. With heroin, users can try to recreate that time, to recapture a childhood they feel they never really had. The anxiety-free state of regression is fine, until the user wants to come off, and then has to work through this stage, through emotional immaturity, among all the other difficulties. The idea that a person grows out of drug use is thus particularly relevant.

Women users and weight

The situation can become even more complicated with female users. Coming off drugs is often accompanied by an increase in weight, because drug users can be underweight as a result of their poor and insufficient diet while using. This applies to straight drug use, without the complication of HIV infection. For women users this weight increase can be undesirable, as it does not fit in with the media-required sexual image.

Susan: 'I still have not touched dope, honest! You can see it anyway, as I'm putting weight on. I'm like a big beached whale.'

Women users can be severely underweight and this gives them an asexual shape. This is no drawback to users, who have little interest in sex if using regularly. The view that they would look much better if they did put on weight, is denied by users, who see themselves as becoming grossly overweight, if they stop using heroin.

Lisa: 'I'm getting fat.'
Me: 'You're what?'
Lisa: 'Getting fat.'
Me: 'You're joking!'
Lisa: 'No, I'm not. I've got a stomach on me.'
Me: 'I can't see it.'
Lisa: 'I have, look!'
Me: 'Well, I can't see anything.'
Lisa: 'But I am fat.'

In fact, Lisa was then weighing seven stone and her concern about possible weight gain was such that soon she only weighed six stone four pounds. Body image can be important as can the accompanying sexual connotations. It is also possible to see the underweight person as someone younger than she really is. If someone is taken as being a lot younger, then again the behaviour towards them is of a type that allows them to be treated as less responsible. To act less responsibly can fit in well with the demands of being a member of the drug subculture. Thus the thought of putting on weight as a result of coming off heroin has implications for female users, implications as regards their sexuality and their relation to the drug subculture. By coming off drugs, users imagine at times that the clock has been turned back and things are going to be as they were, before getting into drugs. However they can also recognize this as being little more than fantasy. Apart from the mere fact that the years will have slipped by, the user's situation will have changed.

Acceptance of the end of use

Firstly, just because the user has stopped taking drugs, there is no certainty that others will believe this change of behaviour. Sometimes others might not even know about the change. So one requirement is to make the change public, at least to relevant persons.

Derek: 'I stopped using, but I didn't tell anyone. Soon I had started again.'

Even when others are aware of the stopping of drug use, users initially might be treated as if they were still using.

Josie: 'I don't know why I stopped. My Mum doesn't believe me and still keeps trying to check up on me all the time. I might as well be using for all the difference it makes.'

This stage is usually a temporary stage, as partners, family and close friends in general want to believe the user has stopped. Only the memories of past 'I'm off' statements produce a suspension of belief. However the situation is likely to be more difficult for users as regards the authorities, whether the persons in authority are in the caring profession or the judicial system.

Esther: 'I get more hassle from the police now that I've stopped than ever I had when dealing. God, I hate them!'

Thus at the time when the former user is trying to establish a new role, even a new identity, the words and actions of others may not be too helpful. Users who have come off need to be believed, even if this takes an effort.

Jane: 'I went to the doctor for a painkiller and he said he didn't give painkillers to addicts. I said, "Ex-addict. I'm an ex-addict now."'

Ironically, we tend to want clients off drugs, but are afraid to believe they really are so. We do not want to feel let down or deceived. However we should also appreciate that these are our problems and should be seen and treated as such.

Other difficulties when off

Drug users have to come to terms with the years they see as having lost, and their perception of themselves as almost unemployable, lacking in skills and having little past work experience. Work is important as many drug users have little idea what they can do in the long term, how to fill their days and become an ordinary working person. They may well have the potential for employment in the future but they seldom believe that fact. Usually their negative attitudes and beliefs make a positive outlook hard to maintain.

Thus some of the difficulties of coming off relate to not only change in behaviour but changes in attitude and beliefs. To make things possible, the ex-user has to believe that they are possible. To believe in possibilities is essential if the user is to make the most of the change from the drug subculture to straight society. The subculture affects not only actual drug use but, perhaps even more importantly, how users relate to other people.

Maggie: 'It's not nice to be a junkie; you're not a real person. You live for yourself when you are using. You are all for yourself. When you are on dope you remember everybody, but bugger the social worker – you have something else to do. You don't mean it as bad. In general you forget how other people think and feel; that's because you have forgotten yourself. You don't bother about people, all love leaves you. But junkies deny this. They say, "I do care". They are in a coccoon and don't want to get out. And they are always finding excuses.'

Adjustment to straight society

This adjustment to different aspects of straight society is a personal process. Professional helpers can try to assist, but users have to want the help offered and they have to be in a position to be able to accept and use it. Even drug users or ex-users are in no better position to help.

Chris: 'It's horrible to see people like that – completely lost – and you want to help but you can't. It's funny how other people cannot really help you. You have to do it yourself.'

When the user has begun the adjustment process and is leaving the subculture to enter fully outside society, then not only is the process itself to be considered but the guilt and other feelings that arise from taking on or acknowledging the different norms and values of straight society.

Tammy: 'I feel bad about what I used to do. When you are using, you are so selfish. You have to be. You steal and you think there is nothing wrong with that, nothing wrong with stealing if you can keep your habit going. Now when I look back, I can't believe the things I used to do.'

The whole adjustment process can be painful. To change from the drugs lifestyle may demand the user leave behind past friends and acquaintances. For users whose circle consists of only other users, coming off may mean leaving behind almost everyone.

Judd: 'I learnt to take more responsibility for myself and found new friends. Now my friends are straight and I know twenty to thirty people. I had to cut many people out of my life, people who used to mean a hell of a lot to me. But I can't afford to be with them, to be with junkies. Hale is my brother but he's a junkie. I don't talk to him. I just say hello, and that's it.'

The hardest people to leave behind might be spouses or partners. However if two users are living together it is very difficult for either or both of them to come off, if they continue to stay together. Two users together will mutually reinforce each other.

Lisa: 'Tommy would look at me and I would look at him, and I knew he was thinking about having a shot. I would nod and he would nod. He would say that we had been off a day. Straightway he would begin to fidget and I could see he was desperate for a shot.'

The situation is even more difficult if the client's partner is still using. Even if the client has stopped, seeing a partner use can bring back the feelings of ambivalence.

Lisa: 'Craig was having a £10 shot and the needle was in his arm. He asked if I wanted a bit. I said "No!", but was thinking, should I or shouldn't I. He said if I wanted some I had better say, as he was about to bang the whole lot up his arm. I told him that I didn't want any.'

Nature of coming off

Coming off is not necessarily a single episode event or a single process. Heroin users may come off several times and this will have its effect. After a time, the idea of going through the process yet again can lead to high anxiety, and the user finding it harder to come off.

Dean: 'It's all right for Beth, she has only come off her habit once, but I've had to come off several times. It doesn't get easier with time.'

The opposite is also possible. The user might remember that coming off was not as difficult as portrayed by other users or the media in general. This can lead to a positive frame of mind that aids the whole process. Coming off is about coming off a whole life-style. Even when the user has stopped using drugs, this does not necessarily mean the life-style has stopped.

Rachel: 'I got these things from town. I can't walk out of a shop without taking something – stupid things, which I don't really want.'

Being part of a definite life-style might have other aspects that are difficult to end.

Tammy: 'It's difficult to go into a shop when you have stopped using and have to pay for things. I picked up some mascara and found it cost four pounds. Previously I always used to lift it. It's hard when you are used to new clothes and the best of things, only to find you cannot afford them.'

At times there can be a curious interlinking of coming off drugs and coming off the life-style.

Bruce: 'Even during the periods when I kicked the habit, I still committed crimes to have more than enough money – money I never needed. I think even then I realized that crime was just another habit as well. It released boredom and I also gained some kind of rush of adrenalin at the time of actually committing the crime. I think 90 per cent of the crimes I have taken part in, when I wasn't into drugs, have been through boredom.'

Although crime may appear to be a certain form of behaviour, yet so much more is entailed. There are the attitudes and beliefs, the way that users relate to themselves.

Jane: 'You get smarter with every new trick that's played on you. I had packets of sugar that cost me ten pounds because I never thought to check them. You get to be a really good con. You'll steal and cheat. You cry a bit, but that's to the outside world: inside, it's as if you are made of stone.'

To illustrate something more of what clients might have to face, we should look at the example of those clients who work in the sex industry.

Sex work

Sex work may have started as new and unknown territory, and one requiring to be learnt.

Maggie: 'I worked in a sauna for three months and couldn't believe it! One of the girls had to take me aside and tell me what "extras" were. I used to say at first that there were no extras. At the end of the week I asked where was my money for the massage, but there was no pay for that. You only got paid for doing the extras.'

The ways in which a drug user can make money to pay for drugs are limited, as only those jobs which pay well will suffice. Crime, sex work and dealing are the principal options. Most drug users will have to force themselves to take up one or more of these options.

Cherie: 'I'm a hopeless shoplifter and I couldn't do cheque books, and I don't believe in house-breaking. So the way I see it, down the Shore – it's a business. He gets what he wants and I'm getting what I need.'
Me: 'So it's just a business.'
Cherie: 'My pussy's like a typewriter: it's a business appliance.'

Apart from getting money for drugs, there is the vicious circle of users having to get drugs in order to be able to do sex work. If they have no drugs, then they cannot work. The drug may be alcohol, but for heroin users it is usually heroin.

Lisa: 'I'm withdrawing and I can't go down the Shore to make money. If I'm not using, then I can't go down there.'

When the drug user is coming off drugs, this often means having to stop sex work. The expectation of others is that having stopped taking street drugs, the user will stop sex work.

Lisa: 'I went down the Shore. I haven't been down there for ages. One guy offered me £60 to go with him, but I couldn't. I felt sick at the idea of it. I don't think I could do it now. I went down there because I was that desperate for money.'

What may not be so obvious is that sex workers can constitute another small subculture, and the drug user involved may experience difficulties in pulling away from it. Prejudice against such work makes sex workers band together, to some extent, and facing the world without this feeling of solidarity can be daunting.

Cherie: 'I haven't worked down the Shore for a couple of years, but some people treat me as if I still was. Men can think you are easy. At least when I was working, I got paid for it. I am always scared that I will meet someone I met down the Shore, and everyone would know what I used to do.'

Thus some drug users have to cope with drug use, the drug life-style and also the way of life resulting from the life-style. As counsellors, we have to be able to understand all three aspects of clents' lives.

MEDICATION

Prescribed drugs and coming off

Frequently, users talk about coming off drugs when what they really mean is being placed on prescribed substitute drugs. This confusion is sometimes reflected in the outlook of drug workers and medical services. Heroin users might be placed on a substitute drug with a view to helping them come off heroin, to stabilize their life-style, to help them lead a less risky life-style or to ensure that there is a less risky life-style for others. Because these different overall aims can overlap, confusion may arise.

Another source of confusion concerns the nature of substitute prescribing. The idea, originally, was that the user who wanted to come off drugs would be put off by the discomfort of withdrawal pains. If the user could be helped with withdrawal pains then this would help the user come off drugs. However to eliminate withdrawal pains completely it is necessary to substitute the street drug by an equivalent amount of prescribed cross-tolerant drug. For opioid drugs such as heroin, the usual substitute drug is methadone which is equally physically addictive. So substitute prescribing does not of itself reduce personal addiction, unless the user is prepared to go through withdrawal pains. Prescribing is not a treatment nor a cure for drug addiction. A user who has been placed on substitute prescription is likely to have as great an addiction as when addicted to street drugs.

Richard: 'When you are using methadone you don't want to use smack. But the methadone is still a substitute and I found it worse to come off. Part of it was I thought methadone was the answer but there is no magic pill. I realize that now.'

So both the drug user and the counsellor have to be realistic about medication. It does not necessarily result in any sudden behavioural change. However it might give time for the user to begin to work through different issues.

Advantages of being prescribed

There are some advantages in prescribing. Though it is not really treatment, drug users may think it to be so and this may help them to look at their situation in a more positive light, which is generally helpful. Another possible advantage is that it provides the user with a regular supply of drugs. This in turn allows the user to begin to exert more control and self-control, useful preparation for coming off. Also being prescribed allows the prevention of possible withdrawals and life is more ordered.

When on medication the user is generally placed on a reducing regime, and brought off heroin over a matter of weeks or months. Being on medication and managing to reduce opioid use opens the avenue to positive feedback from the doctor, which in turn helps the user. Doctors can be a source of support.

The final advantage of substitute medication is simply that the user sees a way of coming off drug use. There is a final end to the process. There may be many underlying difficulties as to why the user has continued to use, but it is hard to address these difficulties until off drugs. The initial step has to be made.

Craig: 'You need someone to help tell you what to do. Coming off by yourself is a load of rubbish.'

The sharing of the process of coming off drugs is helpful, as long as helpers realize that they will be subjected to client distress.

Drawbacks

Firstly, a geat number of users come off without a substitute drug, they merely decrease their drug intake. Indeed, doctors sometimes forget that users can come off without their help, and do not discuss the possibility with patients of their coming off without medication. This reinforces the subcultural fears about coming off, as coming off is seen to require the use of substitute drugs and medical help. Yet offers of medication merely interfere with the user's ability to come off.

Beth: 'It's best to come off on nothing. Methadone just strings it out.'

Paula: 'I was on a gram a day and came off on nothing. I went through cold turkey to prove to my parents I could do it.'

Apart from the achievement of going cold turkey, an achievement recognized by other drug users, the very unpleasantness of the experience does have its good side.

Bill: 'Come off and have nothing, that's the only way. It means you remember your withdrawals. That's why I would not want to do it again, use again.'

And it is not just having substitutes that can be the problem. As many people find out when stopping smoking cigarettes, it can be easier to stop altogether than to cut down. Offering substitutes not merely confuses the picture but make it more difficult, as few drug users are going to turn down the chance of taking free opioids.

Skip: 'I'll have to come off without anything. I can't cut down. I'll have to come right off.'

Prescribing may seem the obvious thing for doctors to do, but this comes from many having a belief in the power of drugs. Drugs are more than chemicals. To help, doctors have to have some idea of what they mean to the user, as well as their drug effects.

Gloria: 'I wanted the methadone in liquid form as you are less likely to sell it compared with the tablets. And methadone is better to take than DFs. I wouldn't sell my methadone, I don't let anyone know I get it. It lasts for a long time, one dose. You go to sleep, no trouble. You don't need sleepers; I wouldn't like to get into them. And methadone still acts after you wake up; your eyes are still pinned the next day.'

The main difficulty lies in the different perceptions of doctors and drug users regarding prescribed medication. To the former, it is a means of treatment, whereas the latter views medication as either a means of coming off, or a means of continuing drug use or as a source of income.

Tina: 'Rita sells her Physeptone on Tuesday for £30, she sells them on Thursday for £30, and sells them for £40 on Saturday. That's £100 a week, and that's besides what she makes working down the Shore.'

Another major difficulty is the relationship between the doctor and user. The doctor might be interested in getting the patient off heroin but the user might be more interested in continuing drug use and using prescribed drugs, rather than street drugs, for various reasons such as their easy availability, they do not have to pay for them, the regularity of supply and the idea that taking prescribed drugs is socially acceptable.

Thus the doctor and user may have quite separate aims, one wanting an end to the illegal drug use and the other to be allowed to continue that use. If this is the case, then it is likely to lead to problems. And these problems are seldom merely confined to drug user and doctor, but indirectly affect all drug users.

Dean: 'I know people who are being maintained and their dosage is not being reduced at all. What makes it worse is that they are not real addicts, they only think they are.'

The obvious answer might be to get the user and doctor to come to some proper working relationship but there are snags in this idea. Doctors may not have had much training in illegal drug use and the training and information they receive might be highly medicalized.

Giselle: 'The doctor didn't understand. He said that by taking heroin I was trying to kill myself. I was taking heroin merely to feel normal.'

The doctor is placed in the role of the expert, but drug users see themselves as the experts on the use of illegal drugs. The result can be a confusion of roles, of perceptions and expectations.

The user and doctor relationship

The normal doctor patient relationship is one where the power lies with the doctor. Doctors are the ones who know best about what is wrong with the patient, they are the ones who tell the patient what should be done. The patient believes in the doctor and tends to act accordingly. However with drug users, this setup may well not be the case. Many doctors are uncertain or feel unsure when faced with illegal drug use.

Giselle: 'The doctor said he was going to cure me by Friday. I told him, "You must be joking!".' I know better than him what should be done. After all, it's my habit.'

Users will suggest or even tell the doctor what is needed. The suggestions are not always misplaced and can be used beneficially.

Rachel: 'They should bring people off slowly. They should bring people down when they are ready, not force them. If doctors force you, then you panic.'

Coming off is sometimes seen as a question of arithmetical reduction, quite separate from the person who is taking the drug. This misses the underlying axiom of drug use: drug use is the intimate fusion of drugs and the persons who use them. If there were no human factors involved, help would be easy and problems negligible.

Annette: 'I was on a reducing dose of methadone starting at 40 mls and was down to 5 mls a day. I was on that for ages, scared to stop completely.'

We might ask why drug users and their ideas receive little serious consideration. Patients giving advice to doctors, rather than the other way round, is seen by doctors as the wrong way of conducting patient consultations. The doctor is seen as the person to take control, even though drug use is behaviour over which the user should take responsibility. Furthermore, if the user feels powerless then the actions of the doctor can be counterproductive.

Richard: 'I didn't go to the Clinic today as I felt intimidated. The doctor kept talking about me cutting down the DFs, and I would agree. But by the next week I would tell him it was impossible. I was having panic attacks and could not face cutting down.'

Yet some doctors will listen to drug using patients, and it has to be said that there is no guarantee that drug users will get things right.

Richard: 'I didn't realize that I depended on the methadone. I found I could keep going all day, so I told the doctor I wanted off it. But in a couple of days I cracked up completely.'

So the relationship is not simple. Moreover, the whole of prescribing can become a game, and a game not played necessarily according to the doctor's rules. For drug users, getting a prescription can be another form of scoring, an activity played according to the normal subcultural behaviour rules.

Doctor C: 'Layna is very convincing. She puts on her little girl lost look and it's very appealing. And she seems to be talking so rationally. It is only afterwards, when she has got her script, that you wonder what's going on.'

In the long run, a measure of two directional information and discussion is helpful and supportive for patients. If this does not happen then the attitudes of both drug users and doctors is likely to be the cause. Doctors may dislike drug users, even before they have been seen, and drug users in turn may take a negative view of doctors.

Annette: 'Doctors are not interested in addiction as it is not an illness and it is self-inflicted.'
Dean: 'Doctors stereotype you. Once they have you down as an addict on your file, that's it.'

For counsellors, these difficulties are not irrelevant, as medication may be termed treatment, but it can also be part of the problem.

Relationship reviewed

It might be thought that the situation as described so far has been unfair to doctors, who have to deal with often unruly and demanding patients. The necessity to doubt what the user patient says, to check up on what he does and to take precautions against possible theft, threats and violence, can make normal doctor-patient relationships difficult at times. There is often a lack of honesty between doctor and patient, as both are working to different rules.

Royce: 'My doctor said to me, "Honestly, Royce, I can't take it any more. You tell so many lies." I told him it wasn't personal; it was just that I wanted more tablets.'

Drug user dishonesty is seen as being common and part of the reason for the difficulty in working with drug users. Yet a lack of honesty can also characterize the working of doctors.

Mary: 'I tried to get on a script for methadone and was told it was impossible. But I know people who are on them.'

Dean: 'I've been told you cannot be put on a maintenance script. So why are some folks' dosage not being reduced at all? What makes it worse is that they are not real addicts, they only think they are.'

Nevertheless, the relationship between doctor and drug user is important, as successful help for drug users may depend on it. Both partners in a doctor–patient relationship have their different aims and different beliefs. One of the beliefs held by doctors is that helping a user come off drugs depends largely on the drug used. What tends to be ignored is the mental aspect of the drug prescribed, as viewed by the user. What is best may be what the patient thinks is best.

Annette: 'Methadone worked for me. It has worked in the past. I've come off using it.'

Danny: 'DFs don't work for me because I don't think they will. It might seem stupid but they are no good for me.'

At times drug users will take control completely to bring themselves off, as they do not see doctors giving adequate help and not allowing them control.

Giselle: 'I came off by using methadone. I bought a bottle on the streets for £10.'

The practice of prescribing

As can be seen there is no simple answer as to what is best, even though doctors and clinics tend to favour simplicity, as in the use of just one substitute drug or ignoring user requests as to what they say they want. It is often assumed that the user is physically addicted, when in fact there might not be such addiction or the user might not even be using an opioid drug. These are not minor considerations because the prescribing of drugs can turn someone into a physically addicted person.

A further problem is to estimate the amount of opioid that the user is taking. If the user is not prescribed enough then there will be withdrawal pains. On the other hand, if more than the required amount is prescribed, the user will end up with an even greater physical addiction.

The prescribing of substitute drugs is difficult in that they work only with the cooperation of the user. Often the user will act in certain ways not because they are chaotic or manipulative persons, but because that is where the individual is along his or her drug career. This makes any work with the user difficult as the doctor has to estimate the reality of what the user is saying.

Josie: 'Tina was at the doctor's. She would have been looking for something, something to get her stoned. She hasn't got a habit; she just wants something for a stone. I know, I've done it myself.'

And there is the worry that the user might not be in the right state of mind to be able to use a prescription properly. Users may abuse their prescribed drugs in a variety of ways. One way is to include prescribed drugs in the total of drugs used. Thus street drugs are still taken, on top of the drugs prescribed.

Rachel: 'I was taking my Physeptone (methadone) in the morning, then a gram of smack in the afternoon and a gram at night.'

Faced with such behaviour there is always the temptation to see it as some product of the patient's personality rather than an indication of where drug users are in their drug careers, how far along the road of drug use they have gone.

Prescribing and user options

There are numerous alternative ways of abusing the prescribing process. The prescription can be sold for money or for drugs. The prescription can be altered to obtain greater amounts of drugs, the prescribed drugs can be exchanged for other street drugs. It is hardly surprising that drug users are seen as potentially trouble.

This view is reinforced by their unpopularity in surgeries or clinics where they can frighten other patients, fail to observe the practice or clinic rules, and be threatening or embarrassing. Under the circumstances, doctors and users often do not get on well, especially at first. The mutual suspicion on both sides may prevent the formation of mutual acceptance and a useful working relationship. If things do not go well then the user can be cut off medication or taken off the practice list. This in turn can have possibly undesired consequences.

Maggie: 'You go round to your doctor, but if he won't help you then you go round to the dealer for a packet; your pains are that bad.'

Robbie: 'If you are cut off, then you go back to using. You build yourself up, you are expecting your medication, and then, if you don't get it, well, you have to have something.'

However, despite all the tribulations, being prescribed can be useful if the relationship is right, as the regular contact can help the user. This usefulness arises from a realization that once they have got beyond a mutual preoccupation with drugs, they can interact well together.

Nicole: 'I changed doctors because my new doctor was offering methadone. I now know it was a mistake. My old doctor, he would never give me that, but I could speak to him and he would listen. He would take time and I would feel better afterwards. My new doctor gives me the prescription, hands it over, but he does not talk to me and I don't think he wants me near him. That's not what I want. I want to be able to speak to my doctor.'

What has to be remembered is that drug users bring not only their present but their past with them to the helping situation. Furthermore, their past can be such that it can initially get in the way of good relationships, a drawback that is seldom improved by the fact that they are taking drugs. However, once the preliminary stages of the relationship with a doctor have been successfully negotiated, which might mean there has been no irredeemable disaster, then there is the chance that further good work can be done.

5 STAYING OFF

RESTARTING DRUG USE

Introduction

The user who has stopped drug use is likely at some point to restart. These restarts or relapses are all part of the overall process of coming off. Sometimes they can occur very soon after stopping, so we might say the person was never really off drugs, as there were drugs still in the user's body. This is not a helpful perspective. If a person has stopped, he or she has stopped, and much more than drugs is involved in the process. Even being off a short time is an achievement.

Ronnie: 'Three days off, that was as long as I could last.'

Such attempts to stop should be seen in total context, as being off for three days and not as failure to come off. Drugs workers often get caught up with their concern about relapses and see them as very decisive points, and as failures. Unfortunately, negative messages can convert a relapse into more than it really is, and actually make a relapse permanent. Perhaps it is helpful to bear in mind an observation by Tina.

Tina: 'I've come off before and I'll come off again. You know me, Paul.'

In fact relapses can seem almost casual in their occurrence as they can happen so easily. We have to remember that the outlook of users may differ from those of drug workers. They can start up again quite easily and that may not particularly bother them.

Josie: 'I've been off five days, except for last night. Well, Tricia couldn't get her hit so I gave her it. She gave me three dike, and I took them. You would have done the same, wouldn't you? Anyone would.'

This being the case, it might not take very much intervention to prevent a relapse by the drug user.

Josie: 'I'm glad you came down as Dick was talking about getting a packet. That's why I was about to go out. If you hadn't come to the house, I'd have ended up going out for a shot.'

Restarting can be casual or it can appear dramatic when linked with other life incidents. It may be easy for the user to link external circumstances with restarting personal drug use, but we should also remember that for this to happen, the user must want it to happen.

David: 'I was OK until Roxanne was murdered down the Shore. I had seen her only the previous night. Then the drug use started up again.'

Drug users can be very good at rationalizing their behaviour so that it seems external to themselves, as if they have no control over what they do. This does not mean that external events are irrelevant, but they are never a determining factor.

Acceptance of relapses

The fact that there are likely to be relapses is understood by drug users, who accordingly have their own perceptions and might make their own preparations for such eventualities.

Tina: 'I don't intend to use, but I'm keeping a set of works just in case I should ever need them.They're in the back of the drawer.I keep them where I can't see them, so I won't be tempted to have a shot.'

This might be seen as little more than an intent to start using again, or as being resigned to failure from the very start, but in fact it denotes a realistic approach. One of the difficulties in the whole process of relapsing is that the equation of drug use will shift once a user has stopped taking drugs, and the balance moves so the user is no longer so keen to stay off drugs. On stopping, the drawbacks of using will appear less as the user begins to feel better.

Rachel: 'When you come out of hospital you feel fit and well, so you think one shot will not do any harm. So you have one and you feel great. But the next day you want the same feeling.'

There is a big build-up to the decision to stop and then less and less interest is shown in the process of staying off, both by the ex-user and by others. The greater the time elapsed, the less the interest. Others may show interest if the ex-user has been off a few days, but after a few months any interest is greatly diminished. The same thing happens with a person who has stopped smoking. Everyone is very supportive for the first couple of weeks, but then their interest may disappear. Thus, for no obvious reason, the process of coming off tends to weaken and become less meaningful with time.

Further changes in the equation

Perhaps the chief complaint of those who have stopped using drugs is that of boredom. Part of the boredom arises from the lack of activity.

Lisa: 'I'm bored, nothing to do. All I do is think about my withdrawal pains.'

But boredom is in the head of the user: it is how the person is feeling. Even continuous activity will not necessarily banish boredom. So ex-drug users are likely to use drugs to change how they feel.

Barbara: 'Richard says that he is bored, but everyone gets bored from time to time. Housewives get bored, but they don't jag up.'

So for some ex-users, boredom is a state which inclines them to contemplate renewed drug use.

Rachel: 'I'm all right after I've stopped, but it's after two or three weeks when I'm bored that I want to start again.'

And while relapsing may appear very significant to outsiders, to drug users it means very much less. The change in behaviour represents a swing back in the equation of drug use, and perhaps a very small swing. Relapse shows the continuing ambivalence the user has about both coming off and staying off.

Maggie: 'I'm bored. I'll probably start up again for something to do.'

So it is not merely the boredom that is the problem but the accompanying knowledge that drug use is a way of ending this state. And it need not be the drug effects alone that counteract such boredom.

Richard: 'I realize now that I actually enjoyed having to get the money for dope. It kept my brain employed.'

Being a drug user is a life-style that has many different positive aspects. For those clients who have come off drugs, this certainly can be how they see it, in retrospect. Counsellors are best advised not to argue against such views but to concentrate on the positive perspectives of the client's present and future.

Boredom reconsidered

Boredom might seem a trifling state to concern us, yet it is one that is frequently mentioned by users after stopping drug use. This state can vary in intensity and we should bear in mind that it can verge into depression. Part of the problem arises from the regained ability to feel emotions more fully and having to deal with them without drugs. But we should also realize that the nature of dependency leads to low self-esteem, a lack of assertiveness and a growing inability to handle stress and feeling low. Boredom might appear to represent a state of generally being fed up; it can also cover a mixture of negative feelings and attributes. Boredom of itself does not determine a restart of drug use. Underlying feelings can lead to a desire to use drugs.

Bev: 'Jessie was off, then started using once a week. Now she has a thirty quid a day habit. She wanted her habit back.'

It is easier to be positive in the presence of friends. But with drug users true friends are not so common.

Jimmy: 'When you are on the stuff, you would rip off anyone. You have no friends and you know only junkies.'
Jenny: 'I've no friends, only acquaintances. I only know junkies, and they are not friends. Well, I have Tina as a friend, but I'm lonely.'

Counsellors have to be aware of what clients really want, as opposed to what they say they want, such as simply complaining about being bored. This does not mean clients should not be believed, merely, that at times what clients say merits close examination. On further investigation, clients will admit their uncertainty as to what exactly they do want. We have to remember that there is always a pressure for clients to say what they think counsellors or others want them to say.

Reinforcement

The chief cause of restarting is that of reinforcement. There are some things that are more likely to set the user taking drugs again. They do not cause the restarting but make it more probable. Ex-users can fight against the pressures to start up again and will do so. Restarting drug use is not a sudden action brought on by external pressure, as part of the pressure is already in the mind of the ex-user. What may seem like a sudden decision to use is in fact the result of many micro-decisions, all resting in the context of how the person was feeling in relation to drug use and self. In the following example, what seems like a chance accident can be seen as being what the client actually wanted, even if the result was later regretted.

Rachel: 'I was really annoyed that I had started again. I was feeling shitey, so had to have something. I would have been alright, but had to go into town to get Easter eggs. I had to go in. I went into the pub and met someone there who said, "There's some really good stuff about", but I said I didn't want any smack. But that put it in my mind. I went out with my brother-in-law and we went for a drink. I thought I would not want anything, but later I did have some. If it hadn't been for meeting that guy, I would have been okay.'

A simple reinforcer might be the local area where drugs are easily available.

Chris: 'The environment, it's like a barman being an alcoholic. The stuff is always available.'

Again, it has to be emphasized that reinforcers do not determine a restart of drug use, only make it more likely. Users are well aware of the pressures and can counteract them.

Lisa: 'I'm trying to come off, I'm doing my best, but you can't come off when the stuff's all around.'
Maggie: 'I did! You can if you really want to.'

The presence of other users and especially dealers living nearby is enough to provide further thoughts about drugs, and these are likely to be followed by actual drug use.

Tina: 'I was doing OK until Gary moved in close. It makes it worse when you keep bumping into folk who ask you when you came off, and then tell you there is barry brown gear about. Once it's in your head, that's it. You have to be awfully determined to stay off.'

The drug subculture is centred on drugs, their buying, selling and exchange, along with information about this illegal market. Thus offers to those who have stopped illegal drug use are common, simply because that is what drug users do. Of course, other users might want to justify their continuing drug use and try to convince themselves that it is impossible to come off, according to the subcultural belief of 'once a junkie, always a junkie'. Those who come off drugs are not so popular in that they reinforce the user's low self-esteem. They show it is indeed possible to stop drug use, and that users who want to come off but have not, can be considered to have failed.

Tina: 'I think I'm getting back into it. It's difficult when someone comes to the door and asks you if you want to go halves on a packet.'

An even stronger reinforcement comes from actually being present when people are using. For most users newly off this is likely to prove too great a reinforcement to resist.

Tina: 'I went to Fiona's, but there were people fixing in there. I had to walk out. I was able to walk out all right, but if I had stayed around for any time then I would have been offered and would have taken some. I don't want to use, I'm not going to use, yet there is a part of me that still wants it.'

Reinforcement might seem as the result of external pressure forcing the drug user to behave in a certain way, but we should see it rather as an interaction, as pressure on a vulnerable person, bearing in mind that the user has a role in the process.

Tina: 'I'm really mad with myself. I was in bed at five o'clock and hadn't had anything. Then Jenny came up to the flat and was asking how I was. I didn't want anything, but she kept on and on, her face hanging on the floor, and then she said she wanted a packet. I said I would look after her bairn and she could go for it, but she wanted me to go. Finally, I got a taxi. I was ill afterwards, shaking and shivering – it must have been a bad shot. And I never wanted it anyway.'

Part of the difficulty for many drug users is simply being able to say, 'No'. This has been the slogan for attempts to stop illegal drug use, but it overlooks the fact that many users will not be able to say this. Their low self-esteem, their past life experiences and their role in the drug subculture make it very difficult to refuse another user. Even when users try to refuse, they can be ambivalent and this ambivalence is picked up by other users. Thus users have to train themselves to be resolute.

Chris: 'I'll just say no, completely. No, period. I will not get involved, as it is the only way.'

There can be positive reinforcement, people can be supportive, but unfortunately, most of the support comes before the person has stopped, rather than afterwards when the need is usually greater. In fact, constant reinforcement is needed, and the people to give it.

Bridget: 'Charlie decided to stop. Everyone said how well he had been doing and kept patting him on the back. But when he had stopped then no-one bothered about him. He said he might as well be using. He wants pats on the back all the time.'

Further difficulties
The user generally has to take action to prevent restarting drug use. Drug users are not likely to be very helpful, partly because they find the user who is coming off or who is off as an uncomfortable reminder that coming off is possible.

Ken: 'It is difficult when people are offering you stuff. I met a guy at the bottom of the tower and I told him I was trying to come off. He said, "That's great!". Then he said there was some good stuff round the corner and did I want to come for some.'

We might see sabotaging a user coming off as a cynical ploy, but we also have to appreciate that, for others, coming off can be an indirect attack not just on user ideology but on user identity. What also has to be understood is that clients trying to come off or stay off heroin do not react as counsellors might expect – with annoyance at the continuing user. Clients still react in accordance with subcultural ways, and so feel bad about refusing any offer.

Tina: 'I met Petra and she asked me if I was through the guilt bit. I said I still felt guilty when someone offered me, and I said "No".'

Even lesser intrusions than offers of drugs can affect the user. For instance, drug agencies might expect those who have recently come off to mix with those who are still using illegal drugs or prescribed drugs. This can be unhelpful, as the user who has come off is likely to be adversely influenced.

Giselle: 'I only have to see another junkie on the street and see their eyes. You can tell that they've had something. That makes you want to have some too, even though you know it's going to make you feel worse in the long run.'

The situation is perhaps more complex than might at first appear. The question as to why the ex-user might want a shot on seeing others under the influence can mirror reasons why that person started drug use. Thus there can be feelings of being excluded and even rejected when not using. So pressure to restart can come from the ex-user rather than users.

Bev: 'I haven't had a thing over the last five days, except that day I had Temgesics because of my toothache. Not using really hasn't bothered me. I have seen junkies in the street and it hasn't bothered me, except when I see someone stoned. That's because I feel a bit jealous.'

In time the user who has stopped can resist such reinforcement, however strong it might be.

Maggie: 'I was in a dealer's house recently and it didn't bother me. I even helped someone with a hit and he asked me if I wanted a bit and I said no.'

Drug users are generally aware of reinforcers and the fact that once the idea of drug use is in a user's mind, then it is difficult to dislodge. One important fact to bear in mind is that talking about drug use is just one way of putting the idea back into full consciousness. The idea that counselling should consist of talking about drug use can be counterproductive and actually worsen the situation.

Long-term non-use

Of course there is a big difference between having just stopped and feeling vulnerable, and having been off a long time. This is not merely a question of time having elapsed, it is a question of how much inner resistance the ex-user has. Such resistance can be built up through forms of desensitization, of limited exposure to reinforcing situations. This is done by ex-users without them fully understanding what they are doing.

Giselle: 'I went into the pub and half the people were stoned. It was a wee test.'

Tina: 'I went to Muirhouse to see a friend, not for a shot. In fact I went past all the dealers' houses and didn't stop. I felt quite proud of myself.'

In this way clients can slowly build up their self-esteem and powers of resistance by allowing themselves exposure to reinforcers, and the fact that they can be resisted is one way of helping the user stay off.

STAYING OFF

Early days

Once the user has stopped taking drugs then life without drugs begins. This is not easy. The reinforcers do not go away, but now they are managed. This still requires ongoing determination, as any single lapse can put the whole process back.

Tina: 'See, when someone says what about a shot, then even if you say no, it eats into your brain. You are aching for it, you think about it – should I, shouldn't I?'

The cravings, the preoccupation with drugs, initially, can be at times almost overwhelming. It helps if the user is occupied in some way to cut down time which can be given to thinking about drugs.

Rachel: 'I've been off a few weeks now. There is no morning I don't wake up and think about a hit.'

The reinforcement need not be direct. There can be a variety of factors that remind the ex-user of drugs.

Lisa: 'Do you know I haven't thought of drugs all day. It is only now and then, when I look at the trackmarks on the back of my hands that I remember.'

Slowly matters do improve. Staying off drugs is a constant battle at first, moving from withdrawals to cravings, from the arm to the head. A lot depends on the user's feelings and perceptions, and these should not be ignored. After all, it is the user's battle more than it is the counsellor's. Allowing client's belief in their feelings, and thus in themselves, is helpful.

Spike: 'I feel different this time. The last time I was off I didn't feel like this. I feel different, better this time. I think I'll be able to stay off.'

The lack of pain, the absence of anxiety about pain and the hassles of the drugs life-style produce a sense of well-being.

Lisa: 'I woke this morning and there were no withdrawal pains. I jumped out of bed. I wouldn't have been able to do that a week ago.'

Being off drugs does not eliminate difficulties, but these tend to lessen over time. Finally, the effect of heroin is the same as when it was taken for the very first time: it is unpleasant.

Sharon: 'I admit I did have a shot but it did nothing for me. David was saying it would make me feel great but it did nothing except make me feel sick.'

Sometimes the problems with specific drug concerns may be less important than other factors. Again, the full context of clients' lives have to be taken into account, as matters other than drugs may be of greater importance.

Cherie: 'Some people make taking drugs their life. They say that it gives them a purpose and a meaning to their life. It's terrible that they have to do that to get any purpose in life.'

So the problem moves from that of a life with drugs to simply the problem of life itself and how to cope.

Aftermath

What is not always obvious to drug takers is that intravenous use has its own legacy, even after the drug use has been ended. Part of this legacy is that of vein scarring or trackmarks. These marks are constant reminder of past use and can be a source of possible embarrassment.

Tina: 'See these marks, bloody disgusting, eh? When you're using you don't notice them. Now I have to hide them when I go into town on the bus.'

Bev: 'It's not so good now. It's not so good as I have to wear long sleeves even though it's summer to cover the trackmarks.'

Wherever possible, positive steps should be taken by users to make themselves feel better. For instance, improving personal appearance is one way of producing a better frame of mind.

Lisa: 'I'll have to go to the dentist to get my teeth seen to. Everyone used to say how they used to shine; they were really white. And now look at them.'

Another legacy of the long-term injecting of street drugs with its adulterants can be blocked veins and poor circulation.

Jane: 'Feel my hands, they are freezing. And they are really painful; I can hardly move them. Can you rub them for me? After they have been rubbed or slapped, they are easier to move.'

Other outcomes can be infections such as hepatitis and HIV, the latter being a separate topic in itself. What may not be quite so apparent is the loss of identity when the drug taker has stopped needle use.

Bev: 'It's funny waking up in the morning and not having to put a needle in my arm. I feel lost without any works, not the same person.'

Thus it is worth talking through with clients who are off drugs their past injecting use and their current thoughts and feelings.

Loss and staying off

Being off drugs leaves a hole in the life of the user. It is not just the lack of drugs but everything that drugs and the drug life-style entails. This includes the effect the loss of drugs has on the person as a person.

Bev: 'This woman told me to fill in a job application. I did that and gave it back to her. She said I had only filled in the name and address. I said it was all I could fill in. There was really nothing else.'

Whatever may be the different effects of stopping drug use, there is always a sense of loss.

Bart: 'When I came off I felt as if there was something missing, something was not there.'

If there is a loss then the person should be allowed to grieve. Time is needed because there is not merely a loss for the user, but a loss that is accompanied by strong feelings.

Josie: 'All those years, and they have been wasted.'

Such time wasted is time that could have been employed differently. Whether it could have been used better very much depends on the attitude taken to past drug use.

Sandy: 'I don't regret getting into drugs at all; I enjoyed it. But you regret the waste of time, or the time you have missed out on, time when you could have been into other things.'

Part of the difficulty is that the world moves on, and stopping drug use means that users may find themselves behind their contemporaries, not having achieved what others may have gained.

Renee: 'When you have stopped, you are afraid to meet other people. People who were no better than you at school, now you feel inferior to them.'

Unfortunately, these matters are seldom talked through. Outsiders think that such talk indicates the ex-user is contemplating restarting drug use. Yet grief has to be worked through, and for those who have come off, there is likely to be a period when grief reactions can be observed.

Sarah: 'I don't see anyone nowadays. I keep out of town, as if I saw people I knew and they asked me to go for a coffee then I would be tempted. Perhaps after a few months I could handle it and would not be tempted. But I know I would be – at the moment. And it is a boring life.'

There are a number of ideas embedded in the last quote, but the first thing is to see it in context. This is how Sarah felt at the time and it was not a permanent state. In time, ex-users begin to feel better and more positive.

Sarah (a few months later): 'Everything used to be boring, but it isn't really. I go skating and I've a holiday to look forward to.'

Boredom does not suddenly vanish, but it does tend to fade over time. However it can still re-emerge and this can happen after a considerable period. Here is a clear similarity with grief, which can reoccur long after the actual loss.

Changing over time
The whole process of coming off and staying off is a lengthy one. We have to realize that the process may not be an even one. There will be times when the user will restart using then come off, restart and come off once more.

Craig: 'You have to expect relapses, and often a relapse after three months after stopping. With time those relapses get less and less frequent.'

An important factor is how these relapses are viewed. If the user sees relapses as part of the whole process of coming off, then the user is less likely to continue using.

Thus we see the process of coming off and staying off drugs is not just a matter of stopping drug use. It also includes the active and positive behaviour by the ex-user. Stopping drug use is the lesser problem compared with the main task of staying off.

Annette: 'You have to make yourself a new life, a new life for yourself.'

Part of the process of making a new life is to leave behind what needs to be left behind. When a person comes off drugs, the drug use alone is left behind but not necessarily all the other aspects. Staying off drugs is not simply a passive state but one where new links have to be forged and old behaviour not merely stopped but buried.

Tina: 'See, I told Andrew about being on the dope and going down the Shore. He says that belongs to the past.'
Maggie: 'That's what Glyn said. I told him about working in a sauna and he was glad I told him, not someone else.'

Having stopped using drugs, there can be the tendency to see the main objective as having been reached and the work as having been done. In truth, the real work comes with the task of staying off drugs and reconstructing a life.

Normalizing
The user who has stopped taking drugs has to work at simply becoming used to normal life. Although it might seem that the ex-user is constantly under pressure to keep off drugs, he or she can appreciate that normalization is not necessarily an unpleasant process.

Tina: 'It's nice being in this pub, nice and a bit funny. It's funny sitting and talking to normal people. You forget there are people like that.'

However, the experiences of normal social interaction might seem strange and even intimidating to ex-users. They might require encouragement to participate in activities that others take for granted.

David: 'I went for a drink with my Dad and met a circle of friends I used to know. I was a bit shy, but it was as if I had never been away. I got on great.'

How ex-users are treated is crucial. Accepting behaviour can have a very positive effect on those who not only might have been poorly treated, but who do not think they should be well treated.

Mary: 'It was great! I met this couple and they took me out for a meal. I was treated like I've never been treated. Going out for a meal!'

It can take some time before the ex-user really begins to see the world as it is, rather than through the eyes of a drug user.

Tina: 'I sat in the pub and it was quite enjoyable. There were all sorts; a few business men and some old wifies, blokes playing pool. You forget that there are ordinary folk, that life's like that.'

With so much stress being placed on the lack of drug use, on a loss of drug effects, the user wants not merely the loss replaced but the replacement to be personally meaningful.

Positively staying off

Instead of staying off drugs being a chore, staying off can be a positive time, a time when good things can happen for the ex-user and acknowledgement made of what is happening. Indeed, the ability to get the most out of what is taking place, to see straight life as liberation and not as an inability to take drugs, adds to the chances of finding enjoyment and readjusting to ordinary life.

Lisa: 'I'm getting on better with my Mum now. Perhaps she was right in what she used to say.'

This time can be used to normalize relationships with those close, particularly the family. Usually such relationships are strained, if not completely broken, and former users have their part to play in righting them. It should be remembered that most families will be far more accepting of difficult behaviour than any stranger would.

Thelma: 'I get on better with Roy now, much better than when he was using drugs and I was giving him money. Now he comes when he wants to see me, not because he wants something. We have a much better relationship.'

The support of significant others is very helpful to the person trying to stay off. However this support may take some time to come as others will probably have felt let down in the past, an experience that can be wounding, especially if that experience has been repeated several times. However no amount of support can replace a determined attitude.

Maggie: 'That's the trouble, my Mum doesn't really believe me now. But then I didn't tell her I was on drugs until I was coming off.'

Tina: 'That's right. My Dad doesn't believe me so now I don't bother telling him how I am.'
Maggie: 'But there is no way I'm going back on it.'
Tina: 'You've done really well for yourself.'
Maggie: 'Once you've started climbing the ladder there's no going back, Tina. Once you're onto that first rung then it's easy. You keep going up and up.'
Tina: 'Well, I think my ladder is missing a few rungs.'

Sometimes old problems that involve the family have to be approached and resolved, or managed as best as possible. Not working on such difficulties usually means the client is more likely to go back to using, so counsellors have to ensure that such work is done.

Tina: 'I saw my Dad and told him how I felt. When I had calmed down a bit, I said I had been depressed and no-one had cared. He said, "You felt nobody loved you?". I said, "No, I had never received any love in the past".'

Although such work may be hard for clients, it is only possible when they are off drugs. Also, clients do feel so much better after starting the task of resolving old problems that it has a positive reinforcing effect.

Reinforcing positive feelings

Staying off, in time, develops into contentment and an increase in self-esteem. The past signs of drug use fade away and the ex-user becomes more a person in her or his own right.

Maggie: 'See my arms, I'm really pleased.'
Me: 'That's really good!'
Maggie: 'Barry, eh? See, that vein has healed completely. Feel them! These here are still thrombosed.'
Me: 'But they look OK. Nobody would know you had used.'

Another change which is a sign of becoming a person is the greater interest in sex. As sex is part of a person's identity, sexual feelings are an important signal of not merely being off but of maturing out of being a user. The situation is probably even more meaningful for female users.

Jane: 'I don't know whether you will understand it, but I feel both good and bad. Bad because I'm having my first period in three years and it's heavy. But I feel good because I feel a real woman once again. Of course when you're a junkie then you are not a woman, you're more an animal. Having a period not only means you are getting back to normal, but all the anxiety, all the irritability flows out of you.'

But for all ex-users there is a need to reassert personal identity, to come from behind the mask of the illegal drug user and to be oneself.

Meaning and staying off

Meaning comes not just from definition, it comes from what the experience feels like to the ex-user. Staying off is about individual ex-drug users experiencing a full return to feelings, having a constant battle against drug use, rediscovering the ability to be self-directed, and having self-belief.

Lynne (nine months after stopping drug use): 'I thought going straight, everything was going to be OK. But there is nothing.'
Lynne (eleven months after stopping): 'I know now that I will not use again. When Gordon was in prison for a year, I said I would not use again, but I knew some day I would. But it's different now.'
Lynne (fifteen months after stopping): 'I felt myself getting dragged back into it over the last few weeks, but I feel better now.'

There will be times when the going becomes tough and drug users have to be prepared to face such times. Counsellors must not assume that when the drug user has been off drugs for a couple of months, there is no further need to offer help.

New identity

Again it should be emphasized that coming off drugs is so much more than ending drug use. In extreme cases it is to do with the discovery or rediscovery of personal identity. Thus the identification or not with the term 'junkie' is not just an academic point.

Tina: 'I would not mind if they called me a junkie bastard because that is what I am. I haven't been off for long. But if after two or three months they call me a junkie bastard then I would tell them, "I'm an ex-addict now. I'm off drugs".'
Maggie: 'See, when I talk about junkies I still say "We". After being off for six months I still think of myself as a junkie.'

The entire process can take a long time and there is no obvious point when the term "ex-user" is no longer applicable. When off drugs, the struggle concens a negotiation away from the old identity.

Josie: 'I'm not really a junkie now, though I'm beginning to feel again as if I am. And I'm begining to like it, and I don't want that. I don't want to be a junkie.'

Identity is not just a matter of how ex-users see themselves, but the result of how clients are affected by being a drug user over the years.

Jane: 'I didn't know how on earth I was going to finance my habit. I had never stolen in my life, but a different Jane had emerged by this time, one that I never knew existed before, one who was cold and calculating. You get to be a really good con, you end up a blasphemous liar. You'll steal and cheat, you cry a lot but that's to the outside world. Inside it's as if you're made of stone.'

Other people will have their effect in the way they react to the drug user identity.

Maggie: 'Cliff said to me that he didn't sleep with junkies, and I said, "Well, you've been sleeping with one for the last few months".'

Part of the job of eliminating the 'junkie' identity is to be able to deal with drug use in a detached manner.

Maggie: 'Using again is like a book. You pick it up, look at the cover and say, "That's not for me". And you put it down. You're just not interested. Of course, that's five years I've been off. Tina, she's only been off two and a half years.'
Me: 'She says you're stronger, or at least have made yourself stronger.'
Maggie: 'That's it! I've made myself strong. Tina isn't so sure, but it doesn't bother me if people are using.'
Me: 'But Tina isn't so sure.'
Maggie: 'Yes, but she knows it. That's why she is wary about coming where people might be using.'

Even the task of talking to ex-users about themselves as people, divorced from all reference to drug taking, is likely to prove helpful. Clients find themselves as persons through interactions with others, but the whole process can be accelerated if they are allowed to reflect on these interactions and work through their feelings and thoughts with a counsellor.

Beyond ex-use

If a person is finally off drugs then it is important to be a person and not just an ex-user. This means that the individual has to engage in a search for personal identity, in order to finally throw off the ex-user role and to be seen by others as an ordinary man or woman.

Sarah: 'No-one sees me as myself; a mother, a wife, a junkie but never as myself.'

Although ex-users cannot necessarily change how others see them, they can re-define how they see the situation and themselves.

Jason: 'I've been off for a few years now and have no problems with drugs, about getting addicted again. Sometimes other people think I've got a problem, but I can work with that. Sometimes it's me who thinks I've got a problem and it's not so easy to dispel that myth ... if you understand what I mean.'

So the ex-user has to define the situation and this is not always simple. Just because someone is not using drugs does not necessarily qualify them as being off.

Marshall: 'I was off eighteen months but I realized that I wasn't really off. I was running away from it.'

People who have been into drugs such as heroin may be unsure whether they are really off. This is not just an abstract point for discussion, it is a sign that the person is still unsure of his or her feelings about drug use and so may still be vulnerable to relapse.

Ray: 'When I was in Fife, I was off for nine months and I used to say to myself, "Am I really off?".'

In fact there seems to be no obvious point in time when heroin users can be said to be totally themselves, partly because it depends on how they see themselves. It is easier to reject the drug user identity than to find a replacement.

Maggie: 'Once a junkie, always a junkie – that's a known fact. I would always class myself as a junkie. It's not nice to be a junkie, you're not a real person. You live for yourself when you are using. You forget how other people think and feel because you have forgotten yourself. You don't bother about people, all love leaves you. But junkies will deny this, they will say they do care. They are in a coccoon and don't want to get out. And they are always finding excuses.'

After many years of drug use it is difficult to get away from the drug role. The very term 'junkie' is significant as it encapsulates for users the different, anti-authority, minority group feeling, and legitimizes the feeling of being the outsider. As others may reinforce this idea, it takes a lot of work for some users to escape the label. So if we return to an earlier quote:

Jenny: 'I don't class myself as a junkie. No, I am a junkie – that was me kidding myself.'
Me: 'But what do you really feel? Do you feel yourself a junkie?'
Jenny: 'Everyone says I am.'
Me: 'And what do you say?'
Jenny: 'I don't know. I don't really think I am a junkie.'

What we understand here is not merely that Jenny is asking a question but she is working through a process of self-discovery and self-reinforcement, finding not just who she is but who she wants to be. Who a person is can be determined in part by what they do, so having something to do is important for ex-users.

Jane: 'I know how stupid I've been. I'm my own worst enemy, but if I had something worthwhile to do, I wouldn't get into so much trouble. I just know I would think twice about it. So help me, Paul. What do you suggest I do with my life?'

For straight people, questions about identity are seldom asked. There is no apparent need to do so. Life is simply lived. But identity is composed through roles pertaining to work, family and recreation. The positive filling of such roles is helpful.

Josh: 'It helps if you are working. You get a high from that. When you are working or active, your endorphins are pumping away.'

Giving, sharing and interacting with others, breaking out of the habit of egocentricity, all help to reconstruct identity. Normalization of self can come through working, playing and relaxing with others and forgetting about self.

SUMMARY

Although the preceding chapters have been used to illustrate what may be called drug theory, that theory is little more than a hypothesis, supported by experience, but not proven. However it is more than a mere descriptive explanation as it goes some way towards explaining drug user ambivalence and relapses, and incorporates non-using into the scheme. It has a practical side and indeed it can be helpful in the work with users who want to come off drugs.

Sometimes work with drug users has little to do with their drug use. They have other more serious problems, serious from their point of view. Drug use is not a problem as such, but the answer to a problem. Though as time goes by, it becomes less of an answer and becomes a problem in itself. Nevertheless, to take away the drug use may be to take away an emotional crutch. Some behaviour connected with drug use cannot be condoned. Yet working with heroin users without any understanding is pointless. If we want heroin users to become fully themselves, then they have to be treated as persons in their own right.

Clearly, the equation of drug use does delineate a number of possible stages that will require work by the client. Moreover the theory is positive. There is no adherence to the idea that heroin use leads to the person being a lifetime user.

6 THE COUNSELLING RELATIONSHIP

INTRODUCTION

Work with drug users involves both drug user clients and their counsellors, and not just drug users. In order to carry out the work, counsellors have to understand drug use in general, but they also have to try and understand what is be happening between them and their clients, and this is discovered through their mutual relationships. These relationships cover mutual expectations, and attitudes, as well as their mutual interactions. For counsellors, the relationship is usually seen as the working or counselling relationship, an essential vehicle for the delivery of help to the client. However, though this relationship may indeed be important in theory, the test is whether the relationship is actually of any help. There may be differences between what is meant to happen, what we think is happening and what actually is going on in the mutual relationship.

Formal nature of relationships

The relationship should follow the precepts of the person-centred approach. The emphasis of this approach is on the counsellors and the qualities they bring to the counselling. Thus the relationship should be characterized by acceptance of the client, and the counsellor being non-judgemental and empathic. But we also have to use other criteria to examine relationships.

Counsellors are expected to be themselves, to be genuine, but there is an immediate difficulty in that counsellors also have a role, that of counsellors. Thus counsellors must come to a compromise between being themselves and taking up a role. Working relationships can vary between a friendly, personal approach to the expert, very professional approach. Both approaches have their advantages and disadvantages.

Personal approach

The personal approach is very acceptable to clients, making it more likely they will return for counselling. Clients may also find it easier to talk about their difficulties, they feel well supported and that they are being treated as individuals rather than cases.

The drawbacks may include the counsellor being seen as too close to the client, unable to be challenging, not providing a channel back to wider society, but reinforcing subcultural attitudes and beliefs, if only by unquestioning acceptance. Indeed, such counsellors may take on the values of the drug user to some extent and find themselves in opposition to doctors and other helpers. Wanting to be acceptable to the drug user client, these counsellors find it difficult to be themselves.

This more personal relationship can be subject to extreme variations, as there is less counsellor control. By taking a personal approach, the counsellor may be tempted to pay less attention to theoretical aspects, have difficulties in long-term work and become upset or even overwhelmed by client behaviour.

Expert approach

The expert approach may be harder for clients to accept, resulting in an early drop-out from counselling. Alternatively, the client might stay but react against the counsellor, so what should be help for the client becomes a struggle between counsellor and client. Even worse, the counsellor can rationalize the situation by describing and labelling the client as chaotic, immature, or narcissistic. Such labels are likely to affect the client's ability to get help from expert sources. Also, expert counsellors, blinded by theory, may experience difficulties in seeing what is actually happening or hearing what the client is actually saying.

All of these difficulties can be aggravated if there is an ignorance of the local drug subculture and its effects, combined with an over-reliance on the medical model of drug use. There may be a retreat to a professional rigidity and resultant non-acceptance of clients which may be reciprocated by the clients.

However the expert approach can lay down firm boundaries, which are often appreciated by clients. Counsellors are able to stand back from the client situation, resist client influence and see the situation differently. The approach also allows more professional attitudes and behaviour.

Aims

The aim of counselling is to help the client and the counselling relationship must fit in with this aim. In person-centred counselling the good counselling relationship denotes not merely how counsellor and client do interact, but how they should interact. However, as may be seen, there are degrees of difficulty with any form of counselling relationship. There are variations as to boundaries, honesty, confidentiality, acceptance, involvement and understanding in all relationships. We should also bear in mind that some clients may react better to certain forms of relationships than others.

Person-centred counselling is not the perfect way of helping clients, nor should we expect it to be. However, in my opinion, it is the most suitable for working with heroin users. Yet even so, there have to be additions to the basic approach to maximize effectiveness.

At one time, it was thought that theory was the determinant of effectiveness in delivering help to clients: pick the right theory and this would ensure the correct method. The contribution of Carl Rogers was to point to the counsellor as a major factor. The help delivered depended on the person who delivered help, as well as the counsellor's understanding and skills. How help was delivered was very much a product of the counselling relationship.

Counsellors tend to pick approaches which suit them, rather than the client. This might seem a selfish choice, but it is actually a realistic choice. One of the axioms of person-centred counselling is that counsellors should be themselves, and this is easier if counsellors practice a method with which they feel happy, a method in which they believe. This also means that working with heroin users may not be for everyone, and there should be acceptance of this fact.

Person-centred counselling

Here the helping relationship is viewed as an amalgam of certain core qualities and skills, those of being non-judgemental, empathic, genuineness and accepting of the client. These are combined with skills such as listening, good communication and being able to challenge the client. To be effective, these have to be used by counsellors possessing the requisite counselling qualities. The combination of skills and qualities will go towards making a useful counselling relationship.

Reviewing the relationship

Sometimes the relationship is seen as dependent on the existence of the core qualities and skills, rather than the relationship being of the essence. An emphasis on skills and qualities can lead to a rather cognitive approach, and the role of feelings in the relationship itself may be overlooked. Yet judging how to apply those qualities and skills within the counselling relationship very much depends on feelings, whether it feels right. Thus the relationship has to be considered as a whole. This does not prevent it being analyzed, but we should remember that it is more than the sum of its parts.

Relationship aims

Another way of looking at the counselling relationship is to look at its aims. Basically, the aim of the working relationship is to further the counselling and so help clients towards what they desire, within an ethical framework. The aim can be broken down into various sub-aims, which might include the following:

- to influence the client
- to act as a channel of help
- to support the client
- to act as a model
- to share of oneself
- to be self-reflexive

Influencing the client

The counselling relationship is non-directive and not a method whereby counsellors tell clients what to do. Clients come for counselling because they are having difficulties in their lives, difficulties that remain unresolved. As counsellors, we have to help them ease, manage or solve those difficulties. Telling a client what to do might or might not solve the difficulties, but unless clients solve difficulties for themselves, they merely become dependent on counselling.

However being non-directive does not mean counsellors do not influence their clients. Indeed, if this was not the case then there would be no point to counselling as an activity. So the question remains as to how the counsellor can best influence clients.

A good relationship is in practice the best way of exerting influence. People are more likely to react positively to others within a good relationship. Counsellors have to accept that they do have such power and thus the role of ethics is very important. Just because counsellors are open and friendly does not mean they do not have considerable power in the counselling relationship.

Rachel's Mum: 'You did a lot to help Rachel.'

Me: 'Me? I did very little. It was Rachel who helped herself.'

Rachel's Mum: 'Yes, you did. You took an interest in her, and without that, she wouldn't have bothered. She changed because someone took an interest.'

Channel of help

Counselling is sometimes seen as what the counsellor can do for the client and there is a danger that this gives a false impression, that the client is passive and can be changed by the counsellor. Most counsellors who work with heroin users will soon find this is not the case, and discover that clients are well able to be active, have their say, and do what they want. Clients are people in their own right and to treat them as anything less is to fail in understanding the counselling situation.

Heroin using clients are capable of being effective. Anyone with a weekly income of, say, £40 a week and who is spending £200 a week on drugs has to exercise certain abilities merely to survive. They are also able to work out difficulties for themselves and so help with the problems of others.

Lynne: 'People used to come and tell me their problems. Gordon used to do that, and Sam after he had been arguing with Layna. I used to talk to them about myself, but never about what I wanted to tell them.'

So clients are not helpless even if they may have difficulties in dealing with their own situations. In this respect they do not differ from most of us. We all tend to find it easier to solve the problems of others, rather than our own.

If we return to the above example, why should Lynne react differently with counsellors as opposed to her friends? The reason is that in counselling she felt secure, accepted and supported, which does not always happen, even with friends. She did not talk with her friends about the things she wanted to talk about, and this was in part a result of how she felt. Conversely, she did talk in counselling sessions because she felt differently, and was able to talk. No amount of telling a client like Lynne that she was free to talk about anything was going to help: she had to feel it. Thus the counselling relationship is a way of allowing the client to feel in certain ways, even before anything important has been said. The relationship is the channel through which help can be given, as it allows the client to feel able to participate in the counselling process.

Furthermore, if the client feels positive about the counsellor and counselling, then what happens in the session is meaningful.

Richard: 'We have spoken before, but it is good to see things from a different point of view. After we spoke, it was the first time I had really seen how Barbara was suffering.'

This channel of help, the relationship, is essential when counselling skills are practiced. To be helpful they must be carried out in the context of a useful relationship. For instance, challenging or confronting the client might or might not be successful. Success largely depends on the nature of the counselling relationship. Being challenged is much more acceptable if it is done within a good relationship. Moreover counsellor misjudgements of when or where to challenge the client, which is likely to happen from time to time, will produce less harmful consequences when done in a good relationship. Mistakes by the counsellor can be soon repaired.

Skills used impersonally are less effective than those used within the context of a good relationship. What the counsellor is doing is perceived in a positive light and is more than a mere action.

Jenny: 'You take it all in, don't you? You remind me of my husband. He doesn't say much, but he listens and doesn't miss a trick.'

Support

Many clients basically know what they want, they simply have trouble in carrying out what they want. What many want is a measure of support, so the counsellor's influence is directed towards supporting the client. This means increasing the client's self-esteem and in turn adding to client self-confidence. But support is not given through impersonal behaviour, it is most efficiently given through a warm relationship, a relationship that is two-way.

Maggie: 'I'm happy now being off. But it helps as I know you're happy that I'm happy.'

This can even include physical contact, especially in cases of bereavement. Physical contact, when appropriate, is important as many clients have been starved of such meaningful contact.

Tina: 'I just want to hug you. (We hug.) It's good to know someone cares.'

Of course, touch has to be carefully used because of possible sexual connotations and the counsellor should remember that some clients have problems with physical contact, either through upbringing or through past physical trauma.

Modelling

Clients in a good working relationship will learn a lot from the counsellor, almost as if by a process of behavioural osmosis, slowly taking on some of the counsellor's behaviour but also the counsellor's perceptions. Sometimes the counsellor is expected to model the right way of doing things or behaving, but this is rarely successful. The counsellor is not there to teach, but is someone from whom the client may want to learn. And in practice, clients take from the experience what they see as useful for themselves.

A few years ago, I met a client, one of seven brothers, with whom I had worked. Over the years he had sorted out his life and was doing very well for himself. Wondering about this transformation, I asked him whether my efforts had been of the slightest use.

Karl: 'Oh, yes! You really helped me. I shall never forgot what you said to me that changed my life around.'

Needless to say, my reaction was one of amazement. He had seemed to me to be hardly a success when he had moved out of the area. And I certainly did not remember saying anything of great significance. My interest was aroused. What was this piece of great insight or interpretation that stayed with him?

Me: 'So, what did I say to you that was so helpful.'
Karl: 'Well, after you took the bairn into care, as you know I was not too happy with you. But you always accepted what I said, and you were fair. So when you said that what I should do was always put money aside, a little each week. I thought you might be a bit of a bastard but you weren't daft. You were always fair to me, so it might work. Since then, I've never looked back. A little each week, and with a bit of money behind me I was able to get out of the rut. Best help I ever had.'

So much for insight! All Karl remembered was a throwaway remark, yet clearly it meant something to him, and it proved useful. So how counsellors behave and what they say can be significant if it touches the spot. Clients learn from counsellors, but in their own way.

Sharing of self

Through self-disclosure, counsellors allow themselves to become more open and more accessible.

Me: 'You were saying it takes some time to know a person. Is this important?'
David: 'Yes, for him to know you and you to know him. This way he can take a completely different view of you. Speaking over a period of time, he gets to know you as a person you are, rather than having an outsider's view.'

Any self-disclosure has to be carefully monitored, both ethically and because counsellors also make themselves more vulnerable. Part of the reason for this sharing of self is that for many clients, relating to people can be difficult in itself.

Jaclyn: 'I preferred my father to my mother, yet I never related properly to either. I did not want to relate to them. I do not relate properly to people, though I relate better to men. I should say I get on with people, but I'm happy not relating that much.'

This does not mean the counsellor relates well to clients to make up for their present relational difficulties, or that the counsellor *makes* them experience a good relationship. But a sharing of self is important for clients who have relational difficulties. Their vulnerability results in the counsellor putting a slightly different emphasis on forming the relationship.

Being self-reflexive

The counselling relationship should allow the participants to look at it and discuss it. By so doing, the counsellor and client should be able to improve it. But there is also a knock-on effect, in that this allows the client to learn how to look not merely at the counselling relationship but at other relationships. Not all clients are fully aware of the relationships of which they are a part. They will benefit from the experience of analyzing them.

More commonly, clients are aware of yet are unable to do anything about their relationships. They learn how to do so within the counselling relationship. But this also depends on the client being allowed to learn through counselling and this takes place even when the process seems totally negative. The counsellor has to persist in the suitable and useful relationship, even though it appears that the client is not reacting to it and not playing to the same rules. The only thing to bear in mind is that it can take a long time for relationships with heroin using clients to become significant.

John: 'How long have we known each other, Paul? Seven, eight years? I was glad I wrote that letter from prison to you, as for the first time I really felt we were on the same side. I knew you meant well but I was a radge teenager at the time. I didn't want to know. I never had anything against you. It's different now and I'm glad we can speak like this.'

Counsellors have to be prepared to work for a long time with some clients, while much of the time the work would appear to produce little success. Frequent client referrals, which result in a client having a succession of counsellors, is not to be recommended. That would merely reinforce client feelings of rejection, feelings that are only too common with drug using clients.

INITIAL RELATIONSHIPS

Before the counselling

The counselling relationship is expected to be the main avenue of help for the client, so we should see how it operates in practice. The relationship might be assumed to start when counsellor and client meet, and this should be the pivotal point. Yet, on reflection, we have to see that the relationship is partly composed of what both parties bring with them.

Suppose counsellors have never worked with heroin users previously. Could they work in a satisfactory manner with them? The immediate answer might be that counsellors have worked with many different clients in the past and there is no reason why heroin users should be any more difficult. The assumption is that counsellors should be able to deal with anyone. To say anything different is to label and denigrate a whole class of clients.

Proper as this attitude may seem, there are counter-arguments. For some helpers, this assumption leads to false expectations which later fail to materialize. Counselling drug users very often seems ineffective to new drug counsellors. There are difficulties between counsellor and client, with the client not being totally honest and making promises which are soon broken. This may be rationalized by counsellors who see such clients are being uncooperative and resistant, an attitude which is unhelpful in counselling terms, though it might make the counsellor feel better.

Initial attitudes

Before blaming the client for what has taken place, we should think a bit more about whom we are counselling. Most white counsellors would think twice about offering to work with, for example, Chinese or Bengali clients. We would not feel sufficiently knowledgable about their culture, we probably could not speak the language. The idea that someone from their own culture and country could counsel them better would not strike us as misplaced. A difficulty arises when we are supposed to counsel those not from another culture but from another subculture. Subcultures, whether heroin users or different subcultures like the gay community, or related subcultures like prison inmates, have links with the outside society, so they are not completely apart. However this can also give the misleading impression that they are no different. We can easily overlook the different norms and values of those subcultures. What is worse, we import our own norms and values and assume they are the same as those of subcultural clients.

Counselling training

Every counsellor comes to counselling with various attitudes, a product of life itself. Person-centred counselling has as one of its core qualities the ability of the counsellor to be non-judgemental, to keep those attitudes under control. The training for counsellors is meant to put trainees in touch with their feelings so that they are able to identify their attitudes and so be better placed to have them under control. Clearly, there are certain difficulties about this approach. Firstly, the training has to be free and trusting enough to allow this to take place and for trainees to be able to say that they dislike, are afraid of, feel sorry for, favour or are sexually attracted to certain clients. Having the proper training is not as easy as may appear.

Further problems arise from trainees' attitudes being frequently hidden until they are in action. Most people think they are relatively nice and acceptable persons, behaving in a humane and reasonable manner. The trouble is that this facade of acceptance tends to disappear in action. The reason is that not merely are attitudes often well hidden until we have to act, but we can largely control our behaviour to show our best side. Only under pressure does the cloak fall, only in arguments or in crisis is our real self revealed. These client encounters are hard to replicate in training, and there are ethical arguments against trainees being submitted to such pressurized training.

The final point is that counselling training often does not deal with actual clients but uses simulation such as role-play. This can be useful if other trainees can easily take over the role of the client, but there are obvious difficulties when dealing with unknown members of a subculture. What is usually presented is a mixture of a non-drug user and a stereotypical drug user. My desire is certainly not to lessen the importance of counsellor training but to point out that it can only take the trainee so far. Much of the learning has to be done with actual clients and this means that attitudes might not have been fully sorted out.

Unresolved counsellor attitudes

The fact that counsellors seem not totally prepared when they start actual counselling need not be a defect as long as they are aware of the fact and take care when they start. They should get to know clients and client lives in detail, and be aware of the client as the subject, not the object, of counselling. Counsellors have to be more than non-judgemental: they have to be open. They have to be open to the experience of what is taking place, which means to a degree of letting go at first, of not being in total control. In this way the client can react and the counsellor can feel more accurately the client's situation. This allows the quality of empathy to come into play, an important outcome, especially at the very beginning of counselling. Sometimes counsellors will switch on later, when counselling has reached an apparently important juncture, rather than being open from the very start.

Client attitudes

Clients also bring their own attitudes to the counselling, and these in turn can affect how the counsellor will feel and react. At the start of counselling both parties can be trying to sense how the other will behave. This can happen so early that often we do not even consider it. The client walks into the office after having had to wait. This is not irrelevant but tells the client something. Then the client enters the counselling room. Does the counsellor sit behind a desk? We have to think what aspects of power, distancing and insecurity this represents. Does the counsellor take notes? What does this mean? Is there a telephone so others can call in or so the counsellor can call out? These represent certain attitudes which can go towards forming part of the counselling relationship.

However initially the client tends to suspend judgement until the counsellor's behaviour confirms certain client attitudes. Now that attitude may well be locked into the counselling. For instance, the very job of social worker was one open to the gravest suspicion from some clients.

Ruth: 'The social workers I had were no use. They were middle-class ladies who sat behind a table.'

The situation is often aggravated by clients having been given little idea of what to expect both as regards the counsellor and the counselling. And counsellors do not always give time for clients to look at their expectations and come to terms with what is really taking place, rather than what they imagine is taking place.

Coming for counselling

Clients who come for counselling will have their own attitudes and past experiences. These are not always very positive and can affect the counselling.

Michael: 'I don't like social workers. I've had them for seventeen years, telling me what to do, and I've had enough.'

As mentioned previously, there can be a lack of clear expectations and instead there are a mixture of feelings and fantasies.

Gordon: 'I'm not coming to the Clinic, having psychotherapy. No-one is going to look into my brain.'

Some of the client behaviour is fashioned by subcultural attitudes, in particular that of suspicion towards anyone they see as an authority figure, and this is likely to include counsellors. The attitude can vary between total rejection of counselling as being controlling and authoritarian, to a quite reasonable suspicion of the counsellor.

Tommy: 'I don't want to say too much. I don't really know you or anything about you.'

In fact, the subcultural reaction to authority presents constant difficulties for the counsellor, as it is not easy to get the correct balance, the balance between caring and control. Part of the difficulty comes from clients and their attempts to come to terms with authority, which they have projected onto the counsellor.

Tina: 'The trouble with you is that you are too soft. It was your fault I used up the insurance money, 'cos you went on holiday.'
Me: 'I know I'm too soft. I should have been stricter.'
Tina: 'But if you were strict then I wouldn't have let you into the house.'

Another attitude, especially among male drug users, is that of not involving anyone else in their affairs, and this applies mostly to those who are not users themselves and who represent authority – which includes all counsellors.

Chris: 'I never involve anyone else in my problems. Drugs made me secretive because using them is illegal.'

Thus clients, arriving from an unfamiliar subculture, come to counselling with their attitudes and their imaginings. The recipient is likely to be the counsellor, but what takes place is not necessarily a personal reaction but a product of the counselling situation.

Tommy: 'I think you are into this junk business. You're probably a dealer on the side and raking it in, laughing at us with our five and ten pound packets.'

The two parties might have known of each other before the counselling, even though they might not have met. Counsellors should bear in mind that a local subculture will have its own good network, and information about counsellors will be circulated. Having the right attitudes and behaving well towards a client will be passed around, as will negative attitudes and behaviour.

Craig: 'You would be surprised, lots of people know you. Not that people say anything bad about you.'

In spite of all the difficulties, as long as the counsellor is sensitive to the situation from the very start, progress can be made. We have to remember that clients come to counselling for help, and the counsellors' task is to make help easy to take.

Dean: 'We just want someone we can relate to.'

Even when the relationship is going through difficult spells, we have to remember that clients come for help, not to annoy the counsellor. If the going is difficult, then counsellors have to reflect on the nature of the relationship, what they are contributing to it, and whether they are part of the difficulty.

The nature of the relationship.

Counsellor and client do not simply come together but meet after a process, whether it be of referral for counselling or that of the client deciding to see a counsellor. This can itself be set in a broader social situation. For the counsellor, there may be kudos in having clients coming for help, and so there is a tendency to want to get drug users in for counselling. This sets up a dynamic which might not be so acceptable from the client perspective.

Chris: 'There should be no "must" when it comes to seeing your counsellor, no need. If there is a need then it is like an addiction. It would be different if I was obliged, if I felt it was to oblige someone and so there was a point in coming. But there should be no "must".'

Heroin users will come for counselling voluntarily, if they feel there is a point in so doing. Counsellors may see counselling very much in perceived client needs, but clients may see the situation differently. They may want something on a personal level, as well as professional assistance. So if the service is client centred and the counsellors approachable, drug users will come.

Maggie: 'Can you help me Paul? I've started, I've had three shots. Here, you can see the marks!'

If clients are not self-referring and coming freely for counselling, then the service has to look to itself and what it is, or is not, providing. Once the service is seen as being good and the counsellors are helpful, clients will come, though admittedly not often for their drug use. It is often easier for clients to come for other reasons, but client choice is still important as part of the overall client empowerment.

Jane: 'You must remember I came to you because I chose you. I wanted you to do a report for Court, not because I thought you would get me off but because I thought you would be fair.'

We should not imagine that such decisions come out of thin air. They represent the result of information in the drug subculture and already the start of a relationship, if a one-sided and tenuous relationship. Thus the relationship that the counsellor has may be with individual clients, but it can also be one with the subculture as a whole. Even before the counsellor has met potential clients, they may know about the counsellor, usually from rather distorted information given by other drug users.

Sharon: 'Some people would say they didn't like you and I didn't think that was right. You were only trying to help them.'

However drug users can be very changeable, abusive at one moment, and claiming to be good friends the next. Counsellors have to be careful not to react or get caught up in these expressed feelings. In the long run, the counsellor should be there for the client and this knowledge in turn may assist the counsellor through difficult times. And when counsellors see themselves as having difficult times in counselling, it has to be borne in mind that it is healthy for clients to let go of their feelings. Counsellors should represent safety and acceptance, persons who can allow clients to begin the process of personal liberation.

Gary: 'I don't know why anyone bothers, you're no fucking use! You've never been any fucking use to me, never been able to help. You're bloody useless!'

How the counsellor reacts to such outbursts may determine progress over the next sessions. There is the temptation to react strongly to these displays of feelings, rather than to understand that the counsellor should be pleased that clients feel safe enough to so express themselves. Of course, no counsellor is employed to act as an emotional punchbag and frequent displays of directed emotion require the counsellor to be assertive and reassert personal boundaries. Counsellors do not help by allowing themselves to be seen as anything else but persons in their own right.

Clients in turn should feel accepted, even when they are being angry or abusive. This is all part of the process whereby they can come to terms with a relationship that may differ from others in their life. It is not a better relationship but a different one. Clients should also be given acceptance, so they can grow and change. It has to be appreciated they also may have difficulties with their own behaviour.

Chris (letter from prison): 'I feel a bit apprehensive while writing this letter, due to all the promises I've made during past sentences. I'm really sorry for all the lies I may have given you. I'm not sure what I wish to say to you in this letter, basically it's a cry of "HELP!!!" '

Client empowerment

If clients are to be allowed to regain their power as people then we have to be ready to allow them to do so, and the service has to be able to cope with it. This means the relationship has to be able to withstand clients who exert their power as persons, often accompanied by the strong expression of feelings, feelings which might put on counsellors or which counsellors take upon themselves.

Matt: 'I'm not bloody staying here. I'm going down the road. I'm not stopping. Don't bother, I won't be back.'

In this case, Matt actually turned up the next day to apologize for his behaviour. However I always tell clients they should not apologize for saying how they feel. On the other hand, they are best helped by saying how they feel after such incidents. Just saying how you feel is rarely enough in itself, and often leaves the client feeling worse if it is not followed up. From time to time, clients will storm out of the office, sometimes through how they feel, sometimes because they are beginning to withdraw.

Josie (note left at the office): 'Dear Paul, I'm sorry I walked out on you, but as you saw I was a wee bit down in the dumps.'

We should understand that at these initial stages mutual misunderstandings are quite possible. Both counsellor and client have their first impressions, impressions which are not always correct. The counsellor is just as likely as the client to get things wrong, so these very early stages can prove difficult.

Lisa: 'When I first met you in the office, I thought you were right cheeky. But you were just saying the truth. I was using and didn't want to listen.'

And it does not matter how the counsellor reacts at first, there is still likely to be misperceptions and consequent misunderstandings. Feedback about the relationship is essential, so the counsellor should ask how the client is feeling and whether he or she feels comfortable with the session. This is usually done at the end of the session, but can be done at any time. Thus the counsellor might detect any difficulties but should not react to them, not before being sure of their nature, and then only react in a useful way. Though clients may see things in a certain light, client perceptions often reflect their low self-esteem, so they can view the session differently from the counsellor.

Nicole: 'Are all junkies so suspicious? When I first met you, I thought no-one could be that nice.'

And clients also have difficulty in believing that they are basically good people. Many of them have been subjected to being told that they are bad for years and so find it difficult to be treated as a person.

Georgina: 'Tell me Paul, are you always this nice or is it part of your job?'

Of course, it is easier to think that counsellors have to be nice, than for clients to see themselves as nice people. Part of the job of counselling from the start is trying to help clients to see themselves as themselves, and not how others want to see them.

So in the very early sessions there is often suspicion with the client trying to come to terms with the counselling and the counsellor. One indication of how things are going is simply whether or not the client comes back for counselling. So actually turning up can reflect a growing relationship and is a positive sign. Counselling, or coming for counselling, has to be set in the context of the heroin user's life.

Chris: 'I got up early – you know that's not like me – and came down to see you. I thought, "The cunt's helped me so I've got to do my bit."'

There can be a grudging acceptance that counselling is 'OK', or 'Not so bad', and counsellors should not be surprised if the early sessions are not rated highly. However, in my experience, though there may be little acceptance of the counselling, yet there may be a more positive reaction to the relationship. Clients may not return for counselling for several months and yet this does not negate the worth of the relationship, and those clients often do return through the memory of that relationship.

ACCEPTANCE

Acceptance of the client is seen as a desirable quality in the counsellor. The counsellor is able to work with the client in a nonjudgemental manner, a necessary requirement as many drug using clients will have committed offences, will have been violent or the victims of violence, will be anti-authoritarian. Thus we have to accept not drug users or thieves, for example, but people who have taken drugs and people who have stolen.

We have to accept the person who steals knowing that others are involved. For example, my practice has been not to leave money in my jacket and then leave the jacket unattended. The reason is simply that drug using clients might well steal any money left.

This is not being judgemental: it is being realistic. On one occasion, when I was called out of my office for thirty seconds I returned to find the client, Josie, gone. Though I could not discover anything missing, I decided to ring reception to stop the client. It was then that I discovered she had stolen my office phone.

Subcultural reality and acceptance

Following on from the last example, we might think we are able to accept anything, but this may reflect merely our ignorance of what is being presented. By working through ideas about injecting heroin use, we are more able to accept such behaviour, despite public attitudes towards it. One area which is less acceptable for most is that of drug dealing. Even the police tend to regard drug users as victims but drug dealers as mere exploiters. It is worthwhile taking a closer look at the situation. The first point is that from clients known to me, about a third have dealt drugs at some time or have been the partners of drug dealers. Thus drug dealing is a more common activity than is usually supposed. Most dealing is on a very small scale and usually starts off as helping friends out.

Josie: 'Spike wasn't dealing, he was only getting it for people in the flat. Well, I suppose, technically, he was dealing.'

Most small dealers are users themselves, and will deal as a means to support their own addiction.

Yvonne: 'I would not call it dealing, more like scoring for his mates. He made a £10 packet out of it to maintain his habit.'

Being both a dealer and a drug user is likely to lead to difficulties, as the temptation is always to use the stock.

Devo: 'Sam gave me two grams to deal, but I ended up fixing the lot myself.'

The net result can be that users who deal are not likely to make a lot of money. And they also have to account to main dealers for the drugs they have got on account, or be subjected to heavy physical reminders to repay.

Dean: 'From all the dealing I've done, I've made nothing. In fact I'm £600 in debt.'

It is easy to see small local dealers as exploiters, but they are themselves exploited by others further up the tree, the main dealers, who are themselves liable to exploitation by suppliers. The higher up the chain a person is, the more he or she is in the business of illegal drugs, brokers and dealers in a commodity.

Vince: 'I'm no dealer, but I know the main suppliers. The way I see it is, if they're daft enough to pay for it, then that's their lookout. It's business, and there's a lot of money to be made. You can't feel sorry for addicts.'

Whatever our views of dealing may be, we also have to be aware of the views of drug users themselves. These also have to be taken into account.

Maggie: 'Dealers provide a service. If it wasn't for them, there would be a lot of chemists broken into.'

Apart from the views of users themselves, we have to bear in mind that users who are off, or are trying to get off drugs, are likely to have quite differing attitudes.

Tina: 'I'm glad they're cracking down on the dealers at last. They should have done that ages ago. It will cut down the number of junkies. The junkies will come off if there is no dope about.'

Thus before counsellors talk about acceptance of clients, they have to be aware of the reality of what they are accepting.

Acceptance and counselling

So acceptance is a complex activity and attribute, which has to be realistic. Acceptance is not a state of mind, of deciding to accept a client as a person, but being able to react usefully to how the client behaves.

> *Maggie*: 'Sometimes I used to come and see you, just to argue. I would argue all the time and then you would say at the end, "Thanks for coming, Maggie" and I would go.'

Part of the process of acceptance is that of being able to accept client feelings. Feelings may be expressed because clients want the counsellor to share them. Clients want the counsellor to know how they feel. In the next example the client was extremely upset and only the more restrained section of what she said is given.

> *Bev*: 'The doctor would not give me anything! How am I going to sleep with the pains? He gave me nothing to take the pains away, he didn't do anything for me! Doctors don't help you at all. I'm not going back. I'm going to get a shot, and fuck him!'

This is a situation common enough to those counselling drug users, a stressful situation for the counsellor who is subjected to the raw fury of client feelings. Acceptance of such feelings is the way to turn the situation into a positive occasion.

Accordingly, after ten minutes of talking with Bev, she had calmed down and appeared to see the situation differently. By accepting her feelings, she was then able to deal with them and act more constructively.

> *Bev*: 'OK, perhaps I will see the doctor. I'll be down for nine o'clock. No, I'll do it and I'll be in tomorrow to see you.'

Ironically, it can be easier to accept the major items such as a client taking illegal drugs and stealing to pay for them, than it is to accept the small things, such as the fact that drug using clients sometimes lie. Some drug workers get caught up in the mesh of deceit, try to get the client to admit the truth. This is a failure to accept the person and where that person is at. Some clients need their lies, they need the defence for themselves. They also need counsellor acceptance.

Jane: 'You seem to understand me a little better than any social worker I've been to. I would come to you and lie to you, and you would know I was lying, and yet you would still help me. To me, when I think back, there were a few days when if you had not helped me, then God knows what would have happened.'

Of course, this does not mean the counsellor has to accept everything that the client says; that would be totally unrealistic and unhelpful. The art of counselling is to maintain the balance between challenging the client usefully in order to make the session realistic, and allowing the client a measure of denial. Constant lying by the client is an infringement on and a disregard of the counsellor as a person. Constant challenging or preoccupation with the truth becomes a game to make the counsellor feel better, and a game which the counsellor will not win. Counselling has to allow clients to be themselves and this requires them to discover or re-discover themselves.

Chris: 'It's important to have one person you may speak to, one person you cannot con. Well, we all try it on, but you miss it, you miss it if there is nobody who can talk back.'

Sometimes counsellors talk about accepting the person but not the person's behaviour. This is easy enough in a case of murder. We can accept that the action, because it happened only once, may be dissociated from the person. However this becomes more difficult if the client is a drug user, exhibits a continual pattern of behaviour, more difficult to dissociate the person and the accompanying regular actions.

Clients are more than their behaviour. They bring along possibly different values, hopes and norms. These also have to be taken into account. This requires the counsellor being in touch with the client's perception of the world and the rules that go towards making up that perspective. For instance, a client might work in the sex industry and we could simply say that we have no difficulty in accepting that fact. This overlooks the possible complexity of what is to be accepted, the acceptance of different norms and values, or acceptance of situations that we simply would never have envisaged.

Tina: 'I wouldn't have a man who sent me down the Shore: I don't know how anyone could do that. I would jump out of the window rather than do that. It's different if it's for yourself or for your bairn. That's OK.'

For counsellors to say they accept people before they know anything about them, before they have had time to accept them, is to be correct but unrealistic.

It should be remembered that there will be implications if there is a lack of acceptance. Clients are quite well aware of how they are regarded. They are people, not cases, but this is not always how they are treated. Clients are also aware of their behaviour and not always happy about that, yet it does not help if they are not accepted. No matter how the client behaves, the client should be accepted.

Marion: 'I can't speak to some people. It's because in the past I've been a pain in the arse.'
Me: 'But you have always been able to speak to me, and you've been a pain to me at times.'
Marion: 'That's different, you're so open. Not snobby.'

The term 'snobby' is used by different drug using clients, and reflects their class position and how others react to them. The term also covers those who do not self-disclose, as this is seen as a way of maintaining not just counselling distance but social distance.

Finally, acceptance is fairly passive behaviour and there is good reason for its quiet nature. Too active an acceptance can be interpreted as threatening by the client, who might then retreat and not appear for further counselling or help. Some clients may have difficulty in dealing with relationships and so find passive acceptance suits them best, until they are ready for a more interactive relationship, which they determine.

EMPATHY

Empathy, the ability of the counsellor to see the world from the client's point of view, to be able to share the same perceptions and experience the same feelings, is a necessary part of forming and maintaining the counselling relationship, and something to be worked on. Empathy tends to diminish under stress or with a lack of concentration, resulting in the client's point of view being harder to see. This can result in poor counselling.

Me: 'Do you have to have a shot just because you are feeling bored?'

Tina: 'It's easy for you to speak! You've got a job and a wife and child to go home to at night. Your time is occupied. I've got nothing to do.'

So access to total understanding exists in varying degrees in counsellors. To relate to others we must be able to empathize at least to some degree. However it would be wrong to imagine that we can totally understand others. For this reason from time to time we have to check out the situation, check out whether we do really understand the client.

In particular, we should realize that it is difficult to understand members of subcultures, as their values, norms and beliefs are likely to vary from that of outside society. Indeed, part of the way subcultures ensure their existence is by defining boundaries, to make sure that there are differences between outside society and the subculture. Subcultural argot, norms and beliefs are intended to be different. However subcultural clients do not have to behave in this manner, they can also behave appropriately in the world outside, if they so wish. So drug using clients can be quite understandable, but they also can be different, though the particular differences may be concealed and not obvious. Counsellors should not imagine that they fully understand clients, and certainly not make the classic mistake of stating that they do, or even make lesser claims.

Giselle: 'The doctor said she knew how I felt. I asked how did she fucking well know. It was my habit, only I knew how I felt.'

This can degenerate, if the counsellor is not careful, into client feelings being ignored. So as counsellors we have to sense how clients are, but we only get a taste of how they might feel. We have to accept that difference. If we are realistic and accept this difference, then we are accepted by clients in turn.

Tina: 'It's bad, really bad. You don't know what it's like. You've never been through it.'
Me: 'No, I haven't.'
Tina: 'But you know what it's like.'

It is sometimes said by ex-users that those who have never taken heroin can never really understand what it is like. But then what is being offered to the user is not a heroin user or an ex-user, but a person and a counsellor. And whether the counsellor has had relevant drug experiences is less important than the relationship and how clients feel about the counsellor.

Sam: 'You understand us. The drugs, the attempted suicides and the virus. You've been through it all with us.'

Empathy is one aspect of the working relationship and is used for the benefit of the relationship and so for the good of the client. Without this proviso, empathy is not merely possibly pointless but counterproductive.

Angela: 'It's no use going there. The counsellor I had used to be into drugs and all he wanted to hear me tell him was what it was like to be fixing, all the time. I think he got some sort of kick listening to me, but it did me no good.'

Empathy is part of the counselling relationship, and trying to see the world from the other person's point of view is a natural desire and part of the dynamics of helping relationships. Thus clients might try to see the world from the counsellor's perspective, and just as counsellors might have problems truly understanding drug users, so clients have difficulties understanding the counsellor, especially in relation to drug use.

Craig: 'You must wonder what all this rush thing is about, why it is so good as people say, and want to try it. You must want to experience it, to see what the rush is like – and it's nothing.'

Empathy is important not merely in the helping process but also in monitoring the relationship, in feeling how the counselling relationship is developing. Thus sensing how the client feels can tell the counsellor if the counsellor is getting too close and making the client feel very vulnerable, or if the client is uneasy through feeling controlled by the counsellor. Accordingly, counsellors also have to see themselves through clients' eyes, and without allowing their own perceptions of themselves to distort the picture.

TRUST IN THE RELATIONSHIP

Trust

As the relationship develops, so trust begins to build up. Much of this depends on the genuineness of counsellors, their ability to be themselves. It is difficult really to accept others if there is difficulty in accepting oneself. And such self-acceptance rests not merely on how people see themselves, but the fact that others will have their own view of the person.

> *Jenny*: 'I was talking to Tina about you and said, "The two-faced bastard ...". You don't mind me saying that? I'm just telling you what I said.'
> *Me*: 'No, no. Go ahead!'
> *Jenny*: 'I said, "The two-faced bastard ...".'

This trust building is a gradual process and there will be limits to such trust – on both sides. As counsellor, my preference is to want to trust clients, but past experience of that trust being much abused has left its mark, and caution has taken over. However, we should realize that a good relationship and trust is essential for counselling, no matter how we, as counsellors, may feel.

> *Tina*: 'Don't lecture me. You've got to show me a bit of trust.'

Part of the process of encouraging mutual trust comes when the counsellor accepts and respects the client. This means coming to know the client at the client's pace. Getting information by direct questioning may seem an efficient way of working, yet in the long run, because it does not respect the client or the relationship sufficiently, it can prove to be unhelpful. The one concern that many drug using clients express is that of the counsellor not respecting personal boundaries and being 'nosey'.

> *Beth*: 'Social workers are too nosey. They know everything about you, or think they do, but they do not know you as a person.'

In practice it is not necessary to impose oneself on clients. Respect for the person leads to client trust and clients talking about themselves. They do not have to be pressurized.

Beth: 'I liked you because the first time you came, you were relaxed and did not ask personal questions. You waited to be told. I trust you, I don't know why.'

Being nosey not merely infringes personal boundaries but can remind clients of authority, with which many of them have problems. Being nosey may sound a fairly trivial comment. In fact it may hide a considerable amount of different feelings.

Tina: 'You're OK, you're not nosey. The last social worker, she was always checking up – like the police.'

And checking up may amount to no more than asking clients what they have been doing. With the absence of trust, perceptions of counsellor and client behaviour can take on negative connotations. The opposite side of this is that with trust, with a good relationship, it is possible to be completely honest with the client and let the client know how the counsellor sees things. The good relationship not merely allows acceptance of the counsellor's actions but allows the client to say how they are perceived.

Tina: 'I got that letter from you and thought, "You fucking bastard!", but also I thought it was a barry letter, it was a good letter, and I wanted a letter like that.'

Trust does not come easily to the drug user. Part of this is the result of the client's past. To this end it can be helpful to check out not only past relationships but how they might affect the present, and this includes the relationship with the counsellor.

Me: 'Look, I know some of the things that have happened in your past and how you have been treated by men. You have said you feel unable to trust men – to trust us. I wonder how you feel about what I say, whether you trust me.'

Cherie: 'Oh, yes, I believe you! You're not like other men I have known. I know I can trust you.'

Some of the difficult phases in the initial relationship between counsellor and client may represent the growing pains of that relationship.

Chris: 'I don't think I've found anybody I could trust. I could be honest to someone if I trusted them but they would have to prove it to me that they could trust me. I would test them out, play wee games.'

The creation of trust with heroin users also reflects back on what has been said about personal boundaries. Encouraging clients to talk about themselves is a process taken for granted by counsellors, without the realization that this is an invasion of those boundaries. We might say it is essential to get clients to talk and for the counsellor to listen, but this still misses the point. The nature of counselling itself is one of personal invasion. From the client's perspective, this is acceptable provided it is to some extent a mutual process.

Craig: 'I told you about myself, now you tell me about yourself!'

This represents more than curiosity about myself as counsellor, it represents feelings about the relationship. As such, it should be attended to. Self-disclosure by the counsellor is not merely permissible but is essential.

Chris: 'I hate it when social workers don't talk about themselves. It's because they are snobby; they don't really want to get to know people like us.'

As ever, self-disclosure is a process best done a little at a time. At first the client wants to get things out and does not want to hear anything about the counsellor. Indeed, to self-disclose too early and too much shows insensitivity to the client's needs.

Frank: 'I went down to see the social worker and talked to her for a while. Then she said she understood and began to tell me her troubles, what happened to her. I told her I had not come to listen to her. It was my time. I didn't want to be burdened with all her shit. I wanted someone to help me, listen to me.'

It is only in the longer term that the client can begin to relax and then expect a more even-handed exchange of information and feelings. The process of self-disclosure if done a little at a time, with the feedback being carefully monitored after each disclosure, allows for a useful outcome.

A GROWING RELATIONSHIP

With increasing mutual trust, clients feel able to be more disclos-ing and more honest with the counsellor. This increases clients' ability to be honest with themselves and so be realistic about their situation, to make decisions about what they truly want. We should note that clients are often quite capable of being honest outside the counselling session, though the lack of skilled help may prevent them from really using that honesty. The difficulty about honesty in the counselling session means that it is not just a client problem. It comes in part from it being a counselling session and involving the counsellor.

Maggie: 'You know me, I don't lie but come right out with it: I don't give a damn. What I'm telling you is not as a social worker but as a friend.'

This way of dissociating the person from the role is one way, a good way, for clients to come to terms with the counsellor. Basi-cally, the counselling relationship is between two persons, who happen to be counsellor and client.

Beth: 'I don't like you as a social worker, I don't like any social workers, but I like you as a friend. Strange, you're a bit strange you know. I mean you don't talk like a social worker.'

Clients do not want a relationship with a role, with a counsellor or any other role. What they want is a relationship with a person, and a person in a certain role. Counsellors who stick emphatically to a role and ignore being themselves, might find that clients will act in the same manner, and be drug users rather than themselves. And as long as they act as drug users, they are more likely to stay as drug users.

Further consequences of the growing relationship

The counselling relationship is sometimes described as if it is always the same, yet it is growing and constantly changing. The relationship can become deeper in the sense that both counsellor and client know more about each other and this has its own con-sequences. Sometimes it is good knowing more about others, sometimes we might wish we did not know them quite so well. Clients might be easier to accept when we hardly know them.

One consequence of the developing relationship might be a drift towards it becoming a friendship rather than a counselling relationship. This means that there will be pressures on the personal and professional boundaries. For clients, the counsellors' ability to be themselves becomes increasingly important. Part of this comes through appropriate disclosure, as most of us like talking about ourselves, and it balances the power within the relationship to some extent. Self-disclosure by the counsellor also increases the normalizing trend of the client. For me, a touch of humour reflects the person as a person, and this can also be helpful.

Giselle: 'I don't know how I'm going to feel now the doctor has cut off my DFs.'
Me: 'Now if you feel really bad during the week, before I see you next, if you get really miserable then let me know. I'll come down and we can be really miserable together.'
Giselle (laughing): 'Your job must be depressing, listening to everyone.'

Humour, if used appropriately, and not overused so clients feel they are not being taken seriously, can usefully open up situations. Perhaps humour is not the right description; perhaps it is more a question of displaying a light touch. Clients, and counsellors as well, can only take so much serious and emotion-laden material. The occasional light touch is helpful.

Me: 'You're hopeless Lisa. "Aren't I doing well Paul?" and you staggering about the place. "I've been off for three days Paul!" and if your pupils were any smaller they would disappear. And you going around the place saying, "Give us a shot Tommy!" '
Lisa (laughing): 'What would anyone do with a social worker like this!'

The developing relationship does not become any easier however, merely more rich and more complicated. For instance, as counsellor and client get to know each other, then client guilt can become more important. Clients, because of their guilt, begin to believe that the counsellor knows everything about them. They may think at times that the counsellor can read their minds or mysteriously know what they are thinking.

Susan (angry, in tears): 'You're looking at me. You think I've had a shot! Don't you believe me? I'll prove ... No, you don't believe me. It's no good, you don't believe me!'

What is happening is that the relationship is moving to a different level, not merely in its complexity but in the abilities of both parties to know each other, or even imagine that they know each other. Getting to know the client, paradoxically, might not make the job of counselling any easier, though it makes it more meaningful.

Also the relationship brings to light other aspects. One might be that the client sees the counsellor as helping, but this helping is one-way. The counsellor is helping the client, and though this is what is intended, yet this leaves the client always in the role of the taker. Not surprising this means clients can feel awkward about this.

Jane: 'I would like to do something for you, give you something, but there is nothing I can do.'

Doing home visits may be welcome in that it does offer the opportunity to even up the balance. It does allow some sort of permitted trade where the client can give something in return, for the client to offer hospitality.

Lisa: 'I'm annoyed when I've got no coffee when you come. I like you to have a cup of coffee. Tommy gets annoyed as I don't offer him one, but he's always about and it's different with you.'

But the more the counsellor gets to know the subculture and what is going on, the more difficult it can become, as the counsellor is now more of a possible threat. This is especially the case if home visits are done. The counsellor soon gets to know more about what is happening and can touch reality. This in turn can affect how the counsellor is perceived and client feelings.

Lisa: 'I was round at Tina's, gasping for a shot, and called up to her. I thought she said someone was there, so we looked for the police, but there was none as far as we could see. So I told Graeme to see if there was a white car round the corner. There was. I thought, "You snide bastard, you are still there, waiting to see if I turn up."'

SEXUAL ASPECTS OF THE RELATIONSHIP

Introduction

The counselling relationship can be complex, and the professionalization of the relationship is one way of trying to keep it simple and under control. Such an approach is quite effective but has general limitations. In particular, it is not very effective in dealing with whole life situations.

Thus the usual counselling relationship has to be carefully monitored. This does not always happen. As with many sensitive subjects, there is a swing to taking up polar positions. On one hand there is a pretence that sexual feelings and even sexual behaviour does not happen. But people are brought together in a relationship and if the counselling lasts any time, then there is the possibility that sexual feelings do arise. Indeed this was recognized by Freud, who referred to patients tending to fall in love with their analysts. This will be taken up in the chapter on working practice. However there seems rather more to the situation than just such transference.

From the very start of counselling, sexual feelings can be a subtext, though in a very minor way.

Lisa (first interview): 'I've never had a man social worker before.'

But the feelings are very undirected and there can also be a mixture of them. There can be feelings that arise from the client being helped, being the centre of attention, of having someone listening. The client feels better but may also be confused by being so treated. Many clients are on the receiving end of life in the raw. To meet someone who treats them 'right', but has no sexual intentions, may cause difficulties in interpretation for the client. Because it is also difficult to describe, clients might use the word 'love' because that is the only feeling that begins to approach how they feel.

Jenny: 'I love you Paul, honest I do, for what you've done to help me. I love you.'

These statements should not be taken at face value. All the time we have to look for the real meaning, and assume nothing.

Jenny: 'I don't know whether I like you or not. Aye, I think I do.'

The age of most clients should be borne in mind, and also that sexual relationships are usually a subject of interest. This tends to be reinforced in the local drug subculture where they become a matter of considerable gossip.

Lisa: 'Have you made it with Tina yet? I just wondered.'

So counsellors have to examine carefully what clients say, and appreciate clients in context. Very often clients are aware that what they are saying is not true, or it is gossip, fantasy and imaginings. , Fantasy and imagination is just another way of coping with a client's situation.

Jane: 'One day you'll take me away and look after me, you will protect me ... it's all fantasy!'

Counsellors should feel easy and comfortable about sexual feelings and behaviour, otherwise not only will clients not talk about their fantasies, which may include the counsellor, but they will also not talk about sexual matters at all. This makes understanding client relationships incomplete. And in view of the concern about HIV infection and the need to talk about sex and sexual relationships, as well as the dangers of needle-sharing, ease and normalizing ability with sexual topics is essential. It is also important that the counsellor understands the nature of clients' reactions as this makes it easier to talk about them.

There can be other forms of sexually-related behaviour. Sexually seductive behaviour can be a defence mechanism, a way of diverting the counsellor away from sensitive issues. Sometimes seduction can be the way clients reassure themselves of their sexuality. Sometimes clients will test out the boundaries of permissible behaviour and use possible counsellor reactions as a way of exerting power in the counselling.

If people are to be themselves, then they are to be sexual persons. This also applies to the counsellor. There may be times when counsellors have sexual feelings towards their clients, and they should be able to speak about them to their supporter or supervisor. It is normal when this happens, so the employing agency should have adequate facilities to deal with it when it does happen. Above all, a culture that is against even the mention of such feelings leaves open the possibility of professional sexual abuse, counsellors taking advantage of their position. This is also more likely to happen when there is a very unequal power position, when the client feels emotionally unable to stop such overtures and unable to talk about their occurrence with outsiders.

ENDING THE RELATIONSHIP

Ironically, the forming of a good counselling relationship can make the ending of the relationship difficult and even traumatic. If there is a stated number of counselling sessions, then work on ending should be started when there is a third of the sessions to go. Often clients will exhibit separation anxiety and not want there to be an ending or even talk about an ending. They will bring new material or new problems or crises to the counselling sessions. It is easy to get tempted into dealing with these new difficulties, especially as clients can inject a sense of desperation or urgency into the procedure. Nevertheless, it is essential that the ending work is done, despite pressure from the client not to do so.

Ending work should also be seen in a positive light. It is not just a way of rounding off the counselling, it is a way of dealing with loss and ending relationships. In more symbolic form it is about dealing with death. Thus the work of reviewing with the client what work has been done, what has been achieved and what might still remain to be worked on in the counselling is important. However this still does not deal with feelings about termination itself and the feelings it can arouse such as anxiety, anger and sadness.

Josie: 'What do you mean you are going? You can't go, you can't leave me!'

If the counsellor has little time to prepare for termination, as can happen if moving to another job or another area, then feelings of rejection can be re-aroused. These in turn can lead to anger against the worker or against all helpers.

Maggie: 'I'm done with social workers when you've gone.'

Alternatively, there can be modified reactions to the termination. Each client resolves their anger as best they can. The expression of such feelings helps the client to come to terms with the ending.

Beth: 'If a social worker comes then I'll say I'll see him in the office, but not in the house. If they come to the house then I'll tell them to get out.'

Clearly, these feelings are not in the client's best interests. It is necessary to explain leaving with all the clients, not such an easy business when the counsellor's mind might be elsewhere. However it is essential to talk through the reasons for leaving, as clients can take leaving as rejection in the absence of such explanation.

Tina: 'If you have to go, you have to go. Is it promotion?' (To Josie) 'Well, you can't expect him not to go, he's got his family to think of.'

The termination is a two-way process, and if it is well done, or done as well as can be done under the circumstances, it helps both clients and the counsellor. All clients should be part of the process. Even if it proves not possible to see some clients face-to-face, they should be contacted in some way.

Susan (extract from letter): 'When I got your letter, I felt I lost the only friend I had, cos you were good to me and gave me a lot of help and support. I will miss you, Paul. I am sitting here thinking of all the things you've done or tried to do, and I just abused you. If I knew you were leaving so soon, I would have told you how sorry I was and grateful for all you've done. I will close now, Paul. Give my love to your wife and kid. God bless and take care.'

If fact though termination can be a short period of time yet it can be enormously productive. The client and counsellor are forced to re-evaluate their positions, and they might also see each other slightly differently. They are no longer just linked through work but as people.

The termination process may not be quite so simple, and part of this arises from clients having separation anxiety and not coming to round off the counselling. The whole idea of separation seems too threatening and the only way clients can deal with the situation is to avoid it. My reaction is to try and make contact at a slightly later date and this has in practice proved useful, both in ending the counselling properly and also dealing with client feelings about not having previously faced up to the ending.

The other aspect that counsellors have to keep in mind is the most appropriate time to end. There is usually no obvious cut-off point. Clients will always be able to present the counsellor with new problems or difficulties, there will never be a time when everything is troublefree. Thus to some extent the termination point is going to be arbitrary, when the counsellor thinks the client will be ready to deal with situations without any help from the counsellor. After being in counselling, few clients feel able or want to be able to move to such a position so ending is never going to be that easy. Sometimes the counsellor will misjudge the situation and the client will not be ready to be without counselling help. This can happen because clients kick against future ending and the counsellor, expecting such a reaction, might ignore client behaviour. Sometimes this can be well merited, but sometimes the client really is unready to move into the ending.

Endings will affect both clients and counsellors, the latter sometimes finding their counselling effectiveness diminished because of experiencing separation anxiety. For this reaction there should be agency or colleague help for terminating counsellors as well as clients.

SUMMARY

One might ask whether the relationship really is so important, and if so, whether we want to know more about the relationship. The reason for this is that knowing what is happening can make counsellors very self-conscious and this leads to self-conscious behaviour, behaviour which is stilted and does not really represent what the counsellor wants. This is not counsellors being themselves.

This objection does not hold up in practice, as counsellors can use knowledge about the relationship to fix new objectives, and self-knowledge can be integrated into ongoing behaviour. A comparison might be with counsellors being videoed; self-consciousness is quickly lost and the counsellor forgets that there is a camera present. Attention gets caught up with the client and the camera is forgotten.

Relationships are all different and they all change over time. As counselling heroin users can be long term, the relationship needs to be monitored carefully. Counsellors need to be self-monitoring, and be properly supervised and supported.

7 WORKING WITH CLIENTS

PRELIMINARY THOUGHTS

Introduction

With a grasp of the reality of illegal drug use and some of the issues and difficulties involved, together with a helpful counselling orientation and thoughts about the preferred counselling relationships, the counsellor is ready to move into the work of counselling heroin and other drug users. As much of counselling requires a giving of self, everyone's approach is likely to be slightly different, as each counsellor is different. Thus there is no absolute way of working with drug users. Everyone has to work out their own counselling style, the style that suits them as well as the clients, and which falls within an ethical framework. The style may well be altered by the actual practice of counselling, so constant self-monitoring is essential, and notice taken of what is happening in the counselling.

The equation of drug use is not merely an explanation of what might be happening but an instrument of work. There should be a close integration of our understanding of drug use with counselling action. Counselling drug users is not something the counsellor should do blind. Counselling drug users may cover several years, off and on, and the need for structured understanding is essential for long-term work to be productive.

Thus counselling in the long term is aligned with objectives taken from the overall theory of drug use. Such objectives are shared with the client and they are to be worked towards, provided the client is in agreement.

Referrals

Clients can come themselves to the counsellor or counselling agency, or be referred by other people or agencies. My preference is for the former, for self-referral, as counselling aims to encourage persons to take decisions for themselves. It is preferable that clients come for counselling because they want to, and not because it is part of a referrer's agenda.

However counselling services are not always well known to

potential clients, so referral by agencies or even mention of the services or their holding of relevant leaflets can be useful. This requires ongoing liaison with agencies, a list of referral criteria for the drug counselling and, what is often overlooked, an understanding by other agencies of the nature and role of counselling.

Counselling setup

Counselling should be a service to clients, and should be established as such. The location should be close to transport routes but does not have to be local. Too localized a service results in there being a lack of anonymity. Appointment systems are generally necessary, as drug using clients brought together may result in users reverting to normal subcultural behaviour, such as swapping drugs or sharing syringes. For those clients who are off drugs or trying to come off, this sort of behaviour is highly upsetting. An appointment system lessens the need for an extended set of behavioural rules for clients and having to ensure that clients abide by them.

Counselling should be tailored to client needs, and in practice many clients prefer counselling to be at home. This is not so convenient for the counsellor, but the service is not primarily for counsellors. We should also remember that many clients are likely to be parents with young children, who might find coming to an office regularly inconvenient or very difficult.

Whatever services agencies or counsellors advertise as being on offer, it is likely that drug users will come but not necessarily for counselling. Instead they might want someone to help them increase their prescription, someone to help them get more money from Social Security or help with accommodation. These quite practical needs have to be satisfied in some way. Failure to do so will prevent clients from looking at other issues and even cause them to drop out of counselling altogether. As the initial client concerns are often of a practical nature, referrals to appropriate outside agencies become important. Alternatively, the service should include a range of services, of which counselling is merely one part.

Who is the client?

Sometimes drug users will be referred by members of the family, sometimes by parents, who are concerned and ask that something be done.

Mother: 'I've got five daughters and four of them are on drugs. Can't you do something for them.'

This can be reinforced by users complaining within the family that no-one ever helps them. However unless the user really wants help, then there will only be resentment that the counsellor has been brought into the situation. For referrals by someone other than the client, it is essential to tell other agencies, referrers and clients that cases are not taken on without client agreement. Often it can be the drug user's parent or a referring agency who really is the client, and not the user.

Length and frequency

Counsellors should have an idea of the length of time of counselling and this is best limited to an hour at maximum. Beyond this, client concentration tends to lessen, as can that of the counsellor. The frequency of counselling preferred by myself is once a week, the same day and time if possible to help clients remember. A greater frequency is more likely to lead to dependence on the counsellor. The sessions may be taken twelve at a time and then I have found that a break afterwards of up to eight weeks can be helpful. The client might or might not then agree with the counsellor to embark on another set of counselling sessions. Such breaks give the clients time to digest counselling input and try to modify their behaviour, if they so wish. Such attempts can then be taken back for further work to the next set of sessions.

Indefinite problems

Drug users may turn up for help with a rather vague idea of what they want. Indeed, practical help may be requested simply because they do not know how to ask for help as regards more intimate or threatening areas of their life. They find it difficult to ask for anything but immediate and practical help. Sometimes heroin users will come along with indefinite problems just to see what counselling is all about. Some clients need help to express what they want from the counsellor. Sometimes clients want someone to talk to or someone to relate to, but feel guilty to admit as much.

Thus it is not always apparent initially why clients have come for counselling or whether there might be underlying issues that are troubling them. However there is no need to rush clients. If they want to tell the counsellor something, and there is a good relationship, then they will do so as soon as they feel comfortable.

Long-term work

As counselling is often longterm, it is worth taking note of the fact, not merely by having rests between sets of counselling sessions, but by paying attention to planned objectives and sub-objectives, steps on the way to the overall aim of the counselling. It is easy to get caught up in client agendas, always reacting to practical demands or the latest crisis. Each set of counselling sessions should have an overall aim to which the counsellor and client should work, despite all the diversions and digressions. This ability to work towards some specific end, though not always welcome at the time, is later seen by many clients to have been useful. Clients have to learn to plan and execute long-term aims for their own benefit.

Another aspect as regards long-term counselling is that it is easy for both client and counsellor to fall into a rut. Clients can learn how to be professional clients, giving the answers that are expected of them or saying the 'correct' things. Anyone who has heard psychiatric patients giving a self-diagnosis will be impressed by how well patients can mimic psychiatric language. Clients are able to fall in with counselling attitudes and ideas, without actually believing them. They can return counsellor language and give the impression of understanding and agreeing with the counsellor. Counsellors in turn can also find that they start seeing work with clients as being routine. It is the counsellor's responsibility to be creative and innovative, to see counselling as an art, as a challenge, and react accordingly.

Contracts and agreements

Counselling is usually accompanied by contractual agreements, both parties agreeing to attend, and to work together in a proper and useful manner. However thought needs to be given to what these agreements really mean. Firstly, they were instituted because counselling was a service which had to be paid for, and contracts were needed to ensure legal payment. Now they have often lost this financial obligation, counselling being free under health and welfare programmes, and under charitable aegis. The contract basis of many current agreements, without such a financial aspect, is of doubtful legality. Nor is it obvious what should take place if the terms of such contracts are broken.

My main concern is to integrate any agreement into the counselling itself and make such an agreement meaningful. Contracts are little understood by heroin using clients and seem to me to be out of place. What is required are agreements that support the counselling and give an outline of what both parties can expect from each other. The emphasis is on what each wants and how it might be achieved, not what each has to do. As client behaviour at the beginning of counselling may be variable, even seeming chaotic, there might be an alternative. The counsellor gives the client a statement of intent, detailing what the counsellor will provide but not requiring any similar statement from the client.

Confidentiality

One aspect of the work that needs to be discussed and confirmed is the meaning of confidentiality in the counselling situation. The simple declaration by the counsellor that 'Everything you say here is in confidence' is seldom sufficient. Although most counsellors do not make videos or tapes of counselling sessions, the usual practice is to have some written notes or précis of the sessions. Confidentiality is never absolute, so counsellors should delineate the relevant boundaries.

Notes or records, even when kept under lock and key, are likely to be accessible to more than the counsellor. They may be typed up or word processed by someone other than the counsellor. Aspects of the counselling may be discussed with colleagues, managers or supervisors, and the counsellor's support person. None of this need produce difficulties, provided clients are informed of these facts, and that confidentiality is kept within the counselling agency and with the support person. It often helps if clients meet other agency persons and the counsellor's supporter.

Another aspect that can be usefully discussed is that of the status of what is said by any one client.

Layna: 'I can talk much more if it's off the record. I would not speak half as much if all of it was on the record.'

Very occasionally, clients will object to the idea that confidentiality is not secrecy, and refuse to go along with the counsellor's ideas. This is perfectly acceptable, and it merely means that the counsellor cannot help. This happens very occasionally, and clients have later changed their minds and accepted the rules.

Most difficulties can be resolved by talking through the rules of confidentiality and these in turn should take on board possible client concerns. For instance, information of clients' drug dealing has to be carefully considered as the police ultimately have the right to examine counselling records in serious criminal cases. On the other hand, records can be usefully employed in counselling if the client is encouraged to read them from time to time.

Confidentiality is very much a professional concept and little understood by some clients, perhaps most clients. Clarifying this area is important, not just in itself, but to bring further structure to the counselling relationship.

STAGE 1: AT THE BEGINNING

Introduction

The following is just one approach to helping clients stop their illegal drug use. As the emphasis is on this aim, the other aspect of building and maintaining the working relationship with the client is not featured. However it is just as important a part of the work and its absence here, though making for a simpler account of the work, is both somewhat misleading and might give the impression of the counsellor moving from one stage to another. In practice, work is never so simple or so clean. One stage will merge into another, or earlier work might have to be repeated. Stages can seem simple but passing through them also depends on forming a satifactory relationship and there can be difficulties in the relationship.

Listing of the various parts of the work may give the appearance of the counsellor having to work in a certain manner. Yet once the counsellor tries to force the client into a set pattern of working, there is the almost inevitable outcome of resistance and then having to repair the working relationship. Thus there are different aspects of work to be covered, but it is through the relationship that counsellors sense when and how the work should be covered.

Desires and expectations

After the formalities of the referral, the counsellor should check out the client's desires and expectations. The desires are what clients want for themselves and many clients are likely to be uncertain. Some clients will want very short-term goals, often little to do directly with the use of drugs. Yet others will mention modifying their drug use without really intending to do so. Thus it is worth taking time to discuss generally what clients say they want at this stage. This is not to say that the counsellor will necessarily help to fulfil the client desires. More work will be required before the counsellor can make any such decision.

Client expectations very much cover what clients see as the counsellor's role, what the counsellor can do to help. Some of the expectations are unrealistic. Another person would be a better one to give help. However the counsellor is able to begin to define the counselling role and help the client to understand it.

Counsellor's approach

Parity demands that the counsellor in turn should discuss desires and expectations. Often counsellors have unstated desires, such as clients should come off drugs but see declaring these desires as being out of place. Alternatively, counsellors will not be concerned about the client's drug use as such. Whatever the unspoken agendas, they should be stated. Accordingly, clients' problems are taken as they come and clients are not pressurized into modifying their use, despite what is known to be possible counsellor agendas.

It seems to me unrealistic to pretend that many of the clients' problems and difficulties are not related to their drug use. Problems with drugs themselves, with finance, with accommodation, with relationships, with violence, with employment, with the Law and with the parental family or families are likely to be linked with long-term and chronic drug use. To attend to individual problems and ignore the main factor, the drug use, merely allows further future difficulties and possible dependency on counselling. Far from helping, ignoring the drug use can further lock clients into dependency.

However to insist that clients should modify their drug use is likely to prove unhelpful. Individual difficulties should be attended to, but work should also be done on the drug use, if that drug use is linked with other problems. We have to realize that drug use might be completely unproblematic, even if it is illegal. Indeed, clients who take heroin occasionally, inject safely, do not share syringes, and are well able to pay for it, may experience no difficulties at all.

So counsellors have to be certain as to what may be useful work and what is irrelevant or distinctly unhelpful. And the perceived remit should be conveyed to clients, to be made subject to negotiation. We should bear in mind that the nature of such negotiations will likely reflect the nature of the overall counselling.

Problems with drugs

Again, the counsellor has to be careful to avoid making assumptions because of preconceptions about drug use. The use of physically addictive drugs or even being physically addicted should not automatically be equated with having problems. Equally, I have had clients with drug problems although they were not physically addicted. Clients who were using cannabis, amphetamine and, most commonly, alcohol and nicotine.

Bearing this in mind, work has been divided into general work on drug use and aspects of work with physical addictions. The dividing line is thin at times, and the division is somewhat arbitrary, yet it can be helpful to keep some such separation in mind.

Assessment by discussion

Often clients are made subject to assessment, a process which rapidly gathers information about drug, relational, financial, accommodation, legal and medical matters. This is one approach but my preference is to let clients talk about their situation. Structured assessments affect the relationship from the start, put the counsellor in a position of dominating power and so inhibit clients. So long as the counsellor bears in mind relevant topics clients might have been overlooked, a discussion about client difficulties is generally more productive.

It can also be argued that formal assessments are not always accurate as clients are not inclined to be very revealing initially. These assessments can label the clients or set up counsellor images before they have started to get to know the clients, and this can affect the degree to which they do know their clients. In fact, counsellors make little use of them in practice.

Referring out

The counsellor can soon tell whether work with the client is appropriate or should really be taken on by another agency or organization. However, even if the client requires counselling help, the counsellor still might have to determine whether other workers or agencies might be of more help. There is often a reluctance to refer out, in preference to recognizing one's own limits. In the following case, the client refused to take off his dark glasses, so it was difficult to say whether the alleged heroin user was on LSD, suffering from amphetamine psychosis or schizophrenia, or whether he was just very strange.

Daniel: 'I want to live a normal life, say the most abstract theory and have it accepted. I want to know why people take offence at abstract thought. People hear what you are thinking. In communication I am not classified as real. I am alienated from society for not thinking the right thing. Perhaps it is my overall movement in space that's different.'

I did at least recognize that assessing this client was beyond me and required more specialized work, and accordingly made an external referral.

Starting the process

The counsellor has arrived at the point when the whole subject of whether the client wants to come off heroin in the long term arises, or whether there are other ways he or she can be helped, which might be determined. The question remains open as to whether the client is at the same stage. Often, clients will be emotionally charged, and simply want to let go, to ventilate.

Chris: 'Some people have to keep talking because it's not what they think, it's how they feel. They don't want to hear what others have got to say.'

So time should be given for ventilation, and this is usually over within ten minutes. However, if this stage is omitted, it is difficult for the client to attend properly to anything that follows. When this ventilation has largely subsided, time can be given to working out what the client really wants. Clients should always be given options, so they are not pressurized into agreeing with the counsellor and taking up the counsellor's agenda. Often clients will say they do want to come off drugs and this should not be accepted at face value. The next question is do they really want to come off drugs? And if clients still answer in the affirmative then the next question is, why do they want to come off?

- Wanting to come off because their partner or family want it is insufficient a reason.
- Wanting to come off because they are in trouble with the Law is insufficient a reason.
- Even wanting to come off because their health is being impaired is insufficient a reason.
- Ultimately, the only satisfactory answer is that they want it for themselves. They want to come off for themselves.

This can sound quite threatening to the client, but it need not be. It is important to ensure that the client does not feel pressurized. This can be done with a light touch, it can be done by asking the client whether he or she feels they are being forced into an unwanted position. The client has also to be brought into the counselling process, and have it explained that the counsellor's underlying concern and the client's long-term aims are to be shared for mutual benefit.

Centring the client

Clients who want to come off, need to put themselves at the centre of the process, at the centre of the work and at the centre of responsibility for themselves. They have to work towards taking responsibility for themselves and not expect the counsellor to do so. This requires the counsellor to get clients to begin to own their feelings, beliefs and actions.

One way of doing this is to get clients to think about their drug use. If they are addicted to heroin, then whose habit do they have? If they experience withdrawals, who feels the pain? And whose drug use is it? I stress that clients' drug use is not bad, it is not good; it is not stupid, nor is it clever. The only thing that can be said is that the drug use belongs to them. This may seem obvious enough, but clients have to tell themselves that it is their drug use, and then they can tell others such as the counsellor that the drug use is theirs. They have to own their own actions.

Honesty and realism

The drug use belongs to the client, and this is the reality of the situation. To maintain this reality, the client must acknowledge this reality. This might seem to be another way of saying that clients should be honest with the counsellor, but to me 'honest' has over-tones of being judgemental and 'dishonest' has even more, signify-ing not telling the truth to someone. As long as clients know the reality of their situation, then they are at liberty to tell me, as counsellor, something else if they so want.

People sometimes wonder why I should want clients to admit their heroin use, then say that clients do not have to tell the truth, if they so desire. What clients want to tell us may, of course, be more than it seems initially.

Me: 'You said you hadn't taken anything today.'
Reg: 'No, nothing.'
Silence
Reg: 'I haven't taken anything, as the doctor said if I start again I'll only have two months to live.'
Silence
Reg: 'Well, I had a smoke (of cannabis), that's all.'
Silence
Reg: 'I was in a house and everyone was having a shot and I was on downers. They offered me one and finally I took it.'

– 163 –

Me: 'Mmmm.'

Reg: 'I overdosed. I wouldn't do it again. I'm feared of overdosing. If it wasn't for my wee sister I would have been dead. She knows how to bring us round. It was the first time I OD'd.'

Me: 'The first time?'

Reg: 'Well, I've OD'd before, but I've been able to bring myself round – but not this time.'

The point is not that clients have to be honest and say what they are doing, but to acknowledge that if they are using drugs then the results of that use belong to them. Clients should allow us to know as much as they want us to know, but once they have let us know, then they cannot escape the logic of the situation, that the counsellor will work from this given point.

Preliminary moves

The counselling has kept with the idea of being non-directive and this may give the impression that counselling drug users is a passive process, whereas there is a need to be active. Drug using clients are often locked into fixed attitudes, beliefs and patterns of behaviour. Sometimes they can benefit from active counselling, even a bit of a jolt to get them out of the rut of routine behaviour patterns. However if the jolt is too extreme, if it is confrontational and diminishing of client self-esteem, then the tactic can well prove counterproductive – apart from any ethical considerations. The clients always have to be respected as people in their own right, but small jolts which aid personal movement, insight, or fresh feelings can be helpful.

For instance, if clients come for help with changing or stopping their drug use, then one approach might be to ask them if this is what they want, then why did they simply not do it yesterday or a week ago or a month ago. Why now?

Sometimes clients say they wanted help but delayed making the change until they came for counselling. Sometimes they will say that they want to come off but cannot do it if they are not pre-scribed substitute medication. Sometimes they will say they were not ready then, but they feel ready now. Sometimes an incident has made it more imperative that they do come off. Sometimes they simply did not think of changing their drug use a month ago.

My reaction is that what has been said is rather negative. And if clients are negative about changing their drug use then they will not be able to change it. In fact the client has demonstrated some quite positive actions.

Moving to the positive

Clients often come for counselling with a fairly negative view of themselves and their actions. Part of the counsellor's role is to help clients see themselves and their actions differently, in a more positive light. Clients are often at a loss to think of anything positive they might have done. They do not see that taking the trouble to come for help is a positive act. They have bothered to stay to this point in the counselling session rather than walking out, and that is positive. They have entered into the work despite hardly knowing the counsellor or the nature of the work, of counselling. They may also have decided that a change in their drug use could be helpful. The client has acknowledged that drug use is his or her drug use. The client has said so to the counsellor. All this is very positive.

At the same time we should also remember that for clients with low self-esteem, positive reinforcement has to be done carefully, as they are unlikely to be able to take too much. And what they see as too much might not strike us as excessive.

Tina: 'Maggie was doing my head in. When we went out, she was saying how everything would be okay, boosting me up all the time. She went on all the time and it went for my head.'

When we talk of giving the client a jolt, we refer to client changes in perception and seeing the world in a positive manner. At this stage, a movement to a positive attitude is important. Little has been said about actual content, what the client is bringing to the counselling. Of course, what clients are bringing is themselves and time should be taken to set up a useful counselling relationship and an arena for personal growth.

Accentuate the positive

Making client perceptions more positive requires reinforcement. This can be done by discussing how the client feels about seeing themselves in a more positive light. At this early stage clients have difficulty in seeing themselves positively, so I ask clients whether they believe me, whether they feel I am unrealistically trying to look for something good in the situation, whether they simply think I am wrong. All these questions lead to discussions that get the client to think about what has happened and different ways of viewing the past.

Counsellors should not expect a sudden conversion. However by starting the process from the very beginning, it is not necessary artificially to introduce positivity at a later stage.

Eliminate the negative

Drug-using clients tend to carry a lot of negative feelings and perceptions, products of their past behaviour. Putting the past into the past, finally ending bits of the past which interfere with the present may be important. One of the possible episodes from the past which can affect present behaviour is that of previous attempts, successful or not, to stop or change drug use.

If we look at past so-called unsuccessful attempts to change personal drug use, then one task is to see what makes the clients label them as not successful. For instance, if the client never managed to modify drug use at all then we should see this as successfully taking a decision to change, a decision that many other drug users might not have taken.

If the client did actually change drug use but then went back to using, then stress should be put on the fact that there was a change and this has to be distinguished from staying off, or maintaining the change. The task will be to stay off or maintain the change. What clients have to appreciate is that they did achieve something, no matter how little it may seem to them.

These small actions have to be seen as part of the whole long-term process of personal change and growth. What may seem as failures to change or change permanently are better seen as successful explorations of change, successful first runs or trials. These are usually necessary before clients are able to do exactly what they want.

STAGE 2: WHERE THE CLIENT IS AT

The equation of use

If clients definitely want to change their drug use then it does not help to hold up the process by talking about it too much. Thus this stage might be very much foreshortened according to the client's situation. However we still have to try and establish where clients are in their drug use.

One possible method is to look at the equation of drug use, as outlined in the discussion about drug theory. This is a much more specific approach compared with trying to estimate how serious the client is about coming off from what they say and how strongly they feel about it. By using the equation of drug use, we can help clients identify relevant factors and how best to deal with such factors.

The equation of drug use is the balance of disadvantages of using drugs compared with the advantages, the resultant balance giving the desire to stop or at least modify drug use. However to avoid the impression of pressing clients towards change, the first task is to see why any particular client should continue to use drugs.

Ongoing advantages of using drugs

As the client may have declared an intention to change drug use, there well may be a disinclination to see any advantages in continuing. However it is important that they should be examined and both client and counsellor not be left with the idea that there are no such advantages.

The counsellor can help the client who is having difficulties trying to identify the advantages. Some of them might be:

The experience of taking the drug is pleasurable

- The drug might produce feelings of euphoria, whether it is from the direct effect of the drugs or not. The client may feel happy or at least content or relieved. Alternatively the mode of use might produce pleasure as with the rush from intravenous use.
- Pleasure can come from a sense of novelty, another new experience, or new experiences and feelings.
- Another advantage comes from the pleasure associated with the excitement of taking the drug. Again, this can refer to the drug effects or the mode of taking the drug.
- Taking risks may be another positive experience for the user, especially if the user feels he or she has somehow won.
- Doing what others may strongly disapprove of may make the user feel better and release some internal anger.
- The whole preparation of taking the drug, the personal ritualism of drug use behaviour can be pleasurable and comforting to some users.

Intoxication of the user

- Many users will take drugs to get intoxicated or stoned. The aim is to get close to unconsciousness, 'to be out of it'. Such behaviour may be interpreted as pleasurable in some way partly as the normal rules of social behaviour can be broken by the user.

- Intoxicated behaviour can give licence to the user to behave in particular ways, to regress and act in a childlike manner, or to feel irresponsible and behave accordingly.
- Intoxication can help with the expression of feelings, so users can say how they really feel. There might also be the advantage that others will be equally intoxicated and so fail to remember what happened or what was said, often an advantage.
- Intoxication by most drugs gives varying degrees of relief from anxiety, and relief may also be given by memory impairment which often accompanies intoxication. Users who are under the influence may well feel better as they have a sense of personal power, both physical and mental.

Anxiety relief
- The advantage of anxiety relief has been mentioned, and this can produce several different pluses. This relief can of itself make the user feel better. A weight is lifted from the user's mind. Relief can be given from current difficulties or more serious underlying problems.
- Further benefits can come from the user feeling more confident and this allows different behaviour and perhaps behaviour closer to that really desired by the user. It may permit the user to display greater abilities in social interaction, helping to form and maintain relationships.
- At times the absence of anxiety can allow the user to relax, and apart from being enjoyable itself, relaxation can allow the user to sleep which might be important.

Subcultural gains
- Part of the advantages of drug use may well be caught up in being part of the local drug subculture. For the young person, the subculture offers a bridge from the parental home to personal independence. Such a bridge may be felt as necessary or helpful, especially if life at home has been unhappy. The subculture can then become itself a second home for the user, and the safety and comfort that this represents – however accurate or inaccurate this client view may actually be.

- The subculture can represent an antidote to boredom and for teenagers, boredom can be a real enemy. We should bear in mind that boredom is a state of mind and is not just avoided by activity, as it can arise from lack of meaningful action.
- The subculture can provide new experiences, excitement and risks for the user. The lack of these can contribute to feelings of boredom.
- The drug market-place with its exchange of drugs, information and gossip provides not merely activity but a place for the expression and reception of feelings.
- The subculture provides a place where status may be gained, skills exercised and a personal identity be formed or reformed. However we might view the outcome, they might be advantageous as far as clients are concerned.

Ongoing disadvantages of continuing drug use

With disadvantages there is always the temptation to moralize, to say why such use is bad rather than why user clients may find continuous use not to their benefit. What is important is the perceptions of the clients, whether we agree with them or not. Each client has to decide for himself or herself what is best.

Health matters

- Continuing drug use does present risks to the user's health in the long term. The precise risk depends on the nature of the drug, the amounts habitually used, the method of use and possible contaminants in the drugs.
- Heroin and other opioids produce surprisingly few direct dangers to the user, the chief one being that of overdosing. Multidrug use considerably increases the chance of overdosing and reduces the likelihood of recovering from the overdose.
- Injecting drug use is the most risky method of use, with increased risks of overdosing, endocarditis and septicaemia. Septic retinitis can occur if lemons, used to acidify the heroin, have been allowed to become fungally infected. In addition there is the risk from sharing syringes and needles, with the resultant infection of HIV and Hepatitis B. Abscesses and blocked veins are further risks of needle use.

General health care

- There are indirect health care risks that might also affect the user. These can range from poor dental care, partly as a result of the high sugar diet, to the presence of trackmarks which can be considered disfiguring, especially by women users. Also heavy drug use can result in users eating irregularly and poorly, so that heavy amphetamine or opioid users can have a 'clapped in' look, with sunken cheeks and extreme thinness. The general medical state leaves the heroin user more open to the ordinary infections.

Legal matters

- The risk of getting involved with the police generally increases with time, as does the chance of getting caught committing an offence, of being known to the police, store detectives and the Drugs Squad. The danger is that users will be eventually convicted of offences and become known as persons who have been in trouble with the Law. This may affect to some extent relationships with straight friends and acquaintances, both how they view the users and how the users think they will be viewed by straight people. The net result can be that users slowly drift away from straight people and are locked more closely into the drug subculture.

- Convictions are a matter of record, and this in turn can affect future hopes, such as hopes of employment or of travelling abroad and staying in certain countries. And if offences increase, then the user is more and more likely to end up in prison, locking the user even closer into the subculture and cutting down on options.

Underlying problems

- With ongoing drug use, the user is prevented and not helped from trying to deal with underlying personal difficulties.

- Thus continuing opioid use prevents to a large extent the user from being upset by underlying difficulties, such as parental loss. It also means that the user is unable to grieve.

The final equation of use

We might think that the final equation of continuing use is merely the disadvantages of continuing less the advantages of continuing. However there are further complexities. What constitutes advantages and disadvantages varies for each user, not merely in how the outside situation can change and affect the use, but also how the user perceptions of the situation can change.

For instance, at first, drug using behaviour can seem exciting and provides advantages for the user. However the same behaviour, going out to get money and then going to score, changes imperceptibly to being less exciting, to becoming mundane, routine, and then being seen as boring or a hassle. Time is one of the variables in the equation. Another variable is the one of the user's age. In time, there might be less of a desire for excitement, or risky behaviour might seem foolhardy rather than exciting.

Another change comes with parenthood. As with criminality in general, the greatest decrease in deviant behaviour results from parenthood and the accompanying different perceptions. This is much more than drug users being afraid that the authorities might act against them, though dislike and distrust of social work authorities is high. Rather the perceptions of parents change. I have yet to meet drug using parents who want their children to become illegal drug users, with the possible exception of smoking cannabis. So, despite their own behaviour, they see their children having a different future and indeed may place their hopes for the future in the children rather than themselves. Also the role of being a parent demands time and attention, specially from women users, which puts a strain on being a user. Finally, with time drug users slowly mature as people and not merely take on different perceptions but become more able to deal with their underlying problems.

Use of the drug equation

The argument against the equation of drug use is that the various components cannot be quantified and so it is not helpful. We cannot say accurately to what extent, for example, in any particular case how much the disadvantages do or do not outweigh the advantages of continuing drug use. This is quite true, and it would be wrong to imply that this way of looking at client motivation *is* very accurate, though to my mind it is more accurate than going along with drug user statements that they want to stop or change their drug use.

An accurate answer to whether a client really wants to change or not change personal drug use is itself irrelevant; the client is either going to change or not. The process of working through the drug use equation by clients helps them to clarify their thoughts and so allow them to choose what they really want. Thus what is happening is a form of client empowerment. This is true only if the counsellor treats the whole process neutrally and does not attempt to influence the client to one conclusion rather than another.

Realism

Working through the equation of drug use, the emphasis has to be on a realistic view of the client's wishes. Having reviewed the advantages and disadvantages of continuing drug use, the client has to decide whether to continue or not. Clients will often say of course they want to change their drug use and that is why they have come for help. My conclusion is that they do indeed want help, otherwise they would not have bothered with outside help. This being the case, the client will best be served by working more closely on his or her own self. As counsellor, my role is to help the client do this and to support whatever decision the client makes. It is not my role to stop the client using drugs or to instruct the client how to use drugs more safely. Naturally, if the client wants to discuss such topics, this will be done. But the present task is that of helping clients discover their true desires and intentions.

On occasions clients see themelves as knowing what they want and the process of counselling as being rather irrelevant, but these clients actually tend to be unsure of themselves. Part of our personal strength is to know our weaknesses and to be able to ask for help. Counselling is a process that clients can find both interesting and enjoyable. But clients also find out things about themselves when undergoing the process. They are sure or surer of themselves at the end. The degree to which this can happen depends in part on the client's involvement. Those wishing to skip through the work, those who tend to give the answer they think they should give, or provide the answer they think will be to their advantage, these clients will not get as much as they could – and that is their choice.

Fully engaging clients is the ideal. This rarely happens when counselling heroin users. Clients have asked, 'Why do you want to know if I am really going to change?'. My reply is, 'It is not important whether I know; it is only important that you know for yourself. You are taking drugs and you are also taking control. This is all for you, not me.'

A provisional decision

Having discussed the varous advantages, disadvantages and relevant thoughts and feelings surrounding their drug use, the clients are in a better position to know their own minds. At times it seems useful if I play, *sotto voce*, the devil's advocate to probe the client's reason for change. This can help clients to firm up their views. Clearly, too challenging a stance will merely confuse clients and this also may put the counselling relationship under strain.

The decision taken by the client now determines where counselling will be going. This has to be stated and reinforced in a positive way. As counsellor I say that I am always unsure what is happening until the client and myself have worked through the equation of drug use, until I feel sure as to what the client really wants. And sometimes clients do not know, though they might say they know.

Client control

Clients who know what they want will find achieving it is possible, if they have control. This means instead of giving the right answer or the answer others want them to give, the answer actually comes from them. Client control can be increased by the counsellor, and this is done partly by encouraging clients to work through difficulties. There is a paradox here, in that the counsellor wants clients to undertake certain work, yet client control is apparently not helped by the counsellor taking such a determining role. Again, the proper use of the relationship is essential. Counselling has to be gentle and not put across in an impersonal manner but in a professional and personal way. Also the client should be informed as to what the counsellor is trying to achieve; that the idea is for the client to take control and that the whole purpose of counselling work is to that end.

Client feedback

Although working through the whole drug use equation is reasonably structured, there has to be flexibility. This can be augmented by asking for feedback, finding out what the client feels about the counselling and what the counsellor is trying to achieve. Feedback is pointless unless it is used, so feedback has to be interwoven into the future planning of client counselling. Feedback also helps the counsellor to judge where the client is at and whether to go on to the next stage or not, whether to review the work to date or move forward.

Cognitive examination

The next stage is to reinforce the client's growing control and perception of that control, perception that the client is moving to what is desired. This is done by looking at the client's beliefs and the client's re-examination of those beliefs.

This process can be done by the counsellor asking questions to elicit information about client beliefs and I usually preface this by asking the client not to answer straight away but think about the question carefully.

- The first question is, 'Do drug users need drugs?'.
- The second question is, 'Will drug users always use drugs if they are available?'.
- The third question is, 'Do drug users do what they want?'.
- The last question is, 'Is it true, once a drug user, always a drug user?'.

The counsellor goes through the questions, asking them in a general way then asking whether they apply to the client, such as 'Do you need drugs?'. The discussion should not be threatening but can be around the meaning of need in this context. The aim is for clients to examine their own beliefs with the counsellor's help. Sometimes there is the need to attend to client language, in particular phrases such as 'I must ...' and 'I can't ...', which usually have to be re-interpreted as 'I want to ...'. Also clients have to own what they say, so that instead of phrases such as 'People say that...', clients say 'What I say is...'. Such attention is needed as so many heroin using clients need to be clear and honest with themselves.

As usual, at the end of a stage of work there should be time for feedback and the concommitant to further building and establishment of the counselling relationship.

STAGE 3: WHERE THE CLIENT WANTS TO BE

Decision time

The counselling time taken so far has basically been used to help the client explore options before coming to a decision, and at the same time to build up the counselling relationship. This allows both counsellor and client to review options together.

The time has now come for the client really to say what he or she desires to do as regards personal drug use, and the counsellor can help by briefly reviewing the options. The main options might be:

- information sharing
- continue to use drugs as before
- continue to use drugs but stabilize use
- continue to use drugs but use them more safely
- continue to use drugs but get the drugs prescribed or substituted
- continue to use drugs but move to legal drugs, usually alcohol
- reduce drug intake in order to come off eventually
- come off on prescribed drugs
- stop using drugs, whether or not this involves withdrawals

What decision

For some clients to make a decision two issues may have to be cleared. Firstly, the question is what do you want? This is not the same as what are you going to do? At this stage there is no more than a declaration of desire, not an intention to act. Thus the client need not feel intimidated or panicked by the thought of having to carry out the declared decision. The second is, it is quite all right if the client feels very unsure what to do or what option to choose. The client is saying only what is desired and it should be stressed that most clients are ambivalent at times about what they want. It is helpful if a choice is made. If the client wants to change that choice at any later date then that is acceptable and, it is hoped, the counsellor will be told of any change.

After the client has chosen then reinforcement is required, no matter what the choice was. The way this can be done is to ask how clients feel at this point, whether they feel better having made their choice of what they want. Sometimes it helps to say things are going well from the counselling point of view, that definite progress has been made and thanking the client for the work put in. For many clients the idea of getting somewhere is quite up-lifting.

No desire to change

Clients come for help and then might decide that they do not want to change, or even they do not want a counsellor or this particular counsellor to help them. Whatever the decision the counsellor has to accept that this is what the client wants at this stage. The decision to continue using drugs might worry the counsellor. Perhaps the expectation by the counsellor has not been fulfilled or the counsellor thinks that the employing agency will not accept the decision.

Clearly the counsellor should know how to handle the client's decision. Moreover knowing is not enough. The counsellor has to be able to accept the decision and react accordingly. And certainly the counsellor should not try immediately to dissuade the client. There is clearly no point in encouraging the client to make a free choice and then not accept that choice.

If clients do not want to change their drug use then counselling might have to be terminated, unless help is being given for other client concerns. Rounding off the ending, reviewing the work done and ending on a mutually positive note is very important. Drug using clients do not forget the counselling experience and will return if they feel the experience has been good. And some of them do return as their circumstances change or after some time has elapsed.

Reinforcing desire

If clients basically do not want to change, then as counsellors we have to accept this fact. However if they want change then it is acceptable to see if that desire can be changed into intent. One way of helping this happen is to ask clients what they want and then ask them to imagine it had actually come about, that they have achieved what they want. Clients usually need help at this point, so counsellors can assist.

For instance, if the clients want to stabilize on a prescribed substitute drug then I might ask them to shut their eyes and imagine this scenario.

> *You have just woken up in the morning.*
> *It's cold and there's snow on the ground.*
> *You think, 'Oh, no! I've got to score, go out on a day like this.'*
> *Then you remember that you are seeing the doctor first thing.*
> *You will be picking up your methadone script.*

I then ask clients how they feel at this point.

> *Do they feel relieved?*
> *Do they feel good?*
> *How do they feel about those who are not scripted*
> *and have to go out to score?*
> *How do they feel about themselves,*
> *for having got on a prescribing regime?*

Then my reaction after positive responses is to say that being scripted is somewhere the client wants to be. And not just in imagination but in actuality. If this is the case then the client has to work towards it. This is not going to happen by itself, so the client has got to make it happen. If that is what the client wants then as counsellor, my job is to help the client try and ensure what the client wants comes about.

Information sharing

Information sharing might seem to produce no change at all. However some drug users will enjoy and benefit from sharing information about drugs and drug use. The sharing aspect is important as not only does it fit in with the mutual approach but one can discover what the user knows, rather than the user being told what are the 'facts'. The facts may be a matter of dispute at times so the purpose is not to impart knowledge specifically, but to increase client awareness.

Many users starting to use are surprisingly ignorant of the effects and initial heroin users have been surprised to experience pain, not being aware of the possibility of withdrawals. Alternatively, some users have imagined that physically addictive drugs are instantly addictive, and taking a shot of heroin is the same as being addicted. Other myths have been that smoking or chasing heroin, rather than injecting it, will prevent physical addiction. Users may think amphetamine stops heroin withdrawal pains or believe that opioids damage the body. If other drugs are considered, and most drug users will use a variety of drugs, then the scope for misinformation is considerably greater.

This information sharing does require that the counsellor has a reasonable knowledge of drugs and their use. Also counsellors should feel comfortable about talking about drug use, and not imagine that such talk will encourage users to try different drugs. Detailed drug knowledge will be required if the subject of safer drug use is discussed.

Stabilizing use

Clients stabilizing drug use is one way of using drugs more safely, lessening the risks of overdoses. However the main benefit is that stabilization can provide a springboard, in due time, for further changes and so can be quite a positive move. It is the first definite movement in regaining personal control and should be recognized by the counsellor as such.

The difficulty with stabilization is the question of how this should be achieved. Either it can be done by the careful use of street drugs or users can be prescribed a substitute drug, if they are physically addicted. The first method is often not easily achieved as the supply of street drugs can vary or stop completely for a time, so a stabilized dose might not be easy to ensure.

Getting a substitute drug prescribed is comparatively easy in metropolitan areas but may prove much more difficult in rural areas. In rural areas there might also be greater difficulty in ensuring confidentiality. If prescribed, the usual substitute in opioid prescribing is methadone mixture. The level agreed with the doctor may well be different from the equivalent amount of street drug used. Thus the user might well be stabilized on a lower or higher dosage of drug than previously.

The drawback of all substitute prescribing is that the user gives up much control over personal use, which might be useful in the short term but disadvantageous in the long term. If the user wants to come off, then personal control is needed as only the user can come off – no-one else can do it. However this assumes that the user really wants to change. We have to remember that most users who request substitute prescribing do not want to come off drugs, they merely do not want to have to pay for their drugs, and avoid associated activities such as having to commit offences to raise money for drugs, or having to go out to score. This can lead to false expectations by prescribers, who may demand a reduction in the substitute drug over time.

Safer drug use

Safer drug use is an option taken up by many drug users, at least in part, as they see what they are doing as merely common sense. Thus one approach is to go through the various safer drug use methods and ask how many the client is already using and get reactions to other ideas. We should also bear in mind that many users may not know everything about drug use, so discussing drug use can be mutually beneficial.

The first point is to use safer drugs. When using opioids it is safer to avoid dextromoramide (Palfium) as the effects tend to be uncertain and overdoses are more common than with other opioids. Diconal when injected can give medical complications. In possible multi-drug use, barbiturates are best rejected in favour of benzo-diazepines as the latter have a low toxicity level and avoid the risks of barbiturate burns and arterial spasms when misinjecting.

Adulterated drugs

The change to prescribed drugs is one way of not taking street drugs. The latter are more risky as they are adulterated and their strength can vary, which makes overdoses much more likely. Also the presence of adulterants, which are put directly into the bloodstream on injection, can cause both damage to the veins and bacterial or fungal infection.

Users can never be sure what they are really getting when they buy drugs on the streets and they might be buying different drugs from those stated by the buyer. Thus barbiturates have been used in street heroin mixtures, with clear risks of overdosing when injected.

Another possibly future danger, and one experienced in the United States, is the synthesis of drugs and of new designer drugs. For example, laboratory synthesis of the designer drug synthetic heroin or MPPP (methylphenylpropionic piperidine) can contain MPTP (methylphenyltetrahydopyridine) which has caused Parkinsonism-like paralysis.

Situational considerations

The third approach is to vary or change completely the method of use. For instance, hallucination producing opioids such as pentazocine or mixtures such as old-style Diconal containing the antihistamines cyclizine, are best taken in places where accidents are less likely, away from open fires, windows, away from roads or open water.

The presence of a few friends, at least one not under the influence, can be reassuring and can help in case of user panics or overdoses. This presumes that others know how to help, and simple First Aid instruction, especially putting those unconscious in the recovery position, can be useful and possibly life-saving. Apart from knowing the correct action to take in cases of overdosing, instruction can prevent users from incorrect or dangerous actions such as injecting the conscious user with amphetamine or saline solution.

Other dangers include those of causing fires, usually by dropping lighted cigarettes when under the influence. The use of drugs by vehicle drivers or motor-bike riders presents accident risks, especially as drugs can also impair judgement, and those who originally had no intention of driving may end up doing so.

Injecting use

Injecting use is almost always intravenous use, and will be assumed to be so here, unless a note is made to the contrary.

The first point is that drugs suitable for illegal intravenous use should be soluble in water, or the drug effects will not be experienced. Thus crushing up diazepam (Valium) or the weak opioid diphenoxylate (Lomotil) tablets and injecting the 'solution' is pointless. Temazepam, a benzodiazepine taken by many opioid users, is dangerous to inject as it precipitates out in the veins and can cause gangrene.

The user has to know how to inject properly. The equipment, all equipment, should be hygienic and it is best if it is new. Syringes are cheap and are intended to be disposable, and not for continual use. Drugs are best if pharmaceutical and dissolved in distilled or boiled water. The injection site is best disinfected. Air bubbles should be removed, the vein pumped up, by clenching the fist for intercubital injections or with the use of a tourniquet. If there is difficulties with getting a vein, they can be enlarged by the use of hot water or having a bath. This assumes the user knows the difference between veins with its bluish blood and the red blood of arteries. This is particularly important if the groin is used, as the femoral veins and arteries are comparatively close together. The syringe, when pushed in, is angled so the needle points towards the heart, as opposed to away from it.

Sharing injection equipment

Counsellors should realize that the nature of the subculture tends to be that of social interaction, accompanied by sharing of drugs and equipment. The usual argument is that users never know when they may be without drugs or equipment, so lending out to others is an investment for the time they find themselves in a similar situation, needing a syringe and needle. But more than this, part of the drug use ritual can be that of sharing. Thus smokers who do not pass cannabis joints around will be seen as very anti-subcultural. The sharing of syringes has tended to be another subcultural norm. Thus the spread of HIV infection is only the last in the line of syringe transmitted infections, the previous being malaria and hepatitis B.

Thus preventing syringe sharing is more than a simple individual behaviour pattern and all drug subcultures need to be properly informed of the risks. Moreover, users should always carry clean spares as some users will pressurize others to give them the use of a syringe, and users cannot always withstand the pressure, which might become physical.

It should not be assumed that users who have been told of the risks of infection will necessarily change their behaviour. Many will, but there does seem a small core who will not, because of the stage of drug use they are at, their particular life-situation, and their particular past and future. Also when users find themselves withdrawing, with drugs but no injecting equipment, then they are likely to use anybody's syringe, whatever the risk.

Part of the difficulty is that ending needle-sharing may be the counsellor's agenda but not that of the user. From the user's viewpoint, the sudden interest in the welfare of drug users is seen, with considerable justification, as being open to suspicion. For years drug users were not offered any help. Thus the help is seen as part of the fear of HIV transmission to others, not any real concern for drug users. This is not an absolute barrier, unless the counsellor refuses to take on such client concerns. The counsellor simply says that mistakes might have been made in the past but it is the present concern for the client that is important. The counsellor should not be afraid to talk through past helping experiences.

By talking through injection practices, it is generally possible to come to a reasonable agreement as to what is best for the client. Alternatively, the user's satisfactory practice is reinforced.

Jane: 'I've never sterilized my works, but as soon as I'd finished, I would draw boiling water into them, and rinse them through five or six times.'

The change from glass to disposable syringes has resulted in few users taking pride in them. However, it is better to try and get clients to see safer injecting behaviour in a positive light, rather than merely trying to frighten them into change. Clients who have insulated themselves from thoughts of death are not likely to respond to threats.

Stopping injecting use
Although taking steps to avoid sharing injection equipment, the only real way to use safely is not to inject drugs at all. Using clean injection equipment still does not avoid the risk of overdosing, and the number of fatalities through overdoses tends to be overlooked.

To end injecting use, we have to try and understand why users inject. And though there are rational reasons for such use, the main feature is that injecting is typical of some local drug subcultures and not of others. Thus Scotland has tended to have injecting drug users subcultures and England does not. However there are some heavy injecting subcultures, such as Merseyside. Similar local variations are also typical of different drug using subcultures in the United States.

Once a culture becomes injection orientated, this becomes the norm. This is also true for other methods such as chasing the dragon. Thus injecting use is more than an individual behaviour pattern. It may reflect that of the local subculture, and be reinforced by that subculture. So group action has its place. However there is no overwhelming reason why users should use by injecting, or, conversely, use by another means. The mode of using, like drug using itself, is ultimately a matter of choice.

Reviewing injecting use

Just as there is an equation for drug use, we can consider there being another equation for injecting use. There are reasons advanced for injecting use which might have some basis in fact or might be myths. It is said that injecting is the quickest way to experience drug effects, and this can be important for the user who is withdrawing or anxious about doing so. Yet the rapidity of injecting applies only to intravenous use, and even this is not as rapid as absorption of drug vapours through the lungs, as commonly used with crack or freebase cocaine. But in practice injecting is very much slower, and in some cases is the slowest method, as it can take a long time for users to get a hit. To my knowledge users with very poor veins can take up to an hour to get a hit. This also overlooks the surprising rapidity by which drug effects can be experienced by methods such as chasing and snorting. Thus it is worthwhile discussing injection use so the client can work out what really are the advantages and disadvantages.

Other reasons for using by injection include the ritualism of use, the pleasure associated with making up the shot. Even the pain that often goes with injecting, especially in the long term, can be a help to those internally aggressive or wanting to portray a macho image. Also there is a demonology of injecting use which for young people can be attractive, and there can be a status in the local drug subculture that goes with injecting use. Needle-buzz is another displaced pleasure that can be an advantage to the user.

There are also the disadvantages, which tend to increase over time. Thus pain, medical complications and the likelihood of infections increase. As veins become blocked, so new and more painful or risky injection sites might have to be used.

The balance of the equation of needle use may indicate a desire to stop but addiction to the needle may prevent an end happening. However this addiction is only psychological, and once the user has stopped needle use for a few days, the addiction is broken.

Multi-drug use

Avoiding multi-drug use is another way to safer drug taking. Some drugs act to reinforce each other, and one of the commonest examples is that of alcohol and opioids, a combination which not only increases the risk of overdosing but makes recovery from the overdose more difficult and death more likely. It should be added that when taking drugs, users often fail to consider alcohol as a drug and so can overlook the risk.

Another form of multi-drug use is drug mixtures such as a snowball, a mixture of cocaine and heroin, where the rush comes mainly from the cocaine, but the smoothness and long-term effects come from the heroin. The difficulty is that the user who wants to stop has now to deal with stopping two drugs simultaneously, more difficult than just one drug.

Generally some users will adjust how they feel with the use of different drugs. But in the long term, this can result in the user being unsure as to what is normality, what it is to be without drug support.

Moving to prescribed drugs

If drug counsellors complain that my approach to action with the client user seems very slow, all that is needed is to get the user on prescribed medication and work from there, then my reaction is to ask them to observe what happens to such clients. Are they really any closer to where they want to be? Moreover the whole system whereby doctors prescribe to drug users has resulted in drug subcultures moving to prescribed drug subcultures. What started off as an answer to a problem has become part of the problem.

This does not mean my reaction is to go against prescribing, merely I am against walking into situations unprepared and with an unsure grasp of the aims and objectives. So before jumping for a prescription, I ask users to think and discuss what this change might mean. Often there is a great desire by users to be prescribed if they are physically addicted, and often when they are not so addicted as they think. This desire may not be completely rational but one born of feelings. Users may want to get drugs without the bother of committing offences and having to score, to avoid constantly being on the wrong side of the Law, but in practice there can be feelings of envy that others are getting scripts and they are not. So what may seem to be a rational decision by clients to get prescribed might reflect in varying degrees client concerns about feeling ignored or rejected if not prescribed. There is also the feeling that somehow prescribed users are putting one over not merely doctors but other users. There is little consideration of the implications of getting prescribed for personal drug use.

Aspects of being prescribed

It might seem that moving to prescribed drug use would appeal to all drug users. Without too much bother, the user is kept as a user – at least for a fairly long time – without the disadvantages of requiring money, committing offences or having to score street drugs. The number of users who are prescribed drugs, where those services are available, points to its apparent usefulness. However we should not jump to conclusions too quickly.

Many drug users do jump at the chance of being prescribed, but then have reservations about the whole process. The routine and hassle of getting money and scoring street drugs is replaced by the lack of personal control, having to wait in surgeries and wondering if the drugs prescribed might be reduced. But it is unrealistic to imagine that these users are then going to stop being prescribed. If they are not prescribed and continue to use, then they have to obtain drugs off the streets, go back to the hassle of having to raise money and then score.

A compromise is for users to be prescribed and then exchange or sell their drugs for street drugs. Alternatively, some drug users stop using but continue to maintain they are still using drugs, and will actually get stoned the day they have to go for a urine test. Thus the numbers of users who are being prescribed does not tell us the whole story. Such behaviour, if it is ever discovered, is taken as typical manipulative drug user behaviour, reinforcing any negative attitudes to illegal drug users.

What the user has to decide are the personal advantages and disadvantages of being prescribed substitute drugs, and in the long term. The chance of being prescribed often varies according to local policies and perceived medical advantages. Certainly the advent of HIV infection locally has made methadone so easily available in some places that those infected find it difficult to refuse, and few drug users can bring themselves to refuse methadone when it is offered. Thus prescriptions can result in an increasing medicalization of the user's life. This has its good points in that it is one way of getting drug users into medical services, and they may need help for medical conditions. On the other hand, gaining total control of life is not easy if the user feels controlled by those medical services.

Move to legal drugs

This is an option that is rarely mentioned by drug workers, but it is one that is probably most used by physically addicted drug users. Indeed, it is arguable that it is the most successful method. The opioid user may stop illegal drug use but cover the effects with large amounts of alcohol. The difficulty is that most drug workers would not recommend such a drug as alcohol, a drug which can produce damage to the body and whose disinhibitory effects can release personal aggression. Indeed, the use of alcohol can become so great that for a month or two it becomes the problem rather than any heroin or opioid use. This is serious for those who have experienced alcohol management difficulties in the past, and counsellors should be conscious of the risk of those likely to become rapidly addicted. Those with liver damage or with peptic ulcers have potentially serious health problems with a high alcohol intake. However the heavy use of alcohol is a passing phase and this self-help method of coming off heroin, in my experience, tends to be more successful than methadone prescribing.

There are several possible reasons. Firstly, the alcohol use is under client control, allowing responsibility and self-action to be taken. This also means that there is no fear of being forced to reduce or stop the use of alcohol before the client is psychologically prepared. The fact that alcohol is easily purchasable eliminates any anxiety that it might not be available. Drinking alcohol does not mark out the client as an illegal drug user, unlike methadone use, an attraction for some clients. Finally, alcohol may direct the client towards pub culture, which might act as a bridge into an acceptable social milieu.

If drug using clients do take alcohol regularly in an attempt to stop opioid use, counsellors should be careful not to interfere automatically in the client's chosen process and end up reinforcing that opioid use rather than assisting the client to stop. On the other hand, there may be ethical and practical reasons against suggesting this method as a viable method of coming off opioid use.

Coming off by reduction

This method involves users simply reducing their drug intake. Sometimes outsiders think that this can only be done by moving to prescribed drugs, that going onto a prescribed drug programme is the only way to come off physically addictive drugs. However the substitute drugs are just as addictive as the street drugs used, so one addiction is replaced by another. Of course, for some users the belief that substitute prescribing makes coming off easier could well be a self-fulfilling prophecy and this is by no means unhelpful.

Going for zero drug use means that there has to be a careful self-monitoring by the user and this is done best when the user has control. The user then has more interest in self-monitoring and acting on the results. The first point to be made is that if the client is using a large amount of drugs then the reduction can be comparatively large and rapid initially. This is worth considering, otherwise the whole process of coming off can be very prolonged. Too rapid reductions however can cause the user to panic and this generally results in a sudden increase in drug use, maybe ruining several weeks of reductions. The user has control but talking about these possible occurrences is useful.

Further points for users are that they should not increase dosages. Sometimes users will say that they have had upsets in their life and have to have more drugs. In fact, upsets are better dealt with by keeping a clear head and not increasing drug use. Besides which, once this has happened, the users' lives will suddenly be filled with 'upsets'. Finally, the hardest part of coming off drugs is the very last bit, coming down from very small dosage to negligible to zero. Sometimes the usage will actually bounce up again as the user gets anxious about the idea of doing without addictive drugs. It will probably take a long time to stop use completely, and this should not be seen by the counsellor as the client putting off the final action for good, rather the client coming to terms with a life free of opioids.

To help the process, providing the client with a diary for private use, not to be shared with the counsellor unless the client so desires, can help clients remember how much they have really taken. Often clients will be surprised at the amounts. The diary has another use in that after a time clients can look back and see the progress they have made, how much they have reduced their drug taking. Also support from the client's partner or family is not merely helpful but tends to be more meaningful in the absence of medical assistance.

Coming off on prescribed medication

This method has the advantage of not being overly painful and medication can be given for interrupted sleep, which is often the reason why coming off drugs is so difficult. However giving medication for interrupted sleep can be a double-edged sword as the user has to stop using this hypnotic drug at some point. The client thus has the task of possibly coming off another prescribed drug. Prescribing has the advantage that there will always be a supply of drugs, but the demand by doctors that reduction should be at prescribed rates can be counterproductive and fails to deal with the psychological difficulties of coming off.

Coming off without drugs

The idea of coming off addictive drugs and going through withdrawals without employing any drugs at all, going cold turkey, is not a popular idea and can seem very threatening to users. However it should be said that for clients who have been using opioids for a short time, this method is not nearly as bad as is so often portrayed. Indeed, novice users have come off quite easily. For such clients, the use of prescribed drugs to 'help' in the process can be of very dubious efficiency and can actually worsen the situation, lock the client into long-term drug use. Long-term heroin users can also come off with nothing, as the process is not life-threatening, unlike coming off the physical addiction to depressant drugs such as alcohol, barbiturates or benzodiazepines. Nevertheless, it is usually a very unpleasant process. Even so, it does have the advantage that its very unpleasantness can be a benefit, as users are not likely to want to repeat the experience. Thus the chance of restarting is diminished and the few cases of users going cold turkey known to me tend to support this.

The two major factors the drug user has to combat in withdrawing are pain and sleeplessness. To overcome pain, the user has to remember that the worst will usually be over after 72 hours, so the immediate objective is to get through those hours. Users imagine that the pain will go on for ever, and keeping a target of three days in mind, even if a bit arbitrary, is often helpful. Pains can be eased a bit by drinking pure orange juice and taking warm baths. As pain is usually better withstood when the person concerned is in good health, it might be better before coming off to institute a good diet and be on it for at least a couple of weeks before coming off. The other aspect to bear in mind is that if the client's attention is sufficiently diverted, no pain at all will be felt. Thus users, rather than treating themselves as if they were ill, should attempt as much as possible to get involved in activities, even though they might not feel like it. Having support, people around all the time, is a good way of diverting the user and this is especially important at night time. The user really wants people about then, as sleep is likely to be poor and unsettling.

Sleeplessness is a very wearing affliction and users have to steel themselves for the lack of sleep and not spend too much time trying to get to sleep. The feelings of tiredness should be ignored and users should simply try to do without it. Also they should not get worried because they are not sleeping; in practice they will snatch brief moments of dozing without realizing it. Finally, milky drinks are useful to help sleep, if the clients can face taking them.

This method, though fearsome in reputation, should also be used by those who are not physically addicted. It should be remembered that even long-term users, who are using poor quality street heroin on an occasional basis, may not actually have a physical addiction. Certainly, discussion about this method is useful and we have to bear in mind that some users will try it as a macho act, reflecting their status in the drug subculture. There are a few users who 'do not have the addiction in their head', are physically addicted but have few psychological problems and so can come off relatively easily. This method, though applicable to merely a few, does leave those persons with a sense of achievement so 'cold turkey' should not be ignored as a method, though we should be sensitive to its threatening image.

STAYING OFF

Introduction
The emphasis on help for drug users generally has tended to be on coming off drugs or using drugs safely, rather than staying off, or not using drugs again. Part of this arises from the medicalized perspective which treats drug use as being purely about the use of drugs.

Ironically, staying off is even ignored medically, so no drugs are given for this purpose, though in practice naltrexone, 150 mg taken orally, can completely block for up to 72 hours the effects of any opioid taken. This drug, to my knowledge, is not used in this country. The general attitude tends to be that once the drug user has been brought off drugs, that is the end of the process, rather than seeing it as the start of another much longer process.

To make matters worse, those who do restart their drug use are often regarded as weak, as failures, as never having had the intention of really coming off drugs, of being ultimately uncooperative or resistant to medical and other forms of help. Such perspectives are not useful to either the drug users nor the helpers themselves. They rest on prejudice rather than any analysis of the situation.

Equation of use

To analyze the situation we have to go back to our equation of drug use. Put in the context of stopping drug use, we see that stopping is merely a particular balance, a state where the advantages of stopping outweigh those of using drugs.

Stopping drug use is a large change in behaviour. This change can itself affect the factors that enter into the equation of drug use. Thus we might anticipate that the drug user might change behaviour and revert to drug use as the balance in the equation of use is shifted.

This can be easier understood by taking an example. A drug user is in poor health as a result of taking drugs and so decides to come off and does so. However after a few weeks the ex-user is enjoying much improved health and so one strong reason for stopping using has gone. The balance has shifted towards using and the person restarts.

Changing factors

When analyzing the situation of the client, we have to take into consideration all relevant factors. The first category of factors are concrete factors, factors which have had a direct effect on the desire to come off. These can include medical factors such as the ongoing medical condition, legal factors such as outstanding Court charges and threatened marital or partner breakup. Other factors can be financial such as outstanding bills and personal debts, and relationships with the user's and the partner's families.

Other factors are those which are not concrete, factors such as those of perceptions. The user has perceptions of certain aspects of taking drugs such as the accompanying risks and excitement of such use. Before coming off, the risks of continuing use may seem high and the excitement low. However after being off drugs for a time, perceptions might change and the ex-user might see the risks of using as being not so high and the associated excitement having been higher than previously viewed when still using. Another example might be that of users wanting to stop using drugs as they do not have sufficient control of their lives. However once they are off, then they feel differently, that life is not so difficult to control and this will now apply to drug use, so there is less reason not to use drugs.

Apart from different perceptions, there can also be different expectations. Thus drug users see coming off as an important stage, which is probably quite correct. They also see it as a change to better times, when life is generally going to be better, only to find this does not seem to be the case when they are off drugs. Similarly, life should be much easier and there should be fewer problems, but this does not seem to be the case either. Part of the reason for this arises from unrealistic expectations. So much hope is placed on what it will be like when off drugs in order to help users through the process of coming off. In addition, the absence of drugs results in the users taking a closer and more perceptive view of what is going on, discovering problems and difficulties that previously were unnoticed or about which they were not concerned. Thus it may seem that coming off drugs results in more problems, not fewer.

Another associated outcome of not taking drugs is that underlying problems are not helped by coming off drugs. Indeed their presence may well be experienced more acutely. Drugs at least took away the emotional pain, which now must be withstood by the ex-user without chemical protection. The snag is that a reliance on drugs has made the user less able to experience difficulties. What others might see as a problem, but a copable problem, has been transmuted into a critical situation for the ex-user.

Reinforcement

After drug users have stopped their drug use, then their lives may well have changed. For example, previously the user experienced little reinforcement to use drugs. In fact the reinforcing factors were present but did not matter as the user wanted to use drugs, so the reinforcement was hardly perceived, or if perceived was felt too be insignificant.

Such reinforcing factors could include other users offering drugs, seeing people under the influence of drugs, walking past dealers' houses, hearing that there was good gear in town, even listening to people talking about drugs. These factors move the balance towards the ex-user restarting drug use. Most ex-users are well aware of the pressure arising from these reinforcers, so they should have a strategy to deal with them. The simplest is to avoid places where the client is likely to encounter one or more of these reinforcers. This is not so easy as may appear. For instance, one client came off heroin but his brother was still using. This meant that he had to avoid his brother and refuse to see him, not easy when his brother was so often in difficulties and wanting help.

Another problem can be that there are so many drug users locally, it is hard to avoid them. And there is also the subcultural social aspect, as one user recognizes another and is likely to talk. This becomes almost a reflex action, and the ex-user has to unlearn the behaviour.

New factors

After the client has stopped taking drugs, there will be new factors that arise. Those relevant and close to the ex-user will react to the change in client behaviour and what they see as the change in the client. They might react quite positively to the change, or adversely. For some families the drug user may have become the family scapegoat and serves the whole family in this role. It is good to have someone to blame, especially if such blaming diverts attention from more fundamental family problems. So families might be ambivalent about the user coming off drugs and this could cut across the user's hope of total family support. Family ambivalence is supported by memories of past hurtful behaviour by the user and now, being off drugs, the ex-user may be more open to reproaches about such behaviour.

In addition, users may come off drugs but no-one believes them, or those close and dear to them do not believe. This may lead to the reaction of 'what did I come off for?', and the ex-user questions the value of having come off drugs. Also support is not forthcoming from those close because they do not believe, or, what often happens, they do not let themselves believe. They have been disillusioned in the past by the user saying he or she was off drugs, only to discover this was not the case or coming off was followed by the ex-user starting up again.

Loss

Finally, stopping drug use leaves clients with feelings of loss. Sometimes it is assumed that the loss of bad times is no great loss and will not trouble those affected. But clients will not necessarily see drug using times as so bad.

There were good times, otherwise the clients would have ended their drug use much earlier. More importantly, the difficulties lie around the fact of a loss having taken place, no matter how good or bad the times might have been. If nothing is done about the loss, unless users come to terms with it, then there are likely to be more difficulties and a greater chance of relapse and the ex-user restarting.

Work on staying off

When working with clients on staying off, the first point for discussion is that this stage, staying off drugs, is the most important stage. It is more important than the process of coming off, and it is the stage that receives little attention but needs the most work. Clients do come off drugs and then start again, later to feel bad about restarting. Most of their problems arose through not appreciating the importance of the staying off stage, of imagining that coming off was the greatest hurdle and afterwards drug users just stayed off drugs, having achieved their objective. The really big advance is to accept the importance of staying off and to be prepared to take the stage seriously.

What was previously seen as the end, when the drug user comes off drugs, is now properly seen as the first major step along the road of totally coming off and staying off, of finally being oneself rather than merely a drug user, merely acting out a role. The individual takes full control and becomes fully himself or herself. To achieve this, clients have to see staying off as a very positive and active stage, a stage where there has to be more work, not less, than when coming off drugs.

The work should be intensive and it should be related to timed objectives, timed over a month, three months or whatever is a relevant time. Clearly, when the client has just come off, objectives are fixed with short time spans, even a day at a time initially but then increasing. Moreover, the user needs support and this means moving from privatized drugs use and behaviour to a more open and sharing mode of behaviour.

Starting the work

The work of staying off drugs should demand a heavy programme, and this in turn demands extensive planning beforehand. The ultimate aim is for clients to stay off drugs, but the counsellor and clients have to be realistic enough to recognize that there may be relapses. This should be seen by all as a likely part of the overall process and not as the end of coming off, not as a client failure. Sometimes clients will restart once, twice, six times, many times before finally coming off. These periods of re-use tend to be spaced further and further apart.

And the first point for the user to accept is that there can be little relaxation after coming off drugs. This is the time when the pace of work accelerates and days should best be filled with various forms of activity, both mental and physical. This amount of work may actually be helpful in itself. The chief enemy for the person off drugs is likely to be boredom, so work has to be done to counter-act this threat.

Physical activity

One simple objective is for the ex-user simply to become fitter, to take lots of physical exercise, something which many users do not do. Swimming, cycling, circuit training, aerobics, going for walks are all ways of being active and filling time. However there are other advantages. Exercise is one way of relieving depression which often appears, in mild form, after ending drug use. Also, by taking such exercise, the client can meet new people and can come to re-experience and appreciate different places, gradually building up a different perceptual system and so being able to re-evaluate what it means to be off drugs.

The taking of constant exercise, though hard at first, is useful if monitored, as clients then get caught up in their physical progress and are not constantly judging their progress merely in drug orien-tated terms. Indeed, some ex-users who take exercise, once they become very fit, can get a high or boost from the exercise itself and the need for drugs is further diminished.

Loss, again

The end of drug use means a loss of a former pattern of behaviour and the user should be allowed to grieve for this loss. This idea may sound strange to some, but the client should be allowed to talk through the whole experience of taking drugs and coming off. Most clients will want to do so, though whether they do so with the counsellor largely depends on the counsellor's reactions. Some drug workers still have difficulties with this work as they feel that clients who talk about their former use are paving the way to trying it again. Alternatively, counsellors who encourage their clients to talk about former drug use could be seen as encouraging or reawakening client interest in drug use.

In practice, the counsellor should wait until clients want to talk about past drug experiences. They should not be forced to do so because the counsellor thinks this is what they should be doing. Equally, the counsellor should be totally receptive to what clients have to say. Often clients will go over some incidents time after time, and this is all part of the grieving process. My reaction is to get clients to expand on what they have to say, and especially to talk about their feelings about their drug past. Clients can also be self-censoring and think they should not admit that there were good times and taking drugs was pleasurable.

Often clients will experience feelings of guilt about their past behaviour and get locked into their guilt. Blaming anyone, whether oneself or others is not constructive. Clients should recognize that people are not blaming them, so they should not blame themselves. They should however recognize the very positive feelings people have about them being off drugs and stay with those feelings.

Clients who have suffered a loss often look for a replacement or substitute, and this process can be quite helpful. Unfortunately, some workers feel that to substitute one behaviour pattern by another is to replace one dependency by another, and this does not denote any great progress. My reaction is that we work with reality, not ideals, and if the replacement is less harmful in the short or long term, then it represents a useful change in behaviour.

Ongoing problems

Even when client drug use has ended, there are likely to be outstanding difficulties which require attention. Sometimes these are financial, as clients often have unpaid bills and outstanding drug debts. It might be imagined that coming off drugs would end most financial worries, but this is rarely the case. Firstly, many drug users are able to raise money when they are using. The drugs they take give them the courage to commit offences, and the feeling that they have to get money for their drugs drives them on. However once they have stopped using, their nerve often goes and they lose the knack of being able to raise money quickly, if dishonestly. What makes the situation worse is that when a person is no longer using, then drug debts are likely to be called in, and failure to pay can result in physical violence against the client. My feeling is that drug debts should be paid as soon as possible, even if they are debatable or represent dealers chancing their arm. It is more important to cut such drug use links than look for equity or justice. Moreover any debt can usually be negotiated. In the end, most people are interested in getting their money, even if they have to wait a bit longer for it.

Other outstanding problems may be legal ones, but these are usually simpler as keeping off drugs never goes against clients in Court, so as long as clients contact their lawyer or a social worker in good time so a proper report can be submitted. If the outstanding offence is grave, then clients have more options by going to prison without a drug addiction.

Underlying problems

Stopping drug use means that underlying problems or difficulties might reappear, the absence of drugs making such problems harder to repress. However the complex nature of these difficulties, possibly covering topics such as past trauma, unresolved loss, difficulties of personal sexuality, and severe family problems make their resolution a long-term task. Clients usually find staying off drugs is as much as they can cope with, initially, so undertaking more heavy work might be too onerous. However the client and counsellor should acknowledge if there is such work to be done, even if it is to be undertaken at a later date.

DIFFICULTIES IN COUNSELLING

Overall difficulties

Counselling drug users will have its ups and downs, there will be problems from time to time as all personal change presents difficulties. However there will be time when there are much more serious difficulties, when client and counsellor seem to be getting nowhere or going round in circles, when the client drops out of counselling or the expected client changes simply do not happen. Sometimes the situation can be retrieved, sometimes it cannot, so it is best that such situations are prevented, but when they arise quick work is essential.

Build-up

Poor counselling situations rarely come out of the blue; rather, they build up slowly, almost undetectably at times, so the counsellor may not be aware of difficulties or is scarcely aware of them. The difficulties lead to clients not obtaining what they desire. Clients who continue to behave as previously, because they have decided that is what they want, are experiencing no difficulties; any problem that exists, exists for the counsellor and it is the counsellor who wants the help, not the client. Clearly, this is a matter that demands help from the support person or the counsellor's supervisor. It is important that difficulties in counselling have to be located either as being with the counsellor, or the client and counsellor.

Recognition of the problem

As problems in counselling are not always easily detected, the counsellor must check to see if they are arising but are hidden. Part of this comes from checking whether client objectives have been met, but the counsellor can also sense when the counselling does not feel right. Both can be indications which point to the counsellor perhaps needing to investigate further. There are three aspects that might be worthy of such investigation: the counselling relationship, the counselling and theory, and counselling and practice.

The counselling relationship

The health of this relationship can be judged from counsellor feelings and behaviour in the counselling session. The counsellor should be able to sense that the relationship is not helpful; it may be cold, distant or there seems no rapport there. These can be reinforced by the behaviour of both client and counsellor. Even little things like whether they smile at each other and other non-verbal communication, which is less easy to control than with verbal communication. General characteristics like the degree of animation or the tone of the voices can indicate how the two are interacting. The other extreme is a relationship that is too friendly and does not take notice of reality.

Layna: 'Mrs McLaren was a terribly nice person but I couldn't tell her everything, like I had had a hit. She would have been so disappointed. I can tell you as you would say, "You stupid bastard"... something like that.'

The counsellor might consider how much effort has been given to building the counselling relationship or whether the counsellor expected it to grow of its own accord. Sometimes the latter does happen, but other times the relationship needs nurturing. Another aspect to consider is that of termination, as some clients can react poorly to the idea, even when termination is a long way off. Difficulties in the relationship can reflect the client's desire to postpone any ending.

The counsellor has to think whether the relationship with the client has been discussed at all. If there are possible difficulties in this area, the sooner they are shared in the counselling, the better. Of course, if the relationship is not so good, discussion of it can prove unproductive.

With clients such as heroin users it can be very tempting to blame them if the relationship is not good, to blame their poor attendance for counselling, their verbal aggression, and their broken promises for making the counselling relationship poor. However it is worth the counsellor considering whether the problems really do proceed just from the client.

Firstly, the counsellor should review again the original expectations of the counselling, and what was said at the start of the counselling about what both expected from it. These expectations have to be related to the nature of drug user counselling and the relevant theory. For example, some counsellors will accept that the client who is coming off is likely to be irritable, yet feel offended when it happens in counselling. The counsellor should accept that there will be hard or difficult times, that the relationship will be stretched on occasions.

If the relationship is not good, then the counsellor should accept this fact. There is no reason why the counsellor should be liked or respected, and once this is accepted then the counsellor is more likely to be liked and respected. Part of this problem springs from counsellors feeling confident about themselves as persons.

Theory of drug use

Difficulties in counselling can come from the counsellor being out of step with the client, going at the wrong pace, and this usually means too fast a pace. It can be helpful to return to considering the equation of drug use, to try and work out at what stage the client is at. This depends not so much on what the client is saying, but the factors that comprise the client's position along that drug use equation. This can include the state of underlying problems, support the client is receiving, the present situation, and future hopes and expectations. It is possible that the counsellor has missed some relevant factor or factors, and so misjudges the client's real desire to change behaviour. Having missed a relevant area may point to poor listening by the counsellor or not giving the client enough space.

Counselling and practice

Counselling is very dependent on the client talking and the counsellor listening. For many clients who have low self-esteem, talking can be difficult in the face of perceived authority, expertise and status.

Marion: 'Why can't I speak to the doctor? I decided to phone him and tell him what the matter was, that there were other things besides the smack that was wrong with me, but I didn't. I have everything in my mind what I wanted to say, but I couldn't say it.'

As the client did turn out to have a serious condition, the inability to talk to helpers and the inability of helpers to be open to clients is of no small importance. And the difficulty in talking freely to helpers is more common than may seem.

> *Me*: 'Who do you find it difficult to talk to?'
> *Lynne*: 'Everyone.'
> *Me*: 'And what is it like, trying to talk to people? Do you feel you have nothing to say, or do you know what you want to say in your mind but can't get it out?'
> *Lynne*: 'Yes, the last. I can't say what I want to say. If people keep asking me questions then I would just say, "I don't know", or "Yes" or "No".'

Resistance

Other difficulties can come with the practice of the counselling, and these can often be termed resistance. Client resistance is resistance to counselling and assumes negative connotations. The client is seen by the counsellor as being difficult or obstructive. Sometimes the lack of cooperation is not obvious but is detectable only because the counsellor becomes aware that agreed objectives are not being attained or the counselling seems to be going round and round in circles.

However resistance may be a way of client coping, of stopping the counsellor from working with issues the client does not feel able to confront. Sometimes resistance can come after advances in counselling and the client feels unable to undergo any more highly charged work, so slows down or stops effective counselling. Sometimes resistance can give useful indications of the counsellor needing to consider all aspects of the counselling.

Forms of client resistance

Client resistance can be exhibited in various forms. The resistance can range from being quite conscious, a deliberate denial of what is happening, to a completely unconscious denial. Often the counsellor has to help clients to be aware of their resistance.

Other forms of resistance can include clients who blame others for their situation and so divert attention from their own difficulties. Sometimes the client can divert attention by treating matters in a superficial or joking manner, sometimes by intellectualizing or rationalizing, sometimes by fantasizing. Sometimes action is taken directly to the counsellor, either by verbal aggression or by playing the victim, so making it more difficult for the counsellor to continue. Sometimes the client will 'seduce' the counsellor by playing the 'good' client, the compliant client, a tactic which can result in the counsellor finding it difficult to challenge what the client says.

Using resistance

Client resistance can be viewed as not just the client trying to cope with a counselling situation, but showing the counsellor what issues are sensitive for the client at any particular time. The client might be able to face these situations at a later date, but not just now. Thus counsellors usually do not help by making clients face up to things, when the client has already indicated difficulty in so doing. Instead, other action is required.

Counsellor action

Useful action tends to be that of slowing down the pace of counselling, and temporarily leaving work with feelings alone. Instead there should be a move towards more support for the client. This requires that the counsellor accepts client resistance, acknowledges possible client discomfort, unease or anxiety. Resistance should be seen positively, and then it can later be discussed with the client. Resistance indicates areas of sensitivity and the counsellor might want to help the client investigate the reasons for such sensitivity and help the client come to terms with whatever caused it. However, the counsellor also has to respect reality, and introduce it when the client will benefit from it.

Sometimes clients can indulge in repeated resistance so that it becomes a pattern of behaviour and becomes maladaptive; resistance becomes almost a reflex reaction in certain situations whether it is useful or not. At such times, resistance should be challenged and discussed if it is becoming unhelpful.

Transference

Transference is when feelings from the client's past are placed on the counsellor. This results in the client behaving towards the counsellor in what seems like an inexplicable manner. Thus the client might be very hostile without reason, because the counsellor has set off feelings applicable to someone else from the client's past. Alternatively, the client can 'fall in love' with the counsellor.

Transference involves a false perception of the situation by the client and may require a counselling investigation to discover the source of such errors. As transference is unconscious, the counsellor helps to bring hidden causes to the surface. As these causes can consist of distorting past trauma, only by coming to terms with them can the client have a clear perception and so deal effectively with reality.

Extreme resistance

If resistance is allowed to become unhelpful, then the counselling situation can begin to fall apart. The client will turn up late or find reasons not to attend. Here the problem is not so much the client's own situation as the counselling itself, and this might ultimately end with the client dropping out of counselling. The counselling situation must be worked on, and consideration be given to transferring the client to another counsellor.

Counsellor resistance

In power-orientated counselling, resistance is typically seen as a client problem, thereby tending to overlook resistance on the part of counsellors. Counsellors are also likely to have their own sensitive areas and though through training they should have come to terms with such areas, the constant pressure of counselling and having to deal with painful feelings, painful to the counsellor as well as the client, makes for extreme sensitivity. Resistance is a way of dealing with this sensitivity, sensitivity that in extreme cases can lead to burnout. Less extreme symptoms can be seen in the counsellor's unrealistic expectations, in perfectionism or difficulties in dealing with needy clients.

Countertransference

Counsellors can experience countertransference, when a reaction to their own personal trauma or difficulties is sparked off by clients. The result is that counsellors react to clients in inappropriate ways. Counsellors are often aware of countertransference when they take a dislike to certain clients for no good reason. Countertransference can interfere with counselling and it may be one of the main contributors to difficulties in counselling.

Recognition of counsellor resistance

Possible signs of counsellor resistance can be the counsellor not paying attention during the sessions and being poor at communicating. This can result from the counsellor's own feelings blocking further feelings from the client. The counsellor's own feelings can make the counselling inflexible, acting as a protection against further feelings. Counsellor feelings can interfere in other ways. They can affect counselling skills, so that feelings are missed, situations misinterpreted and what has been said forgotten.

These effects are not always easily recognized by the counsellor. However other effects such as forming an unreasonable like or dislike of the client, arguing with the client or being defensive, are perhaps more obvious. The counsellor may also become sympathetic rather than empathic, so running the risk of becoming over-involved in the client's situation.

In more extreme cases, resistance can be seen in the counsellor starting late or giving excuses for postponing counselling sessions. The counsellor can become preoccupied with clients and counselling, and may try inappropriately to control the sessions through giving advice.

Resistance reviewed

Difficulties will arise in any counselling, so much rides on how the counsellor reacts to them. What the counsellor should always bear in mind is that these difficulties should be welcomed as providing possible indications of client troubles. They are thus steps to further clients' personal progress – though this view is not always easy to hold if clients are being particularly outspoken or aggressive.

Drugs in counselling

Many clients will come for counselling in varying degrees of drug intoxication. My practice is that any user who bothers or manages to turn up should be seen, though not necessarily be counselled. Clients under a heavy degree of intoxication simply will not easily take in what has been said and almost certainly forget what took place. We should also bear in mind that a lack of drugs can equally interfere in the counselling, though if clients are withdrawing they are unlikely to turn up.

Nicole: 'If a person is withdrawing, then it is no use talking to them as they don't really listen. It doesn't sink in.'

To say that clients under the influence of drugs should not be counselled is too simplistic a rule. Firstly, for the physically addicted, drugs are the means to normal functioning. Secondly, many clients coming for counselling are prescribed methadone or other opioids on medical programmes. To be free of methadone, clients would have had their last dose at least thirty-six hours previously.

Some agencies and counsellors like to differentiate between permissible and inadmissible drugs which clients can take. Apart from requiring urine testing, hardly in keeping with the counselling approach, the main criterion of whether the client can be usefully counselled is ignored. Rules are meaningless unless they are enforced, but this is likely to lead to constant confrontation and becomes a diversion from the task of helping drug users. While there is a need in this time of HIV infection for increased counselling, rules and restrictions are best kept to a minimum.

COUNSELLING IN ACTION

The following is a taped extract of a counselling session and demonstrates some of the aspects referred to in this chapter and others. The recording is interspersed with my thoughts. No attempt has been made to cover Josie's actual manner of speech.

> *Me*: 'Hello, Josie, come in. Thanks for making it in, today.'

Heroin using clients seldom get much positive feedback, and so feel little respected. After all, what is the point of trying if no-one bothers. It has to be appreciated by counsellors that it is quite an achievement for heroin users to make it to an office for counselling.

> *Josie*: 'Thought I wouldn't?'

Josie was suspicious that my remark was sarcasm. My intended opening remark could be better phrased. I forgot for clients with low self-esteem, praise or positive feedback can be interpreted as being threatening or undermining.

> *Me*: 'No, no. It's just that it's not always easy to remember which are counselling days. It's just nice to see you.'

Trying to explain has only resulted in me digging a hole for myself. I realized that I was going nowhere and switched to a more personal remark, which did relax Josie. When counselling it is easy to make mistakes, so knowing how best to recover is important.

> *Josie*: 'Well, I've got the doctor in an hour, so I had to get up early this morning.'
> *Me*: 'You're looking very well. Have things been going better lately? I think last session we agreed to look at your feelings about your addiction.'

Positive comments about appearance, provided that they are true, are usually well received. Heroin using clients are aware when they are going downhill and not blind to their appearance or how others might see them. I also think that it is difficult to overdo positive reinforcement. The aim of this particular session was alluded to, providing some shape to the session.

Josie: 'I'm back at my Mum's, but I don't know how long it will last ...'
Me: 'Still difficult?'

Josie did not pick up on the aim of this session at all but went off at what seemed to me to be a tangent. However I decided that this was not tangental for Josie, who wanted to talk about her mother. It seemed better to get this topic out of the way first, otherwise it was likely to block further progress.

Josie: 'Aye. She's still getting on at me, and she's still drinking.'
Me: 'Umm.'
Josie: 'You don't see her when she's been drinking or when she's drunk, as she only starts in the evening, after eight o'clock. She's all fucking nice when you've seen her, but that's been in the day. You don't know what she's really like. She's a witch! She's evil when she's drunk.'

Josie was quite heated and I felt some of her anger was directed at me. I did not know what it was all about, and this is not unusual when I counsel. Some of the time the counsellor is flying blind, so Josie's anger was remembered to see if enlightenment comes later in the session.

Me: 'And when she's sober?'
Josie: 'She's a moan. She gets on at the younger ones more than me. That annoys me.'
Me: 'You seem to me annoyed right now. Is that right?'
Josie: 'Yes. She's a cow!'
Me: 'You're mad with her right now. Tell me one thing about your Mum that makes you mad.'

Earlier I was prepared to wait and see if Josie's anger towards me made sense. However at this moment in the session I am now feeling that perhaps I took on Josie's anger and that anger was not directed at me. However I have the sense that the anger was not simply directed at her mother, either. When counselling, these feelings arise in the counsellor, but cannot necessarily be explained. The logical answer is to investigate the situation.

Josie: 'One thing! When she's drunk she gets onto Karen.' (Her younger sister.)
Me: 'Thinking about Karen when your mother is drunk, do you feel protective of her or do ...?'
Josie: 'Yes! As the oldest, the oldest girl that is, I have to look after the others. I've always had to do that as Mum's been on the booze from before I was born. Over twenty years.'

It was a lucky guess about Josie being protective, but I knew I had struck something, as she agreed so strongly and so quickly. There is a clear contradiction between her perceived protective role of the younger children and the reality of her drug related behaviour. The question was whether there really was a contradiction and whether Josie was aware of it.

Me: 'Yet you usually do not stay at home.'
Josie: 'With friends. That's because of the smack. If my Mum knows I'm using then she chucks me out. Not that I can stay there long anyway. It never seems to work out.'
Me: 'You mentioned looking after, being protective of Karen. Tell me more about this. How do you feel about this?'
Josie: 'How do you mean?'
Me: 'Do you resent having to be protective of Karen, or are you happy being able to help her?'

I was feeling there was a danger that the session could begin to wander and needed being directed somewhere. However my open questions were perhaps too vague. Some clients feel much happier with precise concrete questions, though from the counsellor's point of view they usually do not go very far.

Josie: 'I want to help, I suppose.'
Me: 'You suppose.'
Josie: 'I'm not her mother.'
Me: 'Does that mean at times you feel almost as if you are?'
Josie: 'Umm. Being on smack does not help. Paul, can you put a good word in for me with the doctor? I would be really grateful if

you could do this for me. You know how to talk to doctors. My last social worker had no idea at all.'

Perhaps Josie had lost interest or maybe she was diverting me away from the subject of her feelings. There is also a degree of resistance through seduction or flattery – praising the counsellor and denigrating past counsellors is one way of getting the counsellor onto the client's side and decreasing objectivity.

    Me: 'We'll come to that later. What I want to confirm just now is that your life at your Mum's is not much fun. She gets drunk at night and is unpleasant to the children. You feel you have to protect them. Yet for much of the time, you do not stay in the house so cannot protect them. Is that the case?'
    Josie: 'That's not my fault, my Mum chucks me out.'
    Me: 'It is not your role, your job, to look after the other children so there is no question of it being your fault. But I wonder why you mentioned fault at all. Do you feel responsible for the children, perhaps guilty if you cannot help them.'

Josie's attempt to divert me to the subject of her doctor was largely ignored. Instead by summarizing, it was possible to get back on track again. Near repetition often seems to elicit a different response, partly because the client is given more time to reflect on the situation. The idea of fault was followed up simply because Josie did not answer my question but seemed to be answering her own unsaid critical statement.

    Josie: 'I feel sorry for Karen ... It's not fair on her. Mum hits her when she is drunk and she just takes it. That's Karen, mind. She's not like me. I wouldn't stand for it.'
    Me: 'What would you do?'
    Josie: 'Kill the bitch!'
    Me: 'Would you do that or would you merely feel like doing that?'
    Josie: 'I would do it ... (long pause) ... I don't know. I would want to do it ... (pause) ... No, I suppose I would stop myself ... walk away.'

Client feelings, however strong, have to be accepted by the counsellor. Josie probably would not have continued if her statement about killing her mother had not been accepted. Statements like 'You don't really mean that!' merely diminish feelings and censor future comments. Having accepted the feeling, then Josie can be asked whether she really meant it. Her actual reply took some time with long silences, so long that she felt obliged to speak. Of course, to use silence is as uncomfortable for the counsellor as it is for the client and takes some practice.

Me: 'It strikes me that you have to get out of the situation when you feel so strongly, and perhaps getting chucked out of the house is in a way a bit of a relief.'
Josie: 'I get annoyed that I get chucked out ... I suppose I'm not sorry to go, though. I suppose you could be right. Yes, at least it gets me away from all the hassle.'
Me: 'And one way to get chucked out is to take smack.'
Josie: 'You're saying I take smack to get chucked out?'
Me: 'You are the only person who knows. I am merely offering a suggestion.'

This is getting dangerously close to putting ideas into the client's head: probably I was too caught up in my own ideas to allow Josie space to come to her own conclusions.

Josie: 'I think you're weird!'
Me: 'That's another possibility!'
Josie: 'You're saying I want at times to be chucked out?'
Me: 'Not if you disagree.'
Josie: 'Why should I want to be chucked out.'
Me: 'Perhaps it is your way of coping with a difficult situation. You get really mad with your Mum every night and finally can't take any more. I can see this is a load of rubbish, you don't agree. Let's forget it.'
Josie: 'I don't know, I've never thought of it like that. No, it's not daft ... You're not daft; fucking weird, perhaps.'

When faced with new perceptions, we often need some time to take them on board – if we ever do. Note that trying to end a discussion can sometimes have the paradoxical effect of ensuring that there will be a continuation.

Me: 'Sometimes strange situations can result in ordinary people having to behave strangely. The whole family has to cope with a mother who might be a bit of a moan. During the day she's OK but at night she changes into – well, how would you describe her?'

Josie: 'Monster! Frankenstein!'

Me: 'You dislike this person of the night, your mother when she's drunk, but how about during the day. Do you dislike her then?'

Josie: 'It's the same person, so I must hate her. I don't know. It's like two different people, like that film, Doctor ... you know, the film.'

Me: 'Doctor Jekyll and Mr Hyde?'

Josie: 'That's it! A bit like that. One changes into another.'

Me: 'How did that happen in the film.'

Josie: 'Well this doctor goes into his lab ...'

Me: 'Laboratory?'

Josie: 'Aye. Then he drinks this stuff he's made up and then he changes into this other person, totally evil.'

Me: 'Mmmmm.'

Josie: 'What's that mean? Mmmmm. Fuck! I get you. That's like my Mum, is that what you are saying, eh? Shit! You're right! She has a drink, actually she needs several, and then she changes. Ha! Why watch the film when you can watch my Mum?'

Me: 'Perhaps there is a bit of Jekyll and Hyde in all of us.'

It is easier to have simple feelings about people, but often feelings are ambivalent. Josie appears to see her mother in purely negative terms, but perhaps this is how she wants it to be. The idea of ambivalence was touched on by herself first and needed further illustration in terms with which she was familiar.

Josie: 'Yes, I can be a bad bastard at times. I lie and steal and con folks, but you have to do that if you're a junkie.'

Me: 'So that is how smack has affected you.'

Josie: 'It is not the smack that does that, it's when you have a habit and have to score.'

Me: 'So it is quite different from booze.'

Josie: 'Smack calms you down. It's not like the bevvy which can make you aggressive. The bevvy is worse.'

Me: 'But both drugs can affect a person's life. One has affected your mother's and the other has affected you.'

Josie: 'Not in the same way though. Besides I don't like the stealing and the lying, it's just something I have to do. I don't like that bit of it.'

Me: 'And how about your Mum? Is she happy with her life?'

Josie: 'I don't think so.'

Me: 'Have you ever thought that you and your Mum might have things in common?'

Josie: 'There! I knew you would come up with something like that. Do you know, there are times when I hate your guts – but I don't really. See what you've done! Got me talking like you.'

This time there was a danger of me sounding as if I am moralizing. Generally though, last session's agreed aim for today is beginning to come into view. The ambivalence is there but now Josie is actually experiencing it herself in regard to myself. The counselling seemed to be going somewhere useful, but Josie then diverted the session into chit-chat about what was happening locally. Many drug using clients do not have a great concentration span and can only take so much counselling. In these circumstances it is best to give them a breather and the actual counselling began again later.

Josie: 'Two years time, I know where I'll be in two years time: I'll be dead. There's nothing for me. I've got no schooling and will never get a job. What is there for someone like me but jagging up?'

Me: 'You sound very down.'

Josie: 'It's just that I know we are all born to be something: we were put here for some reason. I was born to be a junkie.'

Me: 'OK, so you are going to keep using. Will it be regular or occasional?'

When a client is down, there is always the temptation to try and cheer them up rather than acknowledging how they feel. However the situation was more complicated with Josie, as she could also play for sympathy and spontaneously turn on the tears. How to proceed depends on the feelings that the counsellor is picking up.

Josie: 'I would prefer it if I didn't have a habit – just the occasional shot. That way I could control better what I was doing.'

Me: 'So you don't want to feel you have to use. You want to be your own person.'

Josie: 'Dope (heroin) isn't everything. I've been into things since I was 14 and I think of all the things I've missed. I want to do things before I'm too old.'

Me: 'It seems to me that you are not so sure what you want.'

Josie: 'I'm not really a junkie; I don't feel I am. But I'm beginning to like it, and I don't want that. I don't want to be a junkie.'

Me: 'But you don't want to be completely straight either.'

Josie: 'Perhaps if I went out on the peeve (drinking) ... But then I don't see myself doing that, it would not be the same.'

Me: 'It might be better.'

Josie: 'I suppose so.'

Summary

This extract only covered a small part of the total counselling session but it shows some of the aspects of counselling. In particular, there is no question of having to get it all right. Rather, it is a voyage of discovery and there are likely to be many wrong or fruitless directions and turnings. Also counselling varies according to the client. Many different topics for discussion arise and when working with heroin users, they are not necessarily always about the drug. Nor, indeed, is it necessary to warn against drug use, as clients almost certainly have heard it all before. What is required is to give clients time, space and attention. Allow them to come to their own conclusions, even if it is one of uncertainty.

Josie did in fact come off heroin and was off for nearly two years, and was able to live the life she wanted.

8 PREGNANCY AND BEYOND

INTRODUCTION

Apart from actual drug use, one of the common difficulties that heroin using clients may face relates to children. The situations as described are very much seen from the client's, the drug user's perspective, but we should also remember that children are persons as well, and they will have their own perspective, as will other family members.

Orientation

The first necessary step is to look at our attitudes, as attitudes around drug use and children tend to be very strong, but not always justified. For instance, we should not assume drug taking parents are bad parents. There are poor parents: they may or may not take drugs. Similarly, parents may take drugs and be adequate parents. We should appreciate that being an unfit parent means indulging in damaging behaviour or the omission of other sustaining behaviours. It is not a consequence of a person being labelled in a certain way. We might see unsatisfactory parenting as being the result of a lack of emotional bonding with the child, a lack of parenting skills, from problems resulting from the parents own parenting, or from illegal drug use. These factors might or might not be applicable to particular cases, and the effects may or may not be reversible.

Judgements

Similarly, we have to get away from the habit of making judgements about people before really coming to grips with some of the complexities. For my part, I do not condemn nor condone illegal drug use, whether by parents or by anyone else. The counsellor has to accept clients and work with their situations.

My belief is that much thinking about illegal drug use and parenting is surrounded by judgemental attitudes, which may prevent others from seeing the reality. These attitudes are general in society and are shared by both non-drug users and drug users. Thus there is no simple 'us' and 'them' situation, no simple illegal drug users on one side and the rest of society on the other. I have heard heroin users being scathing about the child care of other heroin users, I have heard them being rightly critical of the child care of parents who were not illegal drug users. What is required at this point is to be able to clear one's mind, to be prepared to accept heroin users as people and as themselves. We have to suspend all judgements, we have to try to understand. Sometimes this is not easy, but unless we do we will not be of help.

Coming for help

Heroin users are not likely to come to counsellors to discuss having children directly, though the subject might well arise if they are already in counselling. However they might want to come for slightly different reasons. The reasons might include wanting to come off drugs, wanting to know possible risks to the unborn child of their drug use, asking for help as they are HIV infected, and talking about aspects of the relationship with their partner.

All of these require a fair amount of initial information giving, so it is worth considering doing this initially. As always, the counsellor can usefully check out what the client knows, checking out for gaps in knowledge, for misinformation and for doubtful beliefs. Clearly, it is preferable that the process is done with the partner present, if there is a partner around and willing to come.

INFORMATION

Introduction

Counsellors get clients to talk rather than talking themselves. The following information is used to supplement client knowledge, not to form a lecture to be given to clients. Time should be taken to check out that clients really do understand, and this requires more than clients nodding that they have understood.

Pregnancy and drug use

Drugs can affect the unborn child. In particular, drugs taken between the third and eleventh week of pregnancy can cause congenital abnormalities. This is because the formation of the amniotic sac produces a closed system in which the drugs are concentrated: what is excreted into the amniotic fluid is breathed in or swallowed, causing the concentration of drug to be greater in the foetal organs than in those of the mother. Also the mother might be able to deal with the drugs taken but the unborn child does not have the ability to do so, to break them down in the body, at least not very easily. Heroin itself is not dangerous in this respect but other drugs may be. It is important to remember that many illegal drug users will be using more than one drug, so other drugs as well as heroin should be considered.

Amphetamines may cause cleft palates and cardiac abnormalities, multiple abnormalities may be produced by the excessive use of alcohol and sniffing solvents. Also of possible danger is the heavy use of barbiturates and long term minor tranquillizers such as diazepam. The danger comes from the slow build up of longer acting drugs rather than an overdose or large oral dosages.

Taking drugs later in pregnancy

Drugs taken between the third month to the end of term are not likely to cause abnormalities but they can retard growth. These drugs will include opioid drugs such as heroin, and also alcohol. Smoking, whatever the substance used, also has the same effect, as smoking restricts the amount of oxygen passing through the placenta, and this in turn affects the growth rate. The risk now involved is simply that a small baby, like premature babies, is more liable to contract infections. This possibility is increased with drugs like opioids which increase the likelihood of the baby being born before the end of term.

Much more important are the risks of infection being transmitted to the unborn child, the principal risks coming from HIV and from hepatitis B. If the mother is not known to be HIV positive then she must not put herself and the baby at risk by continuing to take heroin by injection. If the mother is HIV positive then the risks of infection are very much greater just after infection and when the mother is symptomatic; worse when highly symptomatic as when having AIDS. Thus there are times when it is best to have specialist advice as this is an area where knowledge is still uncertain and changing.

Other risks are often of an indirect variety. Drug users might suffer from a poor diet and vitamin lack. Parents' attendance at ante-natal clinics is often very poor. Sometimes the use of drugs is part of a risky life-style, and it is this life-style itself that presents difficulties and dangers.

Addicted babies

Most people are upset at the idea of a baby being born a heroin addict. This raises many strong feelings and to some extent explains the poor response that addicted mothers may receive from the medical and other helping services. The symptoms of neonatal withdrawals are the usual ones of opioid withdrawals such as restlessness, sleeplessness, sneezing, sweating, tremors, diarrhoea and vomiting – though not all symptoms need be present. There can also be more specific symptoms associated with such cases such as high-pitched crying and fist-sucking. Seeing these babies in distress is distressing, but nowadays they are treated relatively easily and do not present a serious medical risk.

COUNSELLING HELP

Introduction

Giving information is essential for clients to be able to work with some basic ideas. Some of the information is subject to variation or is not precisely determined, so the client does have to come to understand that certainties cannot be given, even though this is what anxious clients want. Thus information giving can easily lead on to counselling client anxiety.

Counselling is dealing with client concerns, and merely ensuring clients have adequate knowledge is insufficient. The counsellor has to encourage client feedback and help with client planning.

Pregnancy and drug treatment

One aspect to be discussed is whether the mother who is using wants to reduce or stop her drug use. This is not a necessary step and attempts to force the mother to do so are unhelpful. However many mothers do want to come off at this juncture. This is not merely because they do not want their child to be born possibly with an addiction, but they want an excuse to come off. Being pregnant is recognized within the drug subculture as a time when a user should stop and accordingly it is not advisable to pressurize them to continue to use. The pregnancy gives the mother something else to think about, a new interest in life and all this makes it easier to come off.

Jane: 'When I was pregnant I felt more responsible, there wasn't just me to think about. I had to buckle down and that was quite difficult, but I managed it.'

It should be noted that this time, which is usually a good time and a positive time for the mother, is when outside persons and agencies begin to take an interest in the woman user. The interest is not always so positive or helpful and there can be clashes between the helpers and the would-be helped.

The role of the father can be difficult and his behaviour is not always helpful. The father can be jealous of the attention given to his partner and the unborn child. Such feelings may be aggravated by any drugs taken.

Sarah: 'When Zero was on Diconal he used to stomp around, ready to hook somebody. Usually it was me, so often I did not go to the ante-natal clinic because of the black eyes.'

In fact, drug users are not good attenders at ante-natal clinics, though this should be encouraged as mothers-to-be do not always eat well or look after themselves.

Reducing whilst pregnant

The question arises as to whether the mother should come off heroin or other drugs quickly or relatively slowly. Too violent a reduction, especially for heavy users, can bring on foetal irritability and this can foreshorten the term, with the increased medical risks of a short-term pregnancy.

Lizzie: 'When you're pregnant and withdrawing, you feel the baby as if it's about to come. That's what happened to me when my methadone was reduced too much.'

In extreme cases there is severe irritability, a lack of oxygen and consequent intra-uterine death. However a slow reduction spins out the whole process which can make it harder for some mothers. Also it is difficult to ensure the mother will be off heroin at the time of birth, as one of the effects of heroin use can be to shorten the term of pregnancy so the baby is born prematurely.

Attention must be given to the wishes of the parents, the mother in particular. One mother was reduced quickly, was withdrawing and felt the baby inside her also going through withdrawals. While she was prepared to undergo withdrawals herself, she was not prepared to let her child do the same and so returned to using.

Rachel: 'I was going through double withdrawals. I was withdrawing and the bairn inside me was withdrawing; it was kicking like mad. I couldn't go through double withdrawals so I had to keep using.'

Where pregnancy is concerned, both medical and social work personnel tend at times to see their remit as very much with the unborn
child, excluding the mother if she is a drug user. As most drug using
mothers want the best for their child, this exclusion is not merely
unhelpful but misses a valuable opportunity to help the person.

Counselling help

Heroin users, when they first find out they are pregnant, want support and they do not always get it from helpers. This is because such
helpers see the pregnancy as problematic, and hardly the reason for
congratulating the client, though most other women would be con-
gratulated in these circumstances. Failing to do so for drug users not
merely fails to engage the client but indirectly consigns her into the
category of problem people.

This fails to understand what pregnancy means to the client. It
means the drug user can take up the role of mother and stop using
drugs. Many women drug users want to do precisely that.

Jane: 'I told the doctor that there was no way I was using methadone now I was pregnant, and I poured it down the sink. The doctor
shook me by the hand, though he said it might be dangerous for the
baby if I stopped straightaway. I told him there was no way I was
going to bring a bairn into the world and it have pains to go through.'

And in the above example, Jane's partner confirmed her action and
she had no further prescriptions from her doctor, despite his concern
that stopping so abruptly might be dangerous to the foetus. In fact
Jane did come off and stay off, and her child was and is quite healthy.

Clients may need to stop the helping services from taking over
their lives and making decisions for them. Such 'helping' behaviour
might represent helpers working out their own attitudes and
putting them on clients or patients. Counsellors are not remitted to
take the clients' side, but they should try to ensure that clients are
heard, and client wishes are known. Many clients feel intimidated
or have too low self-esteem to be able to resist official actions.

Unexpected pregnancies

We have been rather presuming that the pregnancies will be planned
or at least not totally unexpected. This need not be the case. In
unexpected pregnancies there can be a variety of reactions. Both
parents can be happy, both unhappy or one happy and the other less
so. What often happens is that if the woman has been using heavily

then her monthly periods may well have stopped or become irregular, so missed periods might not seem very significant. As a result the woman might not be aware of her pregnancy until comparatively well on into term. This gives less time for parents to come to terms with the pregnancy. If termination is an option, for instance, or if the mother is highly HIV symptomatic, then there might remain little time to make a decision.

The sudden pregnancy might come as a small crisis for the parents as it can put a strain on the relationship. This is obviously the case if the husband is not the father, but even if this is not the case yet there can be strains. Firstly, there might be expectations on the part of the father that the mother comes off heroin straightaway, even though he should be allowed to continue his use. If this is the first child to the pair then there can be additional strains as it is a further link binding the two together. Normally this would be seen as an advantage but this is not necessarily so between illegal drug users. Relationships between drug users can be stormy and unsatisfactory, the pair staying together through their interest in drugs, or through fear of starting relationships with anyone else. With the birth of the child, it becomes even more difficult to end the relationship if that is what the parents really want.

Further help

Emphasis is likely to be on the pregnancy, from the point of view of her doctors, and this reinforces her role as a mother rather than as a drug user. Much then depends on how the mother is treated, whether she is allowed at least to participate in decisions or is merely told what to do. The mother might be expected to act responsibly and yet responsibility is taken away from her.

Concentration on the mother can be to the exclusion of the father from the whole process. If one or both parents are using then this exclusion is likely to be counterproductive. Indeed, a rather strange change can enter into official help in that the mother has suddenly been elevated from drug user to mother. The father tends still to be regarded as just a drug user and even made out to be the villain of the situation, to be seen as the person who is uncaring, carrying on using drugs and totally indifferent to the situation.

Help might not be well received if it is directive and if it does not include the whole family. There is a tendency to offer help to the mother for the benefit of the child, help that perhaps was not offered when the parent was not pregnant. Thus the parents do not see themselves being helped, only the child. Clients, being drug users, do not count. In these circumstances their self-esteem is further reduced and this in turn makes it more difficult for them to act decisively, especially if hard decisions have to be made.

Family help

The extended families might also be interested in the forthcoming birth. Whether they actually offer help depends on how the members of the family see the relationship between the would-be father and mother. There is also the particular interest of members wanting to have grandchildren or not wanting the couple to stay together. Sometimes the family will see the birth of a child as bringing the parent back into the extended family, as getting the family back to what it used to be, even if only in the minds of the family. In this respect it should be said that grandparents play a strong and sometimes difficult role in many heroin using families.

Many heroin using parents with small children have not fully become separated from their families of origin, they are emotionally dependent on their parents. Having small children makes them further involved with their own families as they may require babysitters. Indeed, in some cases the grandparents will be the main child carers. This allows parents their freedom and greater ease to continue their drug use.

The pregnancies of illegal drug users have many outcomes. The important factors are not just medical but relate to the relationship between the couple, the two of them as separate individuals and what support there is for the couple, whether from the extended families or from official sources. Much of the help may be attitudinally tinged and so there can be benefits from free and open discussions with clients.

Late in the pregnancy

Once the mother is in hospital, she can relax and her husband can visit her. Although she might now be off drugs or nearly so, this is not to say that he will. Active drug users are often a problem in hospitals and care is usually taken so that they do not try to break into drugs cabinets. Apart from taking drugs out, users might also take drugs in, especially if the mother has not come off heroin. For example, I know of a husband who put heroin into his wife's drip. Such behaviour does not endear drug users to the medical staff. The image of drug users is not improved by the suspicion that anyone on drugs must be HIV positive and should be tested for the virus. The possibilities for confrontation are present and seldom prove helpful.

– 217 –

AFTER THE BIRTH

Immediate concerns

Because the user has been on heroin, there is a greater chance that the baby will be born prematurely. This means that the baby is more likely to be kept in the hospital longer and so separated from the mother. This can have implications for the bonding between mother and child. Sometimes there is concern about the care of the child when returned home with the mother, even though there has been no evidence that the mother cannot look after this child satisfactorily. Thus the period in hospital can be a time of concern for the mother. The actual problem is not whether drug use is a good enough reason to safeguard the welfare of the child, but whether the parents are or can be adequate parents. The latter might have little to do with the effects of drugs as such.

The child born to an addicted mother will soon begin to withdraw. With normal amounts of heroin taken, breast feeding will provide only very small amounts of the drug. However, in one case known to me, the mother was on a very high heroin intake and her child did not start to withdraw until a few months old when the mother substantially reduced her drug use. It should be added that even small amounts of heroin in breast milk can affect the baby as it can induce constipation, babies being very sensitive to the constipating effects of opioids.

Other drugs can interfere with normal child care. Drug users are usually multi-drug users or may switch if they have no access to their preferred drug. Tranquillizers taken by the mother can make the baby lethargic, a poor feeder and liable to lose weight. Barbiturates can interfere with the baby's sucking mechanism and this also makes feeding difficult.

Back home

When the mother returns home, a different phase begins. For the mother whose baby was also addicted there is the special problem. Even by the standards of the drug subculture her behaviour is judged as being barely acceptable. Thus she might have to come to terms with having had an addicted baby, which she may deal with by denying the situation, blaming someone else or blaming herself.

Beth: 'I was on one and a half grams a day when I had Johnny, and he had no withdrawals. All babies vomit and sweat. They tested him afterwards and he had no junk in him; it was all in the afterbirth. The afterbirth disintegrated very quickly afterwards because of all the junk in it. They just say these things about addict children to scare people.'

This is something that in time the drug user would appreciate talking about, and probably will do, as long as the counsellor continues to be supportive and is not seen as blaming the client.

But for most mothers the initial days are good days. They are at the centre of attention with the baby, the family is generally very supportive and the local services are pleased to see things appear to be going well. The mother is reinforced in the role as a mother and there is little temptation at this stage to go back to using drugs.

Relapse to using

If things are so positive then we might ask why so many mothers go back to using after a few months. To outsiders this relapse confirms their fears that the mother is really a poor parent and coming off her drugs was not really intended; the mother always at heart intended to carry on using drugs. I think we have to look at the situation in more detail.

We might note that the positive attitudes of the mother are likely to diminish over time. At first they get a lot of positive reinforcement from those around them but this diminishes with time. Staying off drugs for the first days after coming out of hospital calls for some comment; staying off drugs in the long term elicits less comment and support. Once a person is seen as being off drugs then the expectation is that the person will stay off drugs. But there are factors which work against this belief.

One factor might be the role of the husband who might not have come off but continues to use. Under these circumstances having to be in the presence of a drug user hour after hour, as opposed to the restricted time of hospital visits, inclines the mother to use again. We also have to be aware of the father's possible lack of role and even jealousy of the mother and baby who receive almost all the attention. This might make the father resentful and determined to carry on with his drug use. Finally, the mother who has been off heroin for a bit of time, and is consequently feeling much better, might feel able to control the effects and so risk restarting.

We should appreciate that help is usually offered when the mother first comes out of hospital, when the mother might not need help as the baby is easy to handle, sleeping much of the time. As the baby grows older and becomes more active, after a matter of a few months, then less help might be at hand and the mother has more difficulty in coping. How a mother copes often depends on previous ways of coping, and for drug users this might mean dealing with problems by taking drugs.

Counselling help

Low level help and counselling, visiting the client at home, can be useful in reinforcing the non-drug regime. Working with the partner as well as the mother is another potentially helpful option. Often these ex-users do want to talk things through and this involves talking about the past, the good bits as well as the bad. Whatever happens, the counsellor has to be non-judgemental and overtly reinforce the client's position of being off drugs. The client's past was not good or bad; it is simply the past.

Sometimes, after coming off drugs, clients have to get back in touch with their feelings, or the true nature of their feelings. The years of chemically mediated feelings can make it difficult to judge feelings accurately, or relationships and to know themselves.

Discussions can also cover the future, as users seldom think or want to think very far ahead. But thinking about the future can provide hopes, expectations and planning; it may provide reasons for staying off drugs.

Drug using mothers

Once a mother restarts drug use then there is seldom any quick going back. Mothers are likely to feel bad about having started again. Far from making them stop, it tends to make them continue. With their self-esteem low, they feel unable to control their drug use. The actions of others in telling them to stop is likely to ·be equally counterproductive. And the unfortunate fact is their problems are not solved by taking drugs: in the long term the problems actually increase. Attention here is given to mothers because these clients in practice, whatever sexual equality might ordain, have the care of the child almost exclusively for the first months. Once the mother is using then the strains tend to increase as the role of mother does not fit easily with that of being a drug user.

Layna: 'With Helen I used to be tired. I couldn't get to sleep and then I would have to get up during the night. As well as feeding her, washing nappies, you're not feeling well.'

The only way to overcome quickly the effects of withdrawals is to have another shot, and then the user feels better. For the user who is withdrawing the effect of the shot is not to send them to sleep but to keep straight, to make them feel normal. Indeed, for many users the morning shot acts more like the early cup of coffee and gives them energy.

Vivienne: 'I had to have heroin first thing in the morning. Then I was able to get moving and do all my housework.'

The question now arises as to whether taking heroin is likely to have any adverse effect on the child or children. The general impression is that this must be the case, a judgement arrived at without any real sifting of the evidence.

HEROIN USE AND CHILDREN

Introduction

Heroin use by parents is as varied as the parents themselves. There is no easy generalization that can be made. I will give some illustrations but these are all possibilities, not necessities, and they are often the worst scenarios. For drug workers they represent the kind of things that might happen, things that might be kept at the back of the mind but also kept in balance with other aspects. For instance, the use of heroin relieves anxiety and this might be an advantage when having to care for children. The risk of physical abuse of the children might actually be reduced. Moreover the risks to the children occur when the user is withdrawing, when the user does not have drugs.

Angela: 'I want to come off as it is not fair on the bairn. But if I'm withdrawing then I want to take it out on the bairn as he's the only one around to take it out on.'

However, the risk of these eventualities is generally much smaller than the more common risk of neglect, especially emotional neglect. The drugs taken might insulate the taker from the world but the world includes children. Thus the parent is to some extent insulated from the children and the children distanced from the parents. When the user is withdrawing emotional neglect can occur.

Tina: 'If I am withdrawing then I usually push the bairn away and tell him not to bother me.'

We have to be cautious about seeing withdrawing as a physical danger to the children. Users are generally aware of how they are likely to react and take steps to deal with it, though the steps taken might have other drawbacks. Thus we see that parents might intend to do the best for their children but their heroin use can act against such good intentions.

Sarah: 'My husband used to be aggressive when he was withdrawing and would hit me.'
Me: 'Was he ever aggressive towards the bairns?'
Sarah: 'He would shout at them but he would never hit them. In fact he used to be the opposite, say that Mummy was nasty and he would let them do what they wanted.'
Me: 'He wanted to be Mr Nice Guy?'
Sarah: 'Yes!'

As may be seen, drug use cannot simply be equated with certain behaviour. Drugs affect feelings, but behaviour is affected in a more complex manner.

Wider concerns

Concern about heroin use is usually centred around the medical effects. This is far too narrow a way of looking at the situation. We also have to place the situation in a social context and try to understand the whole of what is happening. This includes not just what is going on but whether those involved have the knowledge or abilities to do things in a different manner. The following is a further description of withdrawing.

Josie: 'When you are withdrawing then you can't be bothered with the bairns ... Guy's bairn would be sat on the sofa and people would be fixing in front of him, almost lying on him. They didn't bother with the bairn, and the bairn was great! He would laugh when I picked him up as he wasn't used to being held. And he was never taken out of the house; he wasn't used to the sunshine when we took him out. And he didn't know what orange-juice was. He spat it out when we gave it to him. They wanted to keep him quiet and would give him his dummy. If that didn't work they would give him his bottle. If that did not work they would give him spoonfuls of Calpol.'

What we see when working with heroin using parents is that the main concern is degrees of neglect by parents. However we also have to see something that might not be immediately apparent. There are users like Josie who do care about children and will help out. In this way the local subculture takes on to some extent the nature of a large extended family and others help out those users who cannot or do not care properly for their children.

Lisa: 'David and Sharon were coming round to score and they brought wee Jamie with them. It was about nine o'clock at night and the poor bairn could hardly keep his eyes open. He hadn't eaten anything so I made him a piece and jam.'

However, just because a mother helps others out does not mean that she necessarily will be able to care for her own children when she is using heavily or withdrawing or caught up in the drug life.

Lisa: 'When I was using there was never anything when Tony came in for his tea. I just used to give him 10p. to get something to eat from the shop.'

Part of work with mothers is to help them arrive at the reality of their situation, despite their feelings of guilt and despite what they would like to believe about themselves.

Review of maternal care

Part of the difficulty is that the upbringing of children by drug users reflects their own upbringing, and this might have been far from good. This might reflect both the caring capacities and behaviour of their parents. It should be noted that many drug users have parents who were heavy drinkers. Also reference should also be made to others, especially those older, in the family.

Tina: 'When I was young, Marie was jagging up downers and I hated it. I used to throw the capsules, Seccies and Nembies, down the toilet; then I was caught and leathered. By the time I was fourteen, I was giving them a hit – I had to.'

Drug use, including alcohol, can cover several generations. Rather than passing judgements, we have to deal with the here-and-now. That means we have to deal with clients who might not be dealing with the role of being parents as we see it, but as they see things.

From the counselling point of view, we can help parents to help themselves, to see the situation from another non-judgemental perspective and they can choose their actions from a variety of possible options. Not all parents will be happy with their role as parents, and this is quite general. However drug users parents will find their roles more difficult.

Drug use role and parents

The problem for the parents is that they have to straddle the straight world, looking after their children, and yet be part of the local drug subculture. This might be possible if the parents are using only at weekends or are using small amounts of heroin. This controlled use is not impossible, though it is difficult for many users to adhere to it in the long run. Usually their drug use will increase from this low use.

Ken: 'We used to wait till the children went to bed before taking smack. That way they did not even know we were using drugs and we would not be disturbed.'

When the drug becomes more important, when it becomes the main priority then standards can decline, mainly because child care and heavy drug use are hard to combine. The greater the involvement in the drug culture, the greater the strains of keeping things together.

Josie: 'Hazel, when she was dealing, she couldn't care about the bairns. She would shout at them to get down the stairs. Wee Janey, she would be kept in the cot all day. The mattress, one of those rubber foam ones, it was bending with the weight of the piss and the blankets were wringing. All they bothered about was their arms and the stuff they could put into them.'

One danger is to assume that the difficulties that drug using parents have in child care must be related to their drug use. Many such parents have difficulties simply because they do not know how best to look after children. No-one has really told them or shown them what is best. Sometimes their own upbringing has not been good and they have problems in how they relate to their children. They are likely to experience problems even if they were not using drugs. Indeed, it could even be argued in some cases that drug use helps them cope with the difficulties they find in looking after children.

Annette: 'I want you to take the bairn into care. When I was using I was able to care for her, but not now that I'm off. I simply cannot cope.'

Strange as it may seem, heroin can help through its anxiety reducing properties in making child care easier.

Drug life-style

Another possibly relevant factor in the standard of child care of drug users is how well organized these parents are. Child care requires organization but life might be preferentially arranged around drug use. Thus children may be fed, but their diet reflects the diet of the parents and might consist mainly of juice and sweets. The rather chaotic life-style, or the life-style where drugs are a priority, may also mean that mealtimes are irregular, even insufficient.

Foster-parent: 'Davie must have been fed irregularly. He grabs at his food and always says aye, when offered a biscuit. We have to keep the dog's dish out of reach as he will eat out of it.'

The life-style of drug users may also mean that other items are either overlooked or the parents do not quite get round to carrying out the appropriate action. Priorities can revolve round those actions which are drug centred. Moreover, the taking of heroin can make the users less anxious, they cannot be bothered.

Relative: 'I asked Susan whether the wee one had had his jags (innoculations) and she said she did not know, she was always going to get it done. She hasn't, of course.'

Generally, the relationships between doctor and parent are good enough for the children to be taken to the surgery when ill, even when the relationships between doctor and heroin using parents are poor. However it should be remembered drug users also get put off doctors lists from time to time because of their difficult behaviour, so a small proportion of drug users have no doctor. This has obvious implications if the users have children.

Relationships can also play their part in how the heroin user will use medical services, and to some extent this is determined by how service providers behave or how their behaviour is interpreted.

Beth: 'Do you have to let your health visitor in? She said I wasn't looking after the children and she is always telling me, "I would not do that", and "Do this". You know what I'm like, I'm going to end up hitting her.'

Another particular risk when parents are using drugs is that of fire. Many heroin users also smoke cigarettes and nod off under the influence whilst still having lit cigarettes in their fingers. The principal risk is to the user but the children can also be at risk.

> *Lisa*: 'Did you see my jeans were burnt down the front? Luckily I woke up, or Tony and I could have been burnt alive.'

This danger may be that much greater if the parents are involved in dealing. Drug dealers who work from houses or flats are likely to protect themselves from raids by the Drugs Squad, barricade themselves in the house so the Drugs Squad cannot gain easy access and so confiscate drugs, which could be used as evidence in Court.

> *Jock*: 'The bairns were playing with matches and no-one was watching. There was dealing in the house and the door was barricaded. When the place caught fire no-one could get in to help.'

Thus there are a variety of difficulties which might be experienced by the children of drug using parents. Some of these difficulties relate to physical care but these are seldom the long lasting problems. Children tend to be very adaptable and can live through hard conditions as long as the family life is happy. If the relationships between parents and children are good then the children are not likely to suffer. However drug use often entails difficulties in these very relationships.

RELATIONSHIPS

Knowledge of parental drug use

Even if the parents are using drugs, their poor child care might still be unrelated to that drug use. We have to be aware of the wider context.

> *Dora*: 'I asked Beia why she did not bother with the bairn. She said she never wanted him in the first place.'

However I am more interested in those cases where heroin or other drug use severely interferes with normal child care. We have seen that drug use might be hidden initially from the child or children and some parents make a point of ensuring that the children are shielded from what is going on.

Maggie: 'Tina never let anyone use in front of Kiernan; I respect her for that. I've seen people gouching with syringes stuck in their arms and children running about, but Tina went mental if anyone tried to do it in front of Kiernan.'

In fact some parents will make sure that the children will not know of the drug use by arranging their drug behaviour to take account of the children. Their drug use is fitted in with their role as parents, though this is easier done if they are using small amounts or they are using occasionally. Whether they manage to stick to these arrangements is another matter.

Vivienne: 'I've been in houses where parents have had a fix in front of their children, but not me. I wait until they are out at school before having anything.'

If parents are going to continue to use heroin then the best option is to see if they do so in a manner that is safest and best for themselves, their children and their partners. Some parents are quite amenable to such a compromise.

Stronger evidence of parental use
However it has to be said that the child's abilities to know what is going on are often underestimated, both by parents and by counsellors. Very young children are often treated in the house by drug user parents as if invisible or their presence is forgotten. So at an early age the child might have some idea of certain aspects of what is happening, even if it is not understood.

Tina: 'Her bairn was one year old, under one year old, and she was by the fire – they had an electric fire – and she picked up a spike (hypodermic needle) and said, "Mummy's. Mummy's". I felt sick.'

Now a child who does not understand what is happening might not be affected at all. In drug using areas young children who find syringes, and this is quite likely to happen, are not at any risk as regards family relationships. Of course there can be a risk of puncture by a needle or even infection with HIV or hepatitis, though these are low risks. So what is the danger to the children of knowing their parents use drugs? Before answering this question it is necessary to point out that parents are likely to protest that their children do not know what is going on in the house but usually the children, after a certain age do know.

Me: 'Bairns know what goes on.'
John: 'Ours didn't. I never had a shot in front of them. I was always careful.'

Heroin using parents will believe that their children do not know what is going on because they do not want to believe, and the effects of the drug help parents not see what is really happening.

Relative: 'Daryl told me that he had seen his Mummy and Daddy tying wool round their hands, and his Mummy stuck things into his Daddy and his Daddy stuck things into his Mummy.'

When the position is put to parents the situation might well be denied and the informants branded as liars. However the number of cases leads me to suspect that children frequently know more than their parents admit or want to admit.

David: 'We have always protected the bairns. We have never had a shot in front of them.'
Relative: 'I saw William playing and he had a handkerchief tied around his arm. I asked him why he had it on and he said it was a tie-up, just like Mummy's.'

From the family perspective, the counsellor has to think whether it is the drug taking itself that is damaging the children, the effects of the drug taking or the fact that the drug taking is 'concealed'.

Children's knowledge
Parents usually do not want to accept that their children do see what is going on and might take things in. Under the influence, the parents may not have noticed that the children were watching. The lack of judgement that drugs can bring about also results in parents talking about drugs when children are in earshot.

Lorraine: 'Violette knew what was going on. When she was four she tied a lace round her arm and was playing with a sewing needle. Only recently she said during a drugs programme on the telly, "You did that, you used to take that stuff." I asked how she knew as she would not have remembered, but she said she remembered.'

What we have to determine is whether the children seeing the parental drug use or being exposed to it does any harm. It might be thought that, at a simple level, the children will imitate the behaviour and end up as drug users themselves.

Layna: 'Bairns do copy you. I saw Helen trying to stick a piece of wood into her arm.'

However this is merely play and not of itself a cause for concern. We could liken the situation to that of a diabetic who has to self-inject. Children who see such self-injection are not considered to be at risk. Yet this does not mean knowledge of parental drug use will not affect the children.

Before proceeding further, we must realize that children being aware that their parents are drug users, and the parents being aware of this fact, can produce a degree of crisis. At this point the parents might have to decide what to do. They may decide to change their behaviour.

Vivienne: 'I never thought about it until James asked me why we were always falling asleep. It was then that I decided I would have to come off for the children's sake.'

In most cases the parents do not stop their use. Instead they will attempt to deny their drug use. Denial is now extended to their own children; their children are being treated as outsiders and they are not treated as before. This change in behaviour can grow to more serious proportions if the denials continue.

Jenny: 'I told Lester that I wasn't taking pills or anything. He didn't believe me. He said, "Liar! You've got liar written right across your face!" '

The possible effects of children knowing

One difficulty is that the child is likely to tell others of the parental drug use. For young children it is completely natural that they will chat about what is happening.

– 229 –

Grandmother: 'I put Darren on my knee and he tells me every-thing that happens in the house. I don't have to ask him, he just tells me. They think I don't know what goes on, but Darren would not lie.'

Outsiders such as the grandmother are not likely to keep quiet. Sooner or later they will let the parents know their drug use is no secret. This not only produces a gulf between grandparents and parents but leads to difficulties for the parents and child or children. If the parents do not stop their drug use then the children might have to be controlled from telling outsiders the situation.

Judy: 'I told Chris not to go talking about what happens in this house, that's none of Gran's business.'

This leads to divided loyalties as far as the children are concerned. Despite the fact that children may be aware that their parents are not telling the truth, their overall loyalty is likely to rest with them.

Involvement in the subculture

Slowly the children can be drawn into the subcultural way of life. Their idea of the normal way of behaving reflects the subcultural norms.

Grandmother: 'The two of them have got the children well trained. They were told not to tell me anything, and not to tell the truth to the Police or social workers.'

Children can also be drawn into knowledge of the drug subculture through their exposure to drug taking. Few drug using parents actually realize this fact.

Tina: 'The eldest child was three years old and said, "Mummy, remember to burn the empty packet", and "Do you want your tie-up, Mummy?".'

Very occasionally the child will be involved in the subculture on a practical basis. This represents the extreme end of the range of pos-sible children's involvement. Though it might be viewed as extreme, this does not necessarily entail that the child would be harmed by such involvement.

Lisa: 'Tony, when he was four years old, used to know how to make up a packet. He used to act as doorman for Craig, push the packets through the door and take the money.'

Nor does this mean that the child will be further drawn into drug use. Whatever is happening, many parents tend to try and cover up as much as possible, even if the children are aware of it.

Tina: 'I used to hide my works above the pipe in the kitchen. It was the only place Kiernan could not reach.'

The effect on child behaviour

It is not the drug use itself that tends to be harmful but the reactions of parents regarding their use and the effect of the drug subculture. For instance, knowledge of parental drug use is little worry to children if that drug is insulin and the parents are diabetic, but the use of heroin has a very different image. It is something to be hidden and it is worrying, even if the child does not exactly fully understand the risks involved. But as the children get older, so they might be more affected by what is going on.

Jenny: 'Lester would say if he saw the two of us going into the toilet, "Come out! I know what the two of you are up to!", and he would bang on the door and try to get in.'

In fact it is difficult to cover up all the time, and eventually children are going to found out what really goes on. Quite early on the children are likely to notice that the moods of the parents change after having a shot. For children the mood changes and the accompanying behaviour are worrying, even frightening, as at first they seem inexplicable. For children it is the abnormality of behaviour that produces anxiety.

Tina: 'Petra gave me a healthy shot on Saturday and then I had another. I was really stoned. The next day Kiernan said, "Don't go over to Glyn's and be in the state you were in yesterday".'

Of course if the mood changes are linked with other aspects of drug use then the children are more likely to begin to realize that something is up. In fact, children can be very quick to notice small details that the parents just accept and do not think about.

Jenny: 'It used to be a giveaway as I used to take the vinegar into the bathroom and the bairn must have wondered about that.'

However the chief sign for children is the way parental moods can change after having a shot. It is this inexplicable variability in the parent or parents that can be upsetting.

Jenny: 'Jason would say, "Don't go to the toilet, Mummy, don't go as you change". That was because my mood would change after a shot.'

Reaction of parents

Knowledge of their drug use on the part of children is hard to take as far as the parents are concerned in that it removes the idea that the children might not be affected. Drug using parents are no different from other mothers; they do not want their children to end up taking drugs.

Tina: 'I couldn't stand it if Kiernan got into drugs. I told him about glue-sniffing. If I caught him with a tube of glue I would stick it down his throat. Mind you, I don't think he would; he knows about it.'

But it is the drug related behaviour that begins to affect the relationship. Even when the parent is not obviously under the influence, behaviour may be affected. The mood changes between having had a shot and not having a shot are observable. There is no need for the amount of drug to be that great.

Richard: 'On Saturday night I used to play with Ricky and would make all sorts of promises. But by Sunday morning I would tell him to go away; I wasn't interested.'

It is the uncertainty in the parent and child relationship that can bring problems. Under the influence of heroin or when out to score, time can be an elastic commodity as far as users are concerned. This the children come to recognize.

Layna: 'I'm just going out for five minutes.'
Helen: 'You always say that, and then you're out for ages.'
Layna: 'But this time I really will be five minutes!'
Helen: 'And you always say that as well!'

These incidents do not help bring stability to what is often an ever changing world for the child. The child's anxiety is understandable. The parent might be picked up by the Police or the Drugs Squad, might overdose or be detained for numerous other reasons. The loss of a parent, even for a time, can affect the child, especially if it recurs.

Layna: 'Helen is a bit disturbed but that's not with me taking smack. It's because of Sam going to prison. Every time he goes, she gets upset.'

Thoughts of death are more common than we might think. The anxiety is more likely to be about the loss of a parent than the process of dying.

Lisa: 'When I was on drugs, Tony asked me if I would be around when he grew up.'

Also it should be understood that young children will react to the idea of loss in a child's way. In particular they are likely to worry about themselves, their own fate rather than the parent, about being left without a parent than the parent dying.

Grandmother: 'Eve was crying and saying, "What will happen to us when my Mummy dies?".'

At first I did not think that death really was a concern of the young children of drug using parents, they did not mention it. However in time I came to recognize it as an underlying anxiety. Drug use does very often bring a change in the relationship between the parents and child.

Tina: 'Before I started using, Kiernan was never out of my sight. People used to say that I spoiled him as any money went on him. When I was using I never used to bother with Kiernan, I would push him away.'

We should not forget that some difficulties arise from activities only indirectly connected to drug use. When parents are part of the sub-culture, the house is visited by drug users at any hour, so children have difficulty in seeing themselves as part of a family, as the 'family' appears to include all local drug users. However the form of the family is additionally different in that the main pressure on the drug user, when using, is to raise money to buy street drugs. This might mean the parents will steal and this can be upsetting, particularly if it involves the extended family.

Grandmother: 'Hugh was given a bike for Christmas, but he never got to use it. They sold it. You can't give the children money as their parents spend it on drugs. We bought clothes for them but I've never seen them on the children. Perhaps they are sold as well.'

Again, some drug users will not steal from the family or sell things from the house. Some have said they would stop using, rather than do such things. As usual, children often know exactly what goes on, whatever their parents might think or say.

Lisa: 'Tony said to me that everything that comes into the house I sell. And he's right.'

Eventually, the children not only know what their parents are like but have to take appropriate steps. It is not just the knowledge and the action that they feel forced to take, it is what all this means to the mutual relationship.

Cora: 'Jackie asked the school to look after his money for the trip to France, as he was afraid his mother would steal it.'

Other ways of raising money such as shoplifting, cheque frauds, prostitution and dealing drugs, can produce their own separate problems, not least of which is the stigma attached to the activities.

Lisa: 'See that laddie there? He turned round to Tony and said, "Your mother's a junkie and a prostitute."'

Reactions to parental behaviour

Such remarks are embarrassing for children and embarrassment affects how they see themselves as relating to other children of their age and to other adults.

Dot: 'I'll have to tell Layna not to come back. She came in stoned, and Scott had his friends in. He was embarrassed. He doesn't know what to say when she is like that.'

As the children grow older they know more about the situation and feel that they have to do more to help. Drug using parents will even fall in with this attitude and expect their children to help.

Darlene: 'My Mum was in the toilet one day having her shot and if it wasn't for me she would be dead.'
Me: 'She overdosed?'
Darlene: 'Yes.'

Added to this is the long term anxiety not only about whether parents are going to be all right but also how long the situation is going to continue.

Jenny: 'I have improved, I am a bit better, aren't I Darlene?'
Darlene: 'I can't tell, I can't tell. Sometimes you seem better and sometimes not.'

Eventually, children might become tired of the strain and want to avoid the vulnerability of being a drug user's child. They might switch off, or exhibit behavioural problems.

Darlene: 'I'm not bothering because my Mum's not bothering.'

CHILDREN WHO ARE UNHAPPY

Signs of unhappiness

The children of drug using parents need not be long term unhappy. By unhappiness is meant the children's feelings become internalized and part of them. The signs of this unhappiness are those of any child under pressure and are not specific to parental drug use. Thus the counsellor has to know the whole picture.

Beth: 'This house is really cold in winter. And Jilly (aged 9) is still wetting the bed; that's awful when it's so cold.'

That unhappiness is sometimes not known about until the child is out of the house, with someone else. The behaviour might be there all the time, the child may be unhappy at home but this was unknown to the outside world.

Janice: 'Tony still has his nightmares. He was crying and screaming last night, and every night he sings himself to sleep.'

Sometimes the child's behaviour changes not merely when leaving the home but also on return. There can even be a pattern of these behaviour changes which points to the definite existence of unhappiness.

Grandmother: 'Now that wee David is back with his parents, he is stammering badly again.'

The unhappiness may be internalized and even transmuted into other feelings, especially anger. This anger may come out directly or it may be observed in uncontrolled behaviour.

Lisa: 'Helen when she was three used to fight the five year olds in the nursery. Finally she was put out of the nursery for biting. She was a terrible biter.'

Sometimes the anger can be intense and expressed quite directly. In the case of the following five year old, his anger was almost tangible and indicates a high degree of disturbance.

Sally's son: 'I want to stab you. I want to stab everyone in the world.'

Another sign of disturbance is failure to mature emotionally or even regression. The retreat to security can become not just an emotional retreat but also a physical one.

Layna: 'Helen still sucks her bottle. In her school uniform, people will think her silly if they saw her.'

Another aspect of the child's lack of security can take the form of closely following a parent around.

However, we should not imagine that these children do not feel loyalty to their parents when threatened or apparently threatened, by outsiders.

Lisa: 'Tony took a bottle to the Drugs Squad as they were getting on at me.'

Other consequences of the drug life

These difficulties are often revealed in a normal or straight environment. Most children, being very adaptable, are able to use the new environment to their advantage and improve. But the child is moving more fully into a world where the norms, values and attitudes are very different. Adjusting to this world, a world where there are different boundaries and different expectations is difficult.

First Year teacher: 'Hugh was different from the others. He didn't play like the others or join in easily. He didn't seem to know what he was about.'

This of course presumes that the child is actually going to make it to school!

Tina: 'Kiernan has been late for school recently because he doesn't bother to wake me up in time.'

Disturbance can extend to the school, and among the possible forms of dysfunction are those of not attending school or of walking out of school. Of course one cannot be emphatic about all difficult behaviour being necessarily linked with parental drug use. However it is difficult to avoid that link.

Jenny: 'What's happening in the house is definitely affecting Jason. He's got very moody lately, though that might be him growing up.'

These situations, like all those involving relationships, are rarely simple. At one level children may be well-cared for, and yet there is still a lack; something is missing.

Vivienne: 'I know the children are well-cared for and fed properly, but there are other things they might have missed. I know they have missed out.'
Me: 'When you were using, did they feel rejected?'
Vivienne: 'Yes. I would sit in front of the television sleeping, or tell them to shut up.'
Me: 'And they would have missed out on things like cuddles.'
Vivienne: 'Oh yes!'

But part of the difficulty is that some parents do not have accurate perceptions of what is going on. Being caught up in their own drug using situation, they are unable to perceive situations from perspectives other than their own.

Tina: 'See Kiernan, he is not behaving himself and he won't listen to what he is told.'
Me: 'He's not the only one. You're exactly the same!'
Tina: 'You know, I've never thought about it that way!'

Because children sometimes feel they are not part of the drugs world they are not interested in it. This indifference may represent more; it might even be a rejection of the drug subculture.

Fanny: 'Mo asked for me to shut the door after Elaine came in, as all she speaks about is drugs and junkies. He doesn't want to hear it.'

However, children of drug users do tend to get on well with other children in the same situation.

Relative: 'Hugh seems to get on well with Jimmy. I think he can understand what it is like. They have a common bond. They know what it is like to have junkie parents.'

This in itself demonstrates that drug taking has affected the children and they do want help for themselves.

ENDING HEROIN USE

Introduction

It might be thought that if the parent or parents came off heroin then their child care problems would be at an end. Admittedly, we have noted that the process of coming off, with the possibility of withdrawals, is likely to be a time of difficulty. But the process of coming off drugs is longer and more complicated than most people think.

Most of those coming off heroin will go back to using; there is rarely a simple and final end to using. The whole process can go through many cycles; this is the normal pattern. For those not closely involved in drugs work, the pattern may be interpreted as the user having a series of failures in trying to come off. This in turn not only affects how the mother is seen and treated, it can reinforce her own feelings of perceived failure, and makes it harder for her to stay off drugs.

Many users will try and succeed in coming off by themselves. One common way is to use large amounts of alcohol to cover the withdrawing process and the heavy drinking may last for several weeks. The heavy drinking is likely to be more harmful as regards the welfare of the children. There is a greater risk of physical abuse under the effect of disinhibiting depressants such as alcohol, compared with the effects of heroin. The apparent change from heroin user to heavy drinker does not seem a beneficial change unless it is viewed in the context of being one way to come off drugs, and the user's next step is to control alcohol intake.

However, it is assumed that once the parents have been off drugs for some time, or even if they are stabilized on prescribed medication, then times would be much easier. In fact parents are likely to find that there seem to be even more problems. The problems that came with being a parent used to be eased to some extent by the use of drugs. This option is no longer open in the same way. Also, the active drug user is used to putting up mental walls against the world, of falling into easy denial. Once the user is off, this defence is much harder to employ.

Sylvia: 'When I was using I was able to switch off, just like that. Now I can't.'

Child behaviour and no drug use

The expectations of the parents are that the children will understand that the parents are off drugs and should improve in their behaviour as there is no reason why they should misbehave. Such expectations are unrealistic.

Tina: 'I thought Kiernan would realize that things are better now and behave, but he is much worse.'

In fact, the child is more likely to misbehave as he or she feels secure. Parental drug use, when it is known to the children, will modify their behaviour and can make them inhibited. This is similar to cases where parents suffer from a long-term illness and then recover. The behaviour of the children is relaxed and much less inhibited. We also have to realize that the parents might have changed but we should not expect the children to do likewise.

Lynne: 'I'm worried about Anna, she won't do as she is told. She's got very sneaky. Perhaps I expected too much; I've changed and she hasn't.'

To some extent we can see coming off heroin as parents becoming more like parents and less like children, and this is accompanied by the children becoming more like children and less like parents. It is not an easy double change for those concerned.

The possible aftermath

Behaviour, some of which is the testing out of the new parental behaviour, tends to calm down after a time. However there is another aspect that takes longer to work out. This is the guilt felt by parents, especially mothers, about how they treated their children when they were using.

Sarah: 'When I look back I can hardly believe the things I used to do. I would take the kids across the road when I was out of my head. God knows how there wasn't an accident.'

But these incidents are small compared with the underlying guilt with which users have to grapple. People come to terms with their past drug use when they start to feel guilty about it.

Judy: 'I'm worried about Christmas as I won't be able to get Earl much this year. Formerly I used to get him, well ... last year I got him a portable telly and lots more but now my bottle has gone and I can't shoplift.'
Me: 'But why are you so bothered? Is it for Earl or is it for yourself, because you feel so guilty?'
Judy: 'Yes, I feel so guilty. Those years I was away and now I want to explain things to him, but he says, "It's alright Mum", and walks away. I want him to say how he is feeling but he keeps it in, keeps it to himself. What goes on in his head? I'm scared, scared Paul, in case he takes the wrong track, in case he ends up taking drugs and wasting his life like I have wasted mine.'
Me: 'You realize that you are not just feeling guilty; you are feeling. For the first time you are experiencing real emotions and it's painful.'
Judy: 'That's what the doctor in London said but, clever, I thought I knew better. He said I would never really feel grief after my father died until my body was clear of opiates.'
Me: 'So for years, while Earl was growing up, you could not express true feelings. Now you are beginning to be able to express them. You cannot blame Earl for not being honest about his feelings if you weren't.'
Judy: 'I hadn't thought of it that way. But I am still scared he is

growing up, he will be out there and I cannot help him all the time.'

Me: 'But all children grow up and Earl is at an age when he is naturally growing away. The trouble is that now you are off, you want to be closer to him. You may have to let him grow up and still try to get rid of your guilt.'

Judy: 'Um.'

Me: 'You're thinking ...?'

Judy: 'Well ...'

Me: 'The past ...'

Judy: 'Perhaps what I want is not Earl as now but those lost five years. I want to live them again ... differently.'

REPRISE

Role of counsellor

Counselling adults can be difficult, but counselling adults where there are children concerned can be much more stressful. We can only deal with what is presented and what the clients desire, yet the temptation to go beyond this and tell the clients what to do remains strong. And strong are the counsellor feelings when having to deal with the reality of the drug using situations involving children. There is always the temptation to give feelings full rein and decide what is best. Advances through counselling, periods of personal growth, often come with crises. Thus although the situations can be very difficult, they can be the launchpad for real help, provided the relationship is in place and the counsellor is prepared to work for a positive outcome. Counsellors have to be sure, in addition, they know who their client is. If the client is the drug using mother, then that is the person to be helped. If the children need help, then that might require a separate referral.

Working it through

All these considerations may seem easy in theory. Practice teaches us the opposite. Counselling has to come out of the office as associated home visits are essential. This alone has implications for counselling itself. Anyone who has worked with heroin users knows better than merely to trust what has been said, but supplements this by observation.

For instance, the new door on the council house or flat usually means the Drugs Squad has broken down the old door in a raid.

The counsellor can detect through the letter-box the smell of people withdrawing. A glance may show the door jammed with a railway sleeper or other material to stop any 'bust'; this might indicate dealing takes place in the house. When the door is unlocked, the number of locks that have to be opened may also give an indication of dealing. The lack of names on the door and a stream of visitors late at night can tell their tale.

When seeing the parents, who might declare they have stopped using, pinned pupils will show if they have had opioids, flicks of blood on shirt cuffs can indicate injecting. A visit to the client's bathroom can reveal old needle-cases, while a lack of dessert spoons in the kitchen drawers may indicate drugs have been prepared at some time.

Implications

Usually counselling is done with individual clients and this leads to a certain reassuring simplicity. However where there are others concerned, especially young children who have little effective power, then the situation is more difficult. The use of observation is little different from observing the person for non-verbal communication. What may seem to some as intrusion into the life of clients may be seen differently by clients themselves, for the counsellor sets up a different dynamic.

The counsellor who has a better idea of the truth of a client's situation is more of a possible threat, can make the client feel more guilty, and yet can also be more of a friend and a help – provided a good counselling relationship is in place and provided the counsellor is sensitive to the demands of the situation at the time. Whatever the client has done or is doing, and this includes reacting to the counsellor, there still has to be counselling acceptance.

Any work that impinges on the children of drug users is likely to be the object of parental suspicion, and this suspicion is not totally misplaced due to attitudes of some workers and services in the past. Yet counsellors, despite possibly strong reactions from parents, should not assume that those parents are as much in opposition as might seem. To some extent action can be what parents desire. This is more than a rationalization, as with a good relationship, it is possible to break through to the stage where parents can admit what they really want.

The counselling relationship is likely to be put under pressure. Moreover strong feelings do not just arise in the parents. Counsellors will have to deal with their own strong feelings. Parents in turn can feel reassured in time that someone cares so much about their situation. By coming through the difficulties, the relationship can be strengthened and made more productive.

9 DEATH

INTRODUCTION

Counselling injecting drug users is bound at some time to cover the subject of dying, death and bereavement. With the advent of AIDS this subject has become even more relevant and familiarity with dying, feeling at ease with death and finding comfort through grief should be part of the counsellor's repertoire. Deaths through drug use, directly or indirectly caused, divide into two broad categories. Those which are very sudden and unexpected like drug overdoses, and those in which the person is dying and known to be dying as in cases of AIDS. Overdoses are unexpected and the person concerned may be unaware that he or she is dying. Thus help can only be given to the family and friends of the user who overdosed.

Overdose

Overdoses occur when too much of a drug has been taken, and in the case of opioids such as heroin, the resultant respiratory depression may be so great that the drug user stops breathing and dies. Such overdoses often occur through multi-drug use or drug users ignoring their likely tolerance level. In addition, users can die from anaphylactic shock when injecting can cause a sudden and massive release of antibody produced vasoactive substances such as histamine, which in turn causes a huge fall in blood-pressure, followed by breathing stopping and death. Anaphylactic reactions are very swift and may occur when virtually none of the drug has been injected.

Most drug users are likely to have encountered overdoses and so have some idea of what to do.

Josie: 'Dave overdosed two days ago and I brought him round, hitting him. It's no good tapping them, you have to punch like fuck. He's still got the bruises on his face.'

Reactions to overdoses

One concern about overdosing, especially for the partner and family of the drug user, is whether the act was accidental or intended.

The question is often put in this form, and it is not easy for the family to appreciate that the overdose may not fall neatly into either category but be the product of a high risk life-style. Overdosing has always been a danger in injecting drug use. It is difficult for those who are not part of the drug culture to understand not just the actual behaviour but the attitudes that lie behind that behaviour.

Bill: 'The doctor had better give me Nembies. That stuff he gave me was no good. I tried to OD, took forty of them and nothing really happened: I'm still here. It shows how weak they were.'

Often outsiders like to apportion blame; they like to be able to say if the death was intended or not. If it was intended then it was suicide, if it was accidental then it was simply an overdose. Often the client does not know what was intended, and there is no reason why others should know better.

Jane: 'I thought I had lost my giro and reckon that Dale would never believe me. So I went round and swallowed every tablet in the house. Later the police found it in the bottom of my bag. Because I had overdosed my doctor cut me off my tranquillizers which I had been on for twelve years, because he heard that I had overdosed. Without them I panicked. I went on the drink and had to have a half a bottle of Vodka to get me to sleep. Dale was out a lot and I got depressed. In the end I stabbed myself with a pair of scissors.'

The temptation is to ascribe reasons for the overdose and not appreciate that associated behaviour can arise from how the client feels.

Overdose and attempted suicide

Thus what we often have is behaviour of a desperate nature. Desperation can come and go, and it is helpful not to let incidents simply slide away. Overdoses in general tend to be ignored in the long term as they are subjects of denial. In the case of those overdoses which do not result in death, there is a tendency for the user to deny the true nature of the act and the accompanying danger. Professional helpers may also go along with such denials and see such acts as annoying mistakes, requiring medical attention, or they see the acts as being little more than attention-seeking devices.

Overdoses are seen as unintended acts whereas attempted suicide is seen as intentional. To me there is often no clear distinction as the attempted suicide is sometimes not a matter of wanting to die, but the drug user not caring whether he or she lives. The user will run risks, and whether he or she survives is left to chance, fate or God. This attitude becomes more understandable when we remember the extreme low self-esteem of some injecting drug users, who might not think it matters if they are alive or dead. Clearly, from the counselling point of view, overdoses should call for a review of how users feel about themselves and how such feelings can be improved.

Depression

Depression is quite common among heroin users, and many users will attempt suicide at some time. The problem is often overlooked as those drug users who do make attempts on their lives tend not to overdose intentionally on heroin or other drugs, partly because drugs are not associated with death but with comfort. More likely, they will cut their wrists or use other methods. Indeed by looking at client wrists, we can often see old scars of past suicide attempts.

Attempted suicide has its own myths. The notion that those who talk about killing themselves will never do so is incorrect. My experience has been that any expressed self-destruction should be treated seriously and time taken to talk through how the person is feeling. Also it is essential to make an appointment to talk again with the client. Clients have to feel that the counsellor is there, actively supporting them, and prepared to talk to them at any time.

The latter always worries some counsellors, who imagine that the client will constantly be in touch, rather than appreciating it is how the client feels that is important. The counsellor has to ensure a definite follow-up, and not leave things indefinite. The following is a quote from a suicidal client on the telephone, as she is persuaded to come into the office the next day.

Claire: 'Yes, that will be great. Don't worry, I wasn't expecting any answer, it was just good to be able to talk to someone. Nine out of ten times I don't want to have answers; I just want to talk and someone to listen. I have to work things out for myself. I wouldn't do what someone else told me, anyway. If I come in tomorrow, that will give me something to hold on to. I thought of taking 240 mls of methadone, that is enough to kill me. But I won't. I will definitely come in to see you.'

Feelings about death

Counsellors will have been trained in dealing with loss, death and bereavement, so will be prepared to some extent for themes around death. For the counsellor the subject of death induces strong feelings, whatever training has been undertaken. My experience has been that the death or even threats of death of clients are hard to take because of the counselling relationship.The fact that clients are almost always younger than myself makes feelings more acute, as death of young people is harder to manage.

As counsellors we are supposed to empathize with clients, but this is not easy at times. For members of the drug culture, death is no stranger and it is difficult for them to feel too much surprise or sorrow, or perhaps the influence of the drugs they are using prevent any such expression of sorrow.

Tina: 'This bloke asked me, "Doesn't it worry you when someone you know dies using dope. What do you feel?" I said you say, "What a shame!" And that's it. That's all.'

And how drug users can react to actual overdoses can also raise difficulties, which in turn can affect feelings towards drug users in general, feelings which if not attended to can spill over into the work with individual users.

Jane: 'The last time I OD'd I was left there. Well, addicts don't want the Police to get involved as they start saying things like "Was your finger on the plunger?" Oh, and my pockets were dipped. I found out who it was and pulled him up about it. He said that he had put me on my side so I wouldn't choke on my vomit before he left.'

Countermeasures

Counsellors can discuss issues about death and can express their own feelings to a support person or to colleagues, and this does help. But the counsellor can also take more active measures. The learning of simple First Aid is very useful. It will probably never be put into practice but the knowledge of what to do in overdose cases is reassuring.

Secondly, one should check whether clients themselves know about First Aid and work with overdose cases. Most drug users think they do, but some of the alleged subcultural treatments such as injecting the user with amphetamine or saline solution can be dangerous. Also some overdoses with barbiturates and multi-drug overdoses can be very deceptive as the user appears to recover, can be conscious for several hours and then collapse into coma.

HIV infection and death

With the advent of AIDS, users have become more aware of their impending death. Death is a taboo subject, we are not encouraged or permitted to discuss it, though it is the one aspect that is common to all of us, the one inevitability in life. This is especially true for the young. The diagnosis of AIDS is significant as it tells the user nothing except he or she is going to die; it puts a label of death on the user.

Fiona:'I think about death all the time. I write letters to people for when I'm gone. That's not normal is it? And I greet all the time. I'm twenty and will never be able to have bairns. I cannot sleep. When you cannot sleep you see things, like things keep flashing past your eyes but there is nothing there. I think about doing away with myself. I would but I haven't got the nerve but I think about it. I wish I was dead.'

Some individuals see themselves as dying and take up the appropriate role, even when there is little likelihood of any immediate death. Such clients believe that nothing is worthwhile and become preoccupied with death. The client may begin to withdraw from life, become isolated. This can become a state of depression and we should not overlook the fact that depression is a common and often overlooked aspect of clients with fatal conditions.

Counsellor feelings and death

Client isolation can be reinforced by the reactions of professional helpers, who reflect back some degree of depression as they themselves have not come to terms with the situation. As helpers we have to be aware of our feelings and not take on the expected feelings of the dying and project them back onto the client. Although some clients may be depressed yet this is not inevitable, so helpers should not feel depressed. In fact the diagnosis of AIDS can bring immediate relief in some cases as it brings to an end the anxiety about whether the user is going to get AIDS and probably die within a relatively short period. There is also relief when the client understands that having AIDS does not entail the user dying within a matter of days or weeks necessarily.

The diagnosis can produce shock but little denial or even blame.

The nature of HIV infection being spread over several years tends to make a degree of acceptance of AIDS easier and many people with AIDS are not so surprised at their diagnosis, they see it as the next stage of infection. This seemed surprising to me as it did not entail the amount of denial that goes with a positive HIV antibody test result.

Final stages

The task of health maintenance is less important here than that of the quality of life. At this stage I see little point in bothering about the client having to avoid cigarettes or alcohol if these are his or her pleasures. Although focus is placed on the person with AIDS, others such as the family or even professional helpers are likely to require a measure of help.

We tend to think that it is the dying person who has to be prepared for death but, to some extent, so do those around the dying person. There is a need for the client to end all unfinished business, to try to come to a satisfactory state with all outstanding and important relationships. Similarly other people might want to come to some understanding with the dying person. This may be seen as less important yet it does point to dying being a two-way process, that others die a bit with the client.

Aspects of helping

There is a general problem concerning the extent a person should be helped to fight and try to resist death, or help the person to accept death. Clearly these can be quite conflicting aims at times. For example the user might ask how long he has to live. The counsellor can avoid the issue, can give a vague reply or even devise a reassuring answer but none of these is likely to be totally satisfying to the client, especially as the client is able to observe the counsellor's discomfort and general evasiveness on further questioning.

An alternative might be to give the minimum expected life-span for a person with AIDS and this does provide time for the clients affairs to be put into some form of order. However giving a person an estimated rather than a minimum life-span can affect how long the person expects and even wants to live. The estimate can become a self-fulfilling prophecy.

Diagnosis of AIDS

The diagnosis of AIDS is usually the result of Pneumocystis infection in drug users and this can involve hospitalization. There should be consideration of how and when the user is to be told of the diagnosis. In particular, there should be recognition of the degree of medicalization that hospitalization involves and the resulting loss of control for the client. If the client is to be allowed to fight the infection and perhaps repeated infections, that client must be given the freedom and the wherewithal to fight.

This is important for drug users who fall all too easily into the habit of dependency. The client has to have a positive attitude to be able to live a full life and this can be difficult because of the user's physical condition, which can cause the person debilitating anxiety, pain and tiredness, and the user's psychological condition of low self-esteem and lack of self-confidence. In addition action may be difficult because the client is worried about the future and gets caught up with what might happen.

Tina: 'I feel fucked, there is nothing that can be done. It's a punishment for using, wherever AIDS came from. After me coming off, this is the result.'

Furthermore there can be a falling back to the dependence on drugs, they are seen as the way of coping with life. And to some extent they do help the client cope, but they also make a constructive and positive approach to a client's final period of life very difficult.

Sam: 'We're going to die. That's why we keep taking drugs, to try and forget about AIDS.'

Sometimes clients with AIDS simply do not plan ahead as the whole practice seems pointless to them. The loss of a long future is seen as the loss of any future, and the client decides to give up.

It is easy for the counsellor to get overwhelmed by what may seem a hopeless client situation, especially when the client sees it as hopeless. We have to look for the positive aspects, and they are always present. For instance, basically clients do not want to die, whatever they say from time to time. There is usually that spark still there. The task is to change our perspective and that of the client to see some hope. Thus what the client says may sound very negative.

Tina: 'It's not fair. Life owes me something, all I've been through. When is it going to be good?'

But we also have to recognize that underlying feelings such as anger can be present. Such anger can be turned to positive effect. The anger that clients feel against themselves or others or life in general can be used to drive themselves on.

Behaviour of people and death

Some people have difficulty dealing with death or the idea of death, and the knowledge that a person has AIDS can act as a constant reminder of death. The client, especially in hospital, can be treated as if he or she is already dead. Friends can talk across the person as if he was not there or they talk in hushed tones. Decisions are made without reference to the person with AIDS, decisions that are rationalized as being for his benefit. It is as if the diagnosis has completely changed the user, whereas the only change has been the label attached to that person. If the diagnosis is so important then the user's physical condition is less so, at least in the short term. Admittedly, the user may be breathless at times, he may be weaker and easily fatigued but these conditions evolve over a period and are not directly related to the diagnosis. With AIDS there is a greater likelihood of neurological impairment such as short-term memory disturbance but this condition does not start with the onset of AIDS. Thus the major factors initially are not the physical condition but the user's self-perception and the reactions of others; these interact, as self-perception is related in part to the reactions of others.

When visiting clients and meeting relatives or partners, the latter not merely require support for themselves but they often need information and reassurance. To help the client, it is helpful if those close are also helped so they reflect positively back onto the client.

Closer to death

The possibility of ensuing death comes with HIV infection; AIDS is merely the last stage in the passage of that infection. There is still much that the user can do to increase the quality of his life. The opposite is equally true; many of the difficulties that take place after clients know of their HIV infection can remain, depending on how the person has been able to handle knowledge of that infection. For instance, the client might feel that any planning ahead is quite pointless because of the possibility of death.

Many clients will say that they do not expect to live another year, that this will be their last Christmas, New Year or birthday.

Often this can be easily dismissed but there are going to be occasions when the ex-user has voiced what the counsellor may have been thinking. In such cases it does not help simply to dismiss the statement but one should accept it, ask the client how he or she feels about it. But we have to attend to our own feelings as well, to recognize that we are undergoing a grief reaction. Once we find statements hard to take or upsetting, then we are part of the grief process.

Reminders of death

For the person with AIDS his eventual wasting appearance can affect his view of himself and this in turn affects how he expects others to react to him. For acquaintances and friends from the drug subculture, the wasting appearance is a frightening reminder of what may be. The person with AIDS is the object of morbid interest.

The reactions of others is not always negative and in my experience this applies particularly to hospital wards where AIDS patients are treated by the nurses and doctors with great sensitivity. This is sometimes in spite of the visits by friends who are drug users and liable to take in drugs, though for most users with AIDS there is the tendency to restrict visits to the family and straight people and to exclude users.

Subcultural difficulties

Death and the fear of death brings a slow breakdown of the subcultural boundaries and norms.

Mother: 'Since Ronnie died, other addicts seemed to have gone to pot. They are going in all directions; they have given up hope.'

Thus part of the difficulty for clients is the change in the subculture and its attendant relationships. Clients who are feeling at a loss now suffer from disorientation as regards other drug users, from the change in the drug subculture. The subculture becomes a frightening place.

James: 'Everyone is so worried by the virus. When you see your friends dying every month, what do you expect?'

One possible result is that clients may have to reassess their relationship with the subculture and subcultural behaviour.

Changing behaviour

As death approaches there can be a return to a non-drug using perspective, a view that often clashes with the demands or wishes of medical personnel who see the person with AIDS as requiring drugs. This becomes especially pointed for the user who due to his wasted body and infections may be in considerable pain and so is given opiates, even heroin, to control the pain at the end. Drug users with AIDS who have ended their drug use may find difficulty in adjusting to ending their life as heroin takers. However the control of pain is important as it can prevent the client from working through the final stages of relationships and coming to terms with feelings.

Clients might want to distance themselves from the subculture, yet it is medical authorities who are pressing them to stay in a drug using state. For some, the decision is about behaviour but for users it can be about identity. Thus coming to the end of life, or, more often, what they see as the ending of their lives, clients try to understand, put meaning to their life. And they then discover there are no answers, none that they find totally satisfactory.

Simone: 'It's unfair! I got the virus from the first person I slept with when I was eighteen. Why me? Now I can't have any children and I'm going to die. All I want is somewhere to stay and someone to love and to love me. Is that too much to ask? ... What's the point of it all?'

The counsellor will soon realize that ongoing work is to do with feelings and the chief feeling is that of anxiety.

Anxiety

Anxiety eats away at client self-esteem and sense of identity. Extreme behaviour can also be linked with such anxiety. In my experience almost all attempted suicides are connected with such anxiety and the diagnosis of AIDS itself is not a precipitating factor.

Maggie: 'When I've got AIDS I'm going to OD. I don't want to be a burden, have someone having to take me to the toilet. I want to go out happy.'

The difficulty in working with client anxiety can be that drug use, whether illegal or prescribed, tends to interfere. This in turn makes counsellor and client attempts to work towards preparation for death that much more difficult. Drug taking can also interfere with the identification of medical symptoms, especially those of neuro-logical impairment. Problems with short-term memory might be the result of anxiety, they might be the result of the use of depres-sant drugs such as tranquillizers or they might be the effect of HIV damage to the brain. The important point is that the client needs to know whether anxiety is a relevant factor or whether there are other factors.

Anxiety tends to get in the way of acceptance of the situation and thus preparation for death. In the end reality cannot be escaped, so counselling help should be directed at bringing the client to see and to appreciate that reality. However this has to be done at the client's pace. The client should not be forced to 'face up to things'.

Contact

Just as clients need and want help, so they may also begin to retreat. Isolation can occur as death is felt to be approaching and the person withdraws from relationships with people and the world. At other times the isolation can occur through a lack of physical contact, that the person is not seen or visited. Other users regard the person with morbid curiosity. They are not supportive. The occasional visit only emphasizes the user's feeling of isolation.

Isolation can be further broken down by actual physical contact, by touching, holding hands or by hugging. This kind of contact may be unusual with drug users and we should remember they may have problems with physical contact. It is always essential to check out and think before breaking isolation in a physical manner. Isolation can also be as a result of the user feeling bad about himself, a result of guilt or self-recrimination. Users can feel guilty about whom they may have infected in the past, guilty about the sorrow they brought to their family, guilt about the strokes they have pulled and guilt about how their children have suffered. This guilt is often accom-panied by feelings of anger, either against themselves or against others. This anger has to be discharged so the guilt can be removed.

The persistance of guilt goes along with the capacity to blame. Once anger has been discharged, then blame should be discussed so that it can be allowed to die.

Religion

Religion may play a part at this stage. Some clients do get a measure of relief through the idea of forgiveness. The idea of going to a new life with misdeeds or sins forgiven can be very comforting. However we should not assume that a person having a faith, even a nominal faith, will be automatically helped. Some clients can become angry at their situation and lose their faith, while those whose faith is remote may suddenly feel guilty about a lack of religion and fear the unknown. They may imagine ultimate damnation or be very unsure as to what might happen to them. Uncertainty is usually more upsetting than certainty, as it encourages the growth of anxiety.

Young people and death

AIDS is presently a condition that affects those who are young; this has various consequences. The young tend to be resilient, even when physically very ill. They have less of an acceptance of death and so can go through a whole series of relapses and recoveries. They have a will-power to fight and this extends to all spheres. Helpers might think that this is a good thing, a quality to be commended. In practice the fighting spirit may be evidenced in ways that helpers might not always appreciate. The clients may be propelled by anger and make insistent and seemingly quite unjustifiable demands on those around. They might exhibit difficult and almost unmanageable behaviour. The fighting spirit may be seen in uncooperative action, argumentativeness and constant demands on the time and patience of everyone. Feelings can run high as they are reinforced by the reactions of helpers who have their own feelings about young people dying. The result can be a strained atmosphere at times which is unhelpful for all concerned.

The client may have to make preparations for death such as the drawing up of a will yet this action is sometimes seen by young people as giving in to the idea of approaching death. Likewise sometimes the client has quite practical thoughts and concerns and the counsellor has to be receptive to them. Clients should be allowed to talk about the practicalities of death and the funeral, as this actually lessens anxiety.

Lisa: 'What I would like to know is how much a plot costs.'
Craig: 'You probably think it a bit peculiar but it is important for Lisa to have a plot to be with her family.'

The client will have a glimmer of hope to the very end, even though the client realizes at heart that such hope may be quite unrealistic. This raises questions about the role of the counsellor. Whether the need for reality demands that the client be totally realistic about such hopes and the counsellor ensures that the client is totally realistic.

Importance of others

The beliefs and actions of the client are seldom to be taken in isolation: they are also to be related to the beliefs and actions of those close to him. In particular, the role of the client's partner is important. As death approaches, the mutual relationship can improve if that relationship is good. If the relationship is poor then impending death can worsen that relationship. Unfortunately many of the relationships of injecting drug users are far from good, and when one of the couple is dying this is not a good time to try to help improve that relationship.

In theory the passage of dying is made easier if there is joint preparation for the death but this is very often extremely difficult. In some relationships or marriages, fear of loss of the other partner is inbuilt. There is a high degree of dependency, personal as opposed to chemical, and the client can often find that his or her main problem is not addiction but dependency. Thus death or the idea of death can resemble that of coming off drugs completely, and it is hard to know at times which is the worst for the client. A dependent relationship is difficult to end, and death for dependent persons is doubly difficult.

Death and relationships

Even limited experience has shown me that the approach of death acts as a release not from life but from aspects of life that a person may wish to do without. People who feel they have little to lose may decide to end relationships and couples split up. Women with HIV have ended relationships because HIV has liberated them from unwanted situations.

Diane: 'I tanned my wrists but the Stanley knife didn't go deep enough. I've been beaten up again and he is taking the pure cunt out of me. I can't live with him any more ... I want to meet someone. Someone I could hold for days in my arms and who would hold me. I would do everything for him, cook his meals and keep the house for him.'

The variable nature of relationships make it impossible to give any simple answer as to what is the best thing to do. Yet there do seem to be some ideas that are generally helpful. The person who is dying should tell his or her partner of the situation. In the case of AIDS it is unlikely that the partner has not been told but in time and changing relationships it might be that a new partner is unaware of what is happening. A dying person can be supported by the partner, the partner can share in the anticipatory grief and may in fact be angry afterwards if that opportunity was not allowed to him or her. But newly relating to a person who is dying also brings its own hard decisions. It becomes more difficult to end such a relationship because of the personal guilt of the partner and because of the feelings and reactions of outsiders. For a relationship that is not good, approaching death can bring crises in many forms.

Couples

The couple has to work hard at resolving what remains unresolved and the new problems that arise. There has to be clear communication. This does not mean that it has to be necessarily direct as these problems can be raised indirectly in the form of hypothetical situations or even as a joke, though both sides are quite clear as to what is really being said. With AIDS I have noticed a variety of issues that surface. Even communication can be difficult, as not only the person with AIDS but the partner has to come to terms with death. The increasing medicalization of the person with AIDS, especially if hospitalized, can open up a gulf between the couple. This gulf can widen under the stress of death, and arguments can increase or undisclosed resentment build up. Two common key issues may be those of the future of the partner and the future of the children.

The client who is dying may have fears of the partner remarrying but there can be inhibitions about voicing this fear. The other fear concerns what is going to happen to the children, in particular worries about the possibility of the children being taken into care if it is the mother who is dying. There are a number of options. The father may be expected to look after the children in the future, but there can be questions as to how realistic this is. Also the question of remarriage or taking another partner arises. Families might be seen as taking a very active role in the future care of the children but this can also lead to problems.

Firstly, injecting drug use and the accompanying life-style and behaviour can result in families ultimately feeling unable to stand the situation any longer and not wanting to have any more to do with their drug using family member. Even if there is no complete split, drug use puts immense strains upon any family. As a consequence, negotiation about the future of the children is made more difficult because of strong antagonistic feelings which make even simple communication into an indirect and coded operation.

Grandparents

Grandparents can take a very active part at this stage and they usually feel that they have some obligation themselves to look after the children, and yet they can also be resentful at having to do so. They felt that their time as parents was over, yet they now themselves having to go through the same life-stage again. And all this occurs at a time in life when they feel themselves less willing to undergo such a life change. Further problems may arise because there are two sets of grandparents and they in turn might not get on. This is often the case. There is a tendency to protect the using family member and blame someone else, usually the user's partner or friends. Gradually blame of the partner can extend, indirectly, to include the user's family. This is a mutual process so that both sets of families and both sets of grandparents end up with strong feelings about each other.

Such mutual antipathy does not make for smooth cooperation. It makes fundamental questions as to which family does what, whether one family should have the major share of child care, the practicalities of dividing the time of the children between families and to what extent the families want to abide by the wishes of the dying person, even the interpretation of those wishes, all very difficult.

Grandparents may be seen as the best persons to make these practical decisions but we should remember that it is rarely easy as one set will be caught up in the grief for the son or daughter who is dying. This tends to be doubly difficult in that parents expect to outlive their children nowadays and when the children die first, there will be additional feelings of unfairness and anger. All these intense feelings may be flying about and yet it is very hard to discharge them, to show them. Part of the reason for this is that the drug user is usually viewed as a failure, the black sheep of the family. This very bad person remains so until, very often, at the diagnosis of AIDS, he or she is suddenly seen as good.

Drug users as saints

Many parents think, as do many people generally, that it is wrong to speak ill of the dying as it is of the dead. Thus the role of the person who is dying is the very opposite to his or her former role. Such a great change leads to true feelings on the part of the family being suppressed and not being set free.

What is not always realized by the family is that a person might have AIDS but it can be a long time before that person dies. Thus the 'canonization' of the user diagnosed as having AIDS begins to wear very thin. Usually the diagnosis does not have a great effect on the user as a person. If the user was seen by the family as a liar, manipulative and self-centred then the family slowly returns to that view. AIDS does not essentially change the person, though it can provide the opportunity for change. As one mother remarked to me, 'He may have AIDS but he is still no better than he ever was.'

Family care

The treatment by the family of the user with AIDS can be deceptive in that much goes unvoiced and it can take a time before the family realizes that they need help as much as anyone. This becomes even more obvious to outsiders when the user with AIDS has infection and reinfection with Pneumocystis. The constant relapses and hospitalizations can lead to immense strain being put on the family, the strain increased by the ambivalence that they feel towards the user. Parents and relations can push themselves to the limits of exhaustion and this state, along with their unresolved feelings, can make them wish that the user was dead. This can lead to feelings of guilt, especially when the user does die.

Towards the end the client might well want those around to be restricted to the immediate family. With perhaps visits from the counsellor or person of religion, or both. The emphasis is now on the drug user coming to terms with life, so that dying is easier.

Hugh: 'I just want peace now. I've given out enough and taken enough – it all evens out. But now I don't want any more of it; I've had enough. I want to go out into the country, as I know it well, having been a poacher long ago. I like seeing the flowers and the deer. There's a lot of beautiful places I know in Scotland. And there's my son Robert; I don't want him to be like me ... well, I want him to be like in part, but not violent like I was. I want to help people now, not because I would get anything out of it, get gold stars or something, but because I want to help. I want to give something back. I want my life to mean something.'

Some helpers may in turn feel rejected or angry that they are not being involved in the end, so they themselves might want some help. In fact help might have to be slowly adjusted so that relatives are offered more support, as they need to adjust to the fact that the user is dying. For close relatives the very appearance of the client, his possible changed behaviour as he is dying, and whether he recognizes family members can bring their own difficulties.

Feelings of relatives can become mixed up and they do not always understand that the client's feelings are the paramount consideration at this time. They too might feel rejected when the client merely wants to be alone with the partner or with the children. Throughout the latter stages of dying, the client may be in both physical and emotional pain and the recipients of that pain are likely to be not merely those who are round and about but those who are nearest and dearest. All relatives and helpers have to come to accept to some extent that there comes a point when the user has decided to die, decided that his time has come and it is the task of others to allow him to die. In the very end, the client's acceptance of death is helped if it is also accepted by others. Such acceptance certainly makes the final passage easier.

Counselling to the very end

When counselling heroin or other drug users with HIV infection, we have to be sure of our own feelings about loss and death. We also have to recognize that counselling those in the latter stages of the infection may well cause the counsellor to go through grief reactions and these have to be worked on with a support person. Failure to do so may result in the counsellor's own grief reactions interfering with counselling.

The client may go through several different stages such as the diagnosis of HIV infection, diagnosis of AIDS, confinement to a wheelchair and confinement to hospital or a hospice. These stages may be accompanied by clients grief reactions. These can be shock, denial, blaming others, self-blame and depression, and a degree of acceptance. Counselling can help the client through these stages, by reassuring that what is happening is normal, and the process of talking through the situation.

The stages of grief are never clearly defined and are usually jumbled, so the main characteristic appears to be that of personal chaos. Part of the counselling is concerned with trying to inject some structure into client lives, to let clients know they are not going mad. Also there is a temptation to think that clients should undergo grief work, that they should be led through certain helpful counselling stages. All this depends on the clients, and whether they want to deal with certain topics. This may mean that the counsellor has to be prepared not to help, to see a client dying without much counselling help.

Subjects for discussion

Topics that can be discussed with the counsellor vary in nature but may include practical items, present relationships and the future. Practical items might cover present finance, and whether the client wants to apply for grants from Social Security or from charities. These also bring the client further into the role of a person with AIDS, they reinforce the dependent role. Accommodation might be a possible or potential issue, especially as breathlessness and muscular weakness can make living high in tower blocks very tiring. Equally, the occurrence of dizziness or fits may require a rethinking of living conditions. Present concerns may also include holidays, hospitals, and hospices. Clients have to decide what they want to do and possible implications.

Relationships are another area of potential work. The client's illness will usually result in the other partner having to take up a greater load, and frequently needing help. This can become an acute problem if the partner is using drugs or has HIV infection as well. The children can present difficulties, in that they may not know the situation of the parent, though they will know something is wrong and that the parent does get ill. Telling children of school age can not only cause depression but can result in stigmatization if they tell anyone at school.

Finally the user's parents and relations can often provide help and want to do so. This may mean work has to be done as relationships can be strained and unhelpful. The family may require support to get through their own attitudes, problems and difficulties.

Personal help

Towards the end, clients can worry about their death for numerous reasons. They can be afraid of what is going to happen to them, whether they will go to Hell. Sometimes there is anxiety about the unknown, of walking into the unimaginable. Other concerns can be about the actual act of dying and whether it is going to be painful. Along with the latter goes a fear of not dying with dignity, of breaking down or being terrified. There is also the anxiety about whether they will be allowed to die with dignity, or whether they will be kept alive in a painful or vegetative state. Some clients want to talk about euthanasia and the possibility of a referral to Exit might be raised. Although some of these topics are painful, yet they should be talked through and everyone be aware of the implications.

Colette: 'I have thought what I would do if Jim was in pain at the end, and I think I would end it for him. I wouldn't want him to suffer any longer and I wouldn't want to suffer any longer.'

Bereavement

The counsellor should also attend to the needs of those left behind, to the bereaved. Again, experiences vary, both personally and across different cultures. It should be noted that the experience of someone close dying can reinvoke previous feelings about death and the general reaction to loss. For users and their families loss is likely to be a major issue and in various forms they will have experienced many aspects in their life. This help is generally best given to the family as a whole.

The only other point to emphasize is that bereavement is for a young person, and funerals often reflect this. The partner of the client may seek another partner comparatively soon after the death, reflecting a young person's reaction.

10 SUPPORT

STRESS

Introduction

Counselling is carried out nowadays with the counsellor receiving structured support and this is increasingly becoming a condition of counselling. This denotes a change from the past when support was seen as an admission of weakness in the counsellor, a cracking of professional competence. Yet although there has been this change, what is not so clear is how support should be delivered.

The best approach to answering the question is to look at the whole area of counselling stress and how best it can be managed.

Tension

Counselling injecting drug users is emotionally demanding; it places strong stimuli or tension on a somewhat vulnerable person, the counsellor. But tension is not necessarily a negative effect. It can be useful as it sharpens the mind of the counsellor, it can be an impetus to action and it can actually give a good feeling. Tension is often seen as a negative characteristic of work, something that the person should avoid. This is a false perception; tension is a natural part of life.

Tension becomes stress when the brain sees a situation as threatening and the parasympathetic nervous system goes into flight-or-fight mode, the body is prepared for action. The stimulatory hormones adrenalin and noradrenalin are produced, causing the muscles to contract ready for action, the breathing to quicken, the heart rate to increase, and the digestion to slow down. After the threat or danger has passed the body returns to its normal state. The whole cycle is the normal way of dealing with threats and causes the person no harm. In fact, it is an essential part of the human survival mechanism.

The real danger comes when the person is not able to escape from the threatened state or one threat is immediately followed by another, so the body does not return to its normal state. The body reacts further, producing more energy by the release of glucose

– 263 –

from the liver and corticosteroids, which break down energy-rich fats. Now there is an excess of sugar in the blood, which makes diabetes more likely, and fats which can clog the arteries and cause heart attacks. The muscles being in continual contraction may ache and headaches can also occur.

Thus stress, the reaction to threatening stimuli, can be a temporary phase or it can be an ongoing long-term state. In the latter case, stress can be medically dangerous. However there are other effects of chronic stress besides those which affect the human body.

Burnout

Continuous high stress can lead to a state of chronic stress syndrome, known as 'burnout'. By examining burnout we can get some idea of the extremes of stress, extremes in which workers may find themselves. Burnout may be attained for a short time and the counsellor subsequently recovers, but often it becomes a permanent and damaging state.

As counsellors can take various degrees of stress and have different ways of coping, we should not simply judge the pressure counsellors feel by the amount or type of work they are doing. We have to look towards the person. The person reacts to what is perceived as a threat, a threat which is inescapable or followed by other threats. Yet what constitutes a threat can in part depend on perception. What is a threat to some people is a challenge to others. What is a threat that cannot be escaped for some, presents no such thing to others. There may be different genetic abilities to withstand stress, past life-experience can have a strong influence, and stress might be more difficult to manage as one's age increases. There is no simple external way of estimating how much stress a counsellor can or should be able to take, so we should not make any assumptions about bearable stress levels. Thus we never know if a person is in danger of burnout but we can look for possible symptoms.

Symptoms of burnout

Burnout can be characterized as a condition observable in a person, either by himself or others, and affecting physical, psychological and social aspects. Though it is seen very much as an individualistic condition, it can apply to groups or whole agencies. However it is easiest understood initially in the individual.

Counsellors when in a state of burnout can be both physically and emotionally exhausted, unable to escape that condition. They can feel continually tired, lethargic, unable to sleep. They may suffer from physical ailments such as frequent headaches, backache, stomach complaints or other often rather vague symptoms. As can be seen, these are a result of the continual muscle contraction, the production of glucose and corticosteroids, and high blood-pressure. These symptoms may seem rather vague at first, counsellors might feel 'under the weather', but this does not reduce their importance.

The worker can suffer from secondary medical symptoms directly associated with stress such as ulcers, high blood-pressure or asthma attacks. In addition, often infections take a long time to clear up and there can be frequent and prolonged periods off work.

Psychological symptoms of burnout

There are also psychological signs such as disillusionment, self-doubt, doubts about the value of personal work and the work of the agency, feelings of helplessness and being trapped in one's job, a sense of not being appreciated and one's hard work being taken for granted. Counsellors can become rigid in their thinking, stubborn and irritable. There can be a loss of enthusiasm, optimism turns to pessimism, ideals to cynicism, and there can be a change from respect for the client to disrespect, even rejection. Drinking or the use of other drugs may increase, counsellors may suffer from a decrease in proper judgement and reasoning, and they may also be liable to act in a more risky, even reckless manner.

Counselling itself is likely to suffer as counsellors become increasingly depressed and relate poorly to clients. They may find that their memory deteriorates and they have to work harder to keep up with the work. This in turn will increase their isolation from work colleagues. Life can become centred round work and there can be increased interpersonal conflicts. This can affect the whole workplace and everyone can start to become increasingly hostile and rigid, arguing endlessly about the boundaries of their work and that of others. Counselling can become a source of competition between counsellors and there may be an increase in authority conflicts.

Thus in the agency there can be signs of agency malaise if several workers are suffering from extreme stress, the organization can itself be dysfunctional and we might find that important organizational decisions are more frequently made by an increasingly isolated, elitist group which has little real communication with other workers. Morale in such organizations can become low, management and counsellors become mutually disrespectful and distrustful. Workers turn up late for work, fail to attend meetings and the management spends more and more time away from the organization. As has been noted, sickness and absences can increase.

The danger of not dealing with stress is that it can affect counsellors and so affect the counselling. Under high stress the accuracy of perceptions, and the quality of empathy and listening skills of counsellors can all be reduced. Thus providing support is one way of ensuring the provision of a high quality service.

Difficulties in recognition

Some counsellors reading the list of possible symptoms may be inclined to think that they must be suffering from stress as, for example, they are lacking in enthusiasm or the communication in their agency could be greatly improved. These symptoms of possible personal or agency dysfunction by themselves do not necessarily indicate burnout. However if these or other symptoms are constant characteristics of personnel and organizations, then there might be cause for concern. However we might also note that often burnout is a state that is not recognized, or if it is recognized no-one acts to alleviate the situation.

A possible reason is that counsellors may know about burnout but they do not recognize the condition when it happens to them. Counsellors may see themselves as employed to serve and help clients, their attention is pointed that way and this is reinforced by the agency. They feel concerned about their clients and may take on some of their values and causes. What counsellors might not understand is that they can only function with their own integrity being respected. Agencies can also take the same view. They see the justification for their functioning as being for the clients and the welfare of counselling employees takes a low priority.

Perceptions of burn-out symptoms

Both counsellors and the agency as a whole may see the counsellor who admits to having troubles, who sees himself as approaching burnout, as someone who has failed. This is augmented by the concept that the counsellor should be a model for the client; the counsellor should not be seen to be anything else except a person who was strong and able to cope. In fact the client often relates well to the counsellor who shows what may be seen as weaknesses, to the counsellor who is not 'perfect'. To clients, counsellor stress may not be a weakness but signs that they really are human, that they are not paragons of virtue and all that is good. In a curious way, some counsellors may feel themselves more effective in relating to the client precisely at the time when their skills and understanding are declining. As a result, counsellors may be further misled as to the quality of their counselling.

The agency can be in an even more difficult position as it sees the true goals as being an ability to deliver a good service and not to present a human face. As a result the reaction of the agency, allegedly devoted to helping those in difficulties, can be quite negative. It might be thought that the counselling agency that does not respond to the voiced difficulties of an employee, a counsellor, is doing a poor job. However agencies, if they are made cognisant of how counsellors are feeling, are likely to respond. The difficulty is that counsellors under extreme stress is not likely to put themselves in the apparently compromising position of being seen unable to cope.

PREVENTATIVE ASPECTS

Prevention of burnout

The best way to deal with burnout is not to wait till it has happened, especially as there is no certainty that it will be recognized for what it really is. Prevention holds the first and major key to the elimination or reduction of unacceptable degrees of stress. Prevention has to work at several levels, it is not just a simple matter of counsellors having to look after themselves. There has to be an understanding, an acknowledgement and action on work where high stress is likely.

Areas of stress

In practice there are areas of likely stress, areas of high tension which counsellors find difficult to manage. These can be divided into the following broad categories.

There are life's potential stress points, applicable to everyone, counsellor or not. Such stress points include deaths of those close, and divorce or separation. Both counsellor and agency have to be aware of these points and then counsellor support can be given. What is not so obvious is that other more mundane situations may also be surprisingly stressful, situations such as moving house or going on holiday.

There are those potential stresses that come directly from working with clients. These stresses can be divided into three categories:

1. Stress originating from picking up the pain or other feelings of the client.

2. Stress originating from the state of particular counselling relationships, such as those that are poor or those which are coming to an end.

3. Reflection about the counselling, such as a lack of progress.

Empathy with clients

When counsellors empathize with clients, they have to really experience the full force of client feelings; to experience anger, sadness, excitement, pleasure or despair. Sometimes more than one feeling is present, so the feeling may also be of ambivalence or chaos, with secondary feelings about how one is feeling. Counsellors do not stay long with such feelings, but empathy, if it is to mean anything, has to be a true experience of the feelings of another – and this can affect the counsellor.

This picking up the feelings of clients can be complicated and only achievable by counsellors allowing themselves to be, for a short time, totally open and vulnerable. In so doing, counsellors may have to relive past similar feeling of their own, and then be able to dissociate what belongs to clients and what belongs to themselves. And everything that is experienced by counsellors must be controlled to the extent that counsellors are touched, but not overwhelmed.

Counselling relationships

Stress can arise from the counselling relationship, or how well counsellors and client get on together. Sometimes counsellors will relegate the importance of the relationship, as long as clients appear to be progressing satisfactorily. In fact, counsellors are bound to be involved with clients to a greater or lesser extent, though counsellors may not perceive this, and so deny the fact. Such denial is not helpful as it is both dishonest and unrealistic. Moreover denial only aggravates difficulties in the relationship when they occur. The relationship comes under stress because two different persons are involved. In this way it is the same as any other relationship, where one person has to be aware of the other person, the other person's needs, perceptions, past experiences, and future aims. It is not easy to have to constantly think and be sensitive to others.

Counselling expectations

There can be further stress from an unrealistic counsellor's expectations of what clients should do or will do. The classic giveaway is the phrase, 'If I were you ...', ignoring the inconvenient fact that the counsellor is not the client. Clients have to find their own solutions, do things in their way, and at times this can be stressful for counsellors.

Stress can also arise from the counsellor's expectation of success, an expectation partly arising from the counsellor not allowing clients to proceed at their own pace. After working for some time, counsellors may expect to have achieved a lot, only to see what 'little' they have achieved. This in turn they interpret as being a lack of success – and a failure for which they are accountable. Indeed, the counselling agency may reinforce this assessment, perceiving problems with the counsellor. Both counsellors and agencies have to be aware of their own agendas and expectations, and subsume these into the greater task of allowing clients to be responsible and self-directed, and so needing to go at their own speed.

Also counsellors may overlook advances that have been made or look for observable behavioural progress and disregard improvements in relationships or the counselling relationship. The desire for accountability tends to rely on examples of verifiable behaviourable change, and the less noticeable changes in relationships are ignored. All of the counsellor's pessimistic perceptions can further become rooted in the counselling owing to the fact that negative perceptions can be picked up by the client, and the client responds in a negative fashion.

Aligned to counsellor expectations are the failure of expectations, which can produce feelings of having been let down. Counsellors may rationally appreciate that their expectations may have been unrealistic, or there was only a chance that the client was going to behave as expected. Nevertheless, counsellors can still be affected by client behaviour.

Lack of counselling progress

Counsellors may not expect success, but they do expect some degree of progress. Rather than interpreting the situation of lack of movement as being unsatisfactory, it is better to try and check what factors may be related to the blocking. There may be client or counsellor resistance, unrealistic expectations, misplaced aims, incorrect appreciation of the client's situation and who may be involved in that situation. Lack of progress may simply be missed or unobservable, or progress has taken place according to the client and it is the counsellor who has the problem.

Reinforcement of stress

Stress is increased by cognitive aspects and the way the counsellor regards them. Thus certain beliefs make client stress much more difficult to sustain, beliefs such as:

- Counsellors should not make mistakes.
- Counsellors should always arrive at the best solutions.
- Counsellors always have to know what they are doing.
- Counsellors are responsible for what happens to their clients.
- Counsellors should be successful in work with clients.

When working with clients it is easy to ignore completely the above beliefs. Then, as difficulties arise, such troubles are interpreted as counsellor failures. These interpretations in turn aggravate the downward spiral, and make a positive view of personal counselling work even harder to sustain.

Cognitive aspects

To deal with such beliefs, counsellors need to work on them with support persons or colleagues. But this will be insufficient unless there is acknowledgement of the danger of such beliefs on the part of both counsellors and counselling agencies. There also has to be a realization that counsellors do not set out to make mistakes, that they want the best for their clients and that at times counsellors will be unsure what is happening in the counselling. Furthermore, counsellors cannot live clients' lives for them and only clients can ensure success, not counsellors. These thoughts should be written down and made public. Counsellors should be realistic, and acknowledging such counselling limits is being realistic.

Personal life-stress

Apart from counselling, stress can be personal, and need not arise from counselling work. Although life-situations are not directly connected to the counselling, counsellors should be aware of their indirect effects and be responsible for coping or having help in coping with the stress produced. If the counsellor works for an agency, then it is helpful if the agency is aware of the counsellor's life-situations.

This is often achieved indirectly, in that the counsellor has to attend regular personal support sessions where these life-situations can be discussed. One area of possible difficulty arises with regard to information obtained by the counsellor's supporter being passed on to the agency. This causes few difficulties if the agency itself is functioning well and relationships in it are good. If this is not the case, then the agency itself might require organizational counselling. An agency which cannot deal properly with itself, is unlikely to be able to respond appropriately to counsellor stress.

Action on stress

It is helpful if counsellors take action from the very start. This means counsellors actually start to discharge counselling stress rather than carrying it around, with the danger that it expresses itself in unhelpful ways during the counselling. In order to begin the process, counsellors should monitor themselves, be aware how they are feeling. This may be easy enough if the client is being very angry or aggressive, but it might be less easy if the client is feeling depressed. Counsellors may not immediately pick up conscious feelings of depression, yet begin to feel low themselves. This can continue to the point of counsellors being unable to pick up depressive feelings, either in the client or in themselves. Thus the reactions of others close to counsellors can be important.

When considering stress action, we should not confine this to action after the counselling has taken place, but build it into the counselling. One preliminary step is that of counsellors monitoring their feelings during counselling, and following this by the process of distancing. Usually so much is happening in counselling that counsellors have little opportunity to make space for themselves. This can be done by stopping the flow of counselling, by simply asking the client for time to reflect and consider what has been said. Though this can be of help to the client, it is probably more helpful to the counsellor.

In this gap in the counselling, counsellors have to remind themselves that the feelings they are experiencing come from the client, not from themselves. Also these feelings are not directed at the counsellor but merely at the world in general. All these thoughts have to be reinforced by communication with the client. Thus counsellors might say,'Just now I'm feeling ...', to be followed up by 'It seems to me that you could be ...', and then,'When you feel like this, where do you put your feelings?'. Thus the feelings are placed where they belong – with the client – and not taken on by the counsellor.

Poor counselling relationships

Counsellors may be conscious that counselling relationships with certain clients do not seem to be very good. This can have a debilitating effect. The counsellor may not look forward to or even like counselling sessions with the client. Under such circumstances counsellors should express how they are feeling and then how they feel about the relationship to the client. This has to be accompanied by positive feelings as well, even if it is merely to reflect that the relationship is good enough for the counsellor to make comments on it.

Relationships are more likely to deteriorate from lack of action than from counsellor action. And if there are difficulties in the relationship, the client is just as likely to be experiencing them. By not talking possible difficulties through with the client, the counsellor is locking in and reinforcing those very difficulties. In my experience, one of the most common faults in counselling is a reluctance to share counselling difficulties with the client.

Assertion

Counsellors should look towards their work with various clients and should try to determine whether they have been on the receiving end of client feelings to an excessive extent. Counsellors should not take too much, as their work will suffer if they make themselves into client victims. Counsellors have to look towards the necessity of being more assertive, of using assertion techniques in their work. This is likely to be needed more when working with injecting drug users than with many other types of clients.

Assertion is linked with the need for counsellors to ensure that there are mutually recognized work boundaries, recognized both by themselves and their clients. The boundaries are of two forms.

The first is that which defines the counsellor as a person; overstepping that boundary would be to fail to respect the counsellor as a person. The second is that which defines the counsellor as a counsellor; overstepping that boundary would be to take advantage of the person as a counsellor. The responsibility of managing these boundary aspects lies with the counsellor. The client might be accused of taking advantage of the counsellor, but this is to be expected. It is part of the client's coping mechanism.

The question of boundaries, what might be expected of both client and counsellor, can sometimes be usefully formalized in a written agreement. Counsellors should not term this a contract as this implies certain legal obligations and the possibility of penalty clauses.

But if there are infringements of boundaries, by either party, then it is useful to refer back to the agreement. The agreement can be extended to include not merely the expectations but the mutually agreed aims and goals. Usually this is a good idea, as clients are more likely to object to rules about boundaries, but not to the notion that both counsellor and client are going along the same road and have similar goals. Where possible, difficulties should not include ideas of blame but be slanted towards possible cooperation and problem resolution.

Not feeling good

Within the relationship there is also counsellors' perception that they have to be at the service of the client, and they should not behave in any way that interferes with that client service. In practice there are going to be times when the counsellor is going to feel quite negative towards the client, yet feel unable to express that negativity. However storing up negative feelings may be unhelpful for both client and counsellor. The counsellor has to be allowed to express his negative feelings and feel safe in so doing. Here the place of an outside supervisor, a supervisor who is not part of the agency, has a lot to commend it.

Yet this is seldom totally sufficient, as the client is kept out of the situation, though the client should very much be part of the situation. What should take place is for counsellors to be able to work constructively with their negative feelings. There is no need to do this often, but telling the client there seems to be a blockage and asking the client's agreement to work on this blockage can be a preliminary step. One way of working might be for counsellor and client to swop places for ten minutes and to act out how each sees the other as operating. This gives both the opportunity to experience the counselling from the other's perspective and some of the other person's feelings and difficulties.

Termination of counselling

Another issue worthy of consideration before counselling starts is that of termination. The counsellor is expected to relate well to the client and then that relationship might be ended, for a variety of reasons. These can include the counsellor having to close a case through the pressure of work, or there being more urgent cases. Whatever the reason for ending, the counsellor is seldom given time to recover from the termination, he is seldom allowed to grieve. Sometimes there may be little sorrow at the ending of the relationship; more often the end is upsetting for the counsellor. However there is an idea that the counsellor has to continue with his work; he is not allowed to feel sad, he is not supposed to feel sad. This overlooks the loss of a relationship for both counsellor and client.

SUPPORT AND COUNSELLING

Ongoing support and counsellor feelings

Support for the counsellor is both for work related matters and for those matters which may impinge on work.

If we begin with the counselling, then it can be helpful to look at the feelings evoked in the counsellor by the counselling. It can be helpful if the counsellor, after each counselling session, makes the briefest of notes on what feelings and thoughts seem relevant. These can be brought along to the support session for discussion. The feelings that may be marked down can include empathic feelings, those feelings such as the client's pain, anger or sadness which are picked up by the counsellor. Other feelings are those directed at the counsellor, for whatever reason, by the client. A third category are those feelings directed maybe at others by the client but taken on by the counsellor.

It is useful to discuss all these feelings, even if this does not seem so relevant at this later date. The process helps to get the counselling into perspective. The major task however is to locate any unresolved feelings from the counselling. The next stage is then to discover any particular reason for the feelings being unresolved.

Work with the client

Other aspects of client work can also be discussed, though the scope depends on the nature of counsellor supervision as opposed to support. However proper supervision can be supportive, if done well.

The work areas to be covered might include those applicable to each counselling case, a review of the aims, objectives and their achievement. Another aspect is encouraging the counsellor to think about the various counselling relationships and what new aspect or nuances the counsellor has discovered.

Yet another approach is for the counsellor to look at what particular skills were used or were attempted, and the results. Finally, when supporting or supervising, it is important that the counsellor feels good about the experience and so support can usefully be ended with the counsellor talking about a recent bit of counselling that left a good feeling. This is more than a morale boosting exercise, as if the counsellor cannot think of anything, then that becomes a matter of concern. It can reflect the counsellor's negative perception of his or her work.

Specific difficulties

There are some difficulties that are perhaps more common with counselling heroin users, which even if they have been covered in training, still deserve consideration.

The first is client verbal aggression. For some counsellors the difficulty arises from their own life experience and how well they deal with aggression. Aggression should not present a difficulty, but in practice the vehemence of client feelings can overwhelm the unsuspecting counsellor. We should bear in mind that some of the difficulty in working with heroin users can arise not from their drug use but from their working-class origins, as compared to the middle-class counsellor. The same difficulty has been noted with doctor and patient communication during consultations. Thus what the counsellor sees as aggressive might be quite normal to the client. The degree of aggression is reinforced in these clients by their subcultural norms: aggression is a common form of behaviour for drug users.

Assertion may still be required but it has to be done carefully. Much aggression comes from client anxiety and the client will be helped if that anxiety is relieved. Thus when clients are aggressive it is best to deal with the feeling, acknowledge how the client is feeling, and then let him or her safely blow off steam. Clients will cool off in under ten minutes.

Another difficulty can arise from clients not wanting to talk about anything but their prescriptions and how they want their doctor to increase them. This is what the client wants to discuss and seldom takes the hint to go beyond it, so the session can end up with the client moaning about something he or she can do little or nothing about. This sounds a quite trivial difficulty, yet in practice it can be very hard to move the client on. It is helpful when there are these troubles, if the counsellor shares them with the client, makes some remark about feeling frustrated about how the session is going and beginning to feel annoyed with the client for going on about prescriptions. Then the counsellor might add that this counsellor annoyance is not fair to the client and is likely to get in the way of being helpful. Again, anxiety is so often a linked factor and needs attention.

Further difficulties

Counsellors following the equation of drug use should expect relapses and clients to restart drug use. However this does not make relapses any easier for counsellors to take. Counsellors usually want clients at least to come off injecting street drugs, for their own sake. They then feel let down by client relapses. Often counsellors will deny this, saying they accept relapses, but usually this is not completely true. So counsellors should say how they really feel, and then realize that how they feel is probably little different from how the client feels. Clients are likely to be upset about restarting drug use and feel no better about relapses than counsellors. Thus counsellors have to determine exactly how they feel. This can include feelings of sadness and also anger. Counsellors then have to acknowledge to whom the feelings are directed, whether at the client or at themselves.

Threatened suicide

One situation that is likely to occur at some time is that of the client threatening suicide. The counsellor has to decide quickly what this means. Is the client serious or not? Here being empathic can help, and counsellors should allow themselves to share in the client feelings. Is the client feeling desperate, anxious or angry? Is the client displaying firmly controlled feelings?

Further clues are given by acknowledging the client's feelings and then observing the client's reactions. The latter is only possible if counsellors are able to be in control of themselves and not be precipitated into action or to see the client's behaviour as 'manipulative'. Clearly, the client is trying to communicate something and we are interested in the message. We also have to monitor our own reactions. There is a temptation, when the client says, 'If you don't do something, I'm going to do myself in', to be angry with the way help is being requested. It is worth considering why clients should have to resort to such methods, and see such messages as forms of communication rather than threats.

If clients are determined to kill themselves, then they cannot be stopped. However this is rarely the case. What is required is help and boundary-setting, as extreme anxiety can also bring feelings of things out of control and setting boundaries introduces greater control.

STRESS AND THE AGENCY

Management

The counsellor is usually part of an agency and excess stress can be associated with work management within the agency. Account should be taken of the number of cases any counsellor is carrying and their intensity. An ex-drug user who is seen only occasionally is likely to cause less stress than a user who is in the terminal care state of HIV infection. Consideration should be given additionally to how well counsellor and clients relate. Inevitably the counsellor will relate to some clients better than to others, or the counsellor through agency pressure takes on clients with whom he might not have been so keen to work. All these factors can affect the stress and working efficiency of individual counsellors and thereby the agency itself.

Workload

Perhaps the greatest problem is that of the number of clients seen by any one counsellor and the through-put of clients. Many of the difficulties reflect not only problems counsellors might have as regards the criteria for taking on and closing cases; the agency may also be experiencing similar difficulties with the total number of cases. However there has to be a recognition of the differing criteria that individual counsellors and the agency might employ. For instance the criteria for closing cases for counsellors tend to be counselling and goal orientated, whereas the agency criteria will be management orientated and tend to veer towards making space for new cases. Both counsellors and the agency have to be very precise and conscious of their possibly differing aims and goals, evaluating them on a regular basis.

External stress

The counsellor is a person who spends most of his time away from work. Accordingly, what he does outside work can greatly affect stress levels. Stress can be affected by events in his personal life such as the death of someone close or the end of a relationship. Such stresses have to be added to that engendered at work. The important factor is the total amount of stress they are experiencing, from whatever source.

Counsellors can alleviate stress by ensuring that there are strict boundaries between what counsellors should do and what the client should do. The counsellor should not feel obliged to do everything for the client; indeed it is bad practice so to do, as this can increase client feelings of dependency and reduce the chances of clients being able to initiate self-change. These boundaries are better recognized and maintained if counsellors receive good supervision and support. It should be noted that though supervision and support are related, yet they should be kept conceptually distinct. Supervision relates to the management of cases by the counsellor, whereas support relates to how the counsellor is feeling as a person and as a worker. There is often a difficulty if a worker is supported by anyone who is in a position of authority in the agency. The reason is that support can be restricted by authority which prevents the counsellor reacting as a person. In these circumstances the counsellor can find it difficult to voice complaints against the agency, and difficult to admit to behaviour that might be interpreted by the agency as possible signs of weaknesses. Even if the agency person does not view the situation adversely, counsellors may feel inhibited from freely expressing themselves.

METHODS OF SUPPORT

Ventilation

Support should allow counsellors to ventilate their feelings about their personal life, their clients and their agency, if they so desire. They should feel safe and thus able to discuss their hopes and aspirations for themselves as persons, and not just in work terms. Also counsellors should be able to discuss the boundaries between work and home life, to define the situation so work does not overly impinge on the home. This intrusion can consist of excessive work outside normal working hours or it can be counsellors worrying about their work when at home.

What is required is the employment of a trained facilitator or counsellor to be able to use such ventilation usefully. Ventilation without proper takeup can actually be unhelpful, leading to frustrating complaining sessions and a decline in agency morale. This lack of work self-esteem in turn makes it very difficult for the counsellors to get into a positive frame of mind and to be constructive.

Other de-stressing methods

The alleviation of high stress can be helped through the use of relaxation techniques, yoga, meditation or bio-feedback methods. There are two points to be remembered. The counsellor is often told to use these relaxation and allied techniques to diminish personal stress but little attention is given to the causes of stress and the wider agency context. Also these techniques are not universally helpful. I find that some relaxation methods can actually increase rather than decrease stress in myself. On the other hand, I do find that active physical exercise is generally helpful, both for directing interest away from work and as a way of lessening depression.

AGENCY STRESS

Agency difficulties

Burnout is not merely related to the individual, it reflects on the agency. Accordingly, the agency has a responsibility to prevent, recognize and work sensitively with cases of burnout. Agencies should not only be supported but should be helped by the agency planning. Counsellors should be allowed time out, especially in the event of counselling clients dying. Counsellors should be fitted into a scheme of job progression, so that they feel they are advancing personally and are not trapped by their job. Realistically, counselling injecting drug users as a job tends to be time-limited. The counsellor can only counsel usefully for so long, even with measures taken to reduce stress. The agency has to be able to give a sense to the counselling workers of life after counselling injecting drug users. There has to come a time when it becomes unrealistic to expect counsellors to give of themselves any more.

Training

Workers must have sufficient good, relevant training in order to be able to counsel adequately. As much of counsellor training involves the counsellor exploring his own attitudes, opinions and beliefs, we should understand that training is not a single block event. It is a continuous ongoing process as attitudes, opinions and beliefs can alter over time. Information can also alter over time, or simply increases in amount and the counsellor needs to check out new knowledge. So training is an integral part of the agency's functioning, aimed at the preparation, maintenance and improvement of counselling.

Positive agencies

Agencies have a further obligation, one which is equally applicable to counsellors, but one which is more rarely seen in helping organizations. The obligation is that of giving and receiving positive feedback. Too often the organization is defensive about itself, too worried about avoiding mistakes rather than taking risks and achieving progress for clients. Mistakes are sought out but the good done by counsellors is not sought out. It is not appreciated. This marks some of the difficulty in recognizing burnout. Feelings of not being appreciated are burnout symptoms yet they may also be well placed: counsellors might indeed not be appreciated.

Agency burnout

Agencies are capable of poor functioning and in extreme cases they can also suffer from burnout. They feel unappreciated, they fail to cooperate with other agencies and suffer from institutional fatigue. They are unable to change, unable to come up with new ideas and become increasingly bureaucratic and territorial. Such agencies are no longer able to serve a useful purpose, they are unable to service clients properly but keep functioning only through their own momentum. The best thing to be done is to close down the agency for a time until total restructuring and renorming can be achieved.

Support groups

These groups are composed of counsellors, and the idea is that they function as one means of keeping counsellor stress under control. At present there is an almost unquestioning belief in the usefulness of these groups, though in practice many support groups fold or run into major difficulties within six months. One possible reason is that there is an assumption that embers of the group know how to accept and give support, that they can use the group usefully.

Being a counsellor does not entail that the person necessarily knows how to use a group situation to his and others' advantage. If a counsellor is under stress this puts up a barrier, as intense stress can prevent the counsellor from asking for help or giving help: this applies equally to the group situation. What is best for support groups is a facilitator who is chosen from outside the agency, someone to aid the functioning of the group and its members.

The greatest need for support groups is the inclusion of someone who possesses group skills. For instance there is the belief that counsellors all together in the group, having the same interests and the same kind of problems will naturely get on well. This happens at first but then, as members gain confidence, they can afford to act as individuals. Members then might discover that they do not get on. Group functioning can become unhelpful unless there is someone to ease the situation. Generally, there are many assumptions made about how these groups can benefit counsellors: they are assumptions. If the group is dysfunctional, then the stress on the counsellors may be increased rather than decreased, and counsellors would have been better off if they had never gone to the group at all. The same can be said of other stress relieving methods. They have to be right for the situation and the people concerned.

Working with the stress

If counsellors experience stress then they are expected to get help for themselves directly afterwards, but this is seldom possible in practice. The result is that counsellors may be carrying stress around with them. For example, the counsellor may have seen several clients but not have had the opportunity to see a support person, and have had the opportunity to discharge accumulated stress. Admittedly, counsellors do tend to recover somewhat after each counselling session, but there will be a slow build up of stress. In these situations most counsellors have their own informal methods of de-stressing, often involving talking to colleagues. This is quite acceptable as long as it is done in at least a semi-structured manner, in a form of co-counselling. Too often workers talk about their work together but this does not really deal with stress. Dealing with stress requires work.

SUMMARY

Perception of counselling drug using clients

Counselling and working with injecting heroin users may seem dangerous, frustrating and, with the advent of HIV infection, depressing. Support may be needed to deal with these aspects. However support should be an individual not a blanket provision, as the areas of required support will vary from one counsellor to another. The first thing to realize is that support is often needed because of inadequate training and false understanding and expectations. Drug counsellors may feel that the work is dangerous and so take measures, either individually or through the agency. The agency might also take measures for the protection of staff. Thus security cameras, panic buttons and rules for the exclusion of drug using clients are put into use. However these are seldom supportive to staff and frequently give a message to clients about their perceived worth. The result can be that they actually increase the likelihood of incidents. This does not mean outrageous behaviour should be accepted by counsellors or anyone else.

What is important is to have good counselling relationships with clients and to understand clients, as themselves, as family members and as members of a local drug community. Counsellors have to understand that they are also part of the illegal drug using world themselves, albeit in a rather peripheral capacity.

That world has norms such as not 'grassing', paying your debts or risk physical violence, and helping out other members. It is unimportant that not all drug users adhere to such rules. Counsellors, as interlopers in this world, should adhere to them. If we take the first rule of not grassing or informing, then this has implications for counsellors. For instance, some amount of information is kept about clients. As a social worker, I kept case files and allowed clients to read them up to three months of the current date. The provision was retained as reading files could help with the counselling. Clients could read what I had written about them and, as long as it was not too recent, this could be put into a working context. Sometimes I insisted clients read their files to put the relationship on an honest basis. Of course, not everything written down proved pleasant for clients, but the object was to be honest – not nice.

Violence is another fear and I have been the object of threats from time to time, from being beaten up by a client who could scarcely stand to having a gun pointed at my head. Threats are a common currency in the drug subculture. My concern is to try and understand exactly what was troubling such clients, and the difficulties they were experiencing with myself. There is considerable room for client misunderstanding. As counsellors, we have to realize that the more a counsellor knows and understands about drug users and the local drug subculture, the greater potential threat he could appear to be to drug users. The lack of a fixed position of counsellors in the drug subculture hierarchy also leads to uncertainty and possible anxiety. Making one's own position clear can be helpful, as is having a realistic view of the clients. Counsellors are not likely to be subjected to violence as they are not important enough. However a counsellor with access to drugs would be in a slightly different position. Generally, training around the theme of violence is helpful as it reduces possible counsellor induced aggression and even violence.

The work of counsellors with drug users is seen as being frustrating, and counsellors may be given advice about how to advance sessional work. Yet this might not prove successful. Injecting heroin using clients can have so many problems that counselling can last several years in total, and counsellors require patience. Frustration is also the product of what has been put as the working base-line. With some clients, my base-line is survival, whether related to their drug use or HIV infection. If they are still alive, then this is rewarding. There need be no more than this.

HIV infection has given counselling injecting clients a depressing air – wrongly, in my opinion, as this ignores the pleasure and satisfaction for the counsellor that comes through the counselling relationship. And it is the quality of the client's life that is more important than the length of that life.

Support as required

It is imperative that support should be based on understanding and realistic attitudes and beliefs. This understanding should cover both the counsellor, the service and the clients. There are a number of ways of increasing this total understanding and these may vary from individual agency and counsellor. Some support methods will diminish anxiety and difficulties in the short term, but not change the underlying situation. This means support does little more than contain the situation. Rather than maintain any situation, my preference would be to improve it, to put understanding into ethical practice and so advance counselling itself.

BIBLIOGRAPHY

All publishers are in London unless stated otherwise.

DRUGS A

BMA and Royal Pharmaceutical Society of Great Britain (1993) *British National Formulary*, no. 25.

Ball, J. and Chambers, C. (1970) *The epidemiology of opiate addiction in the US*. Springfield, Illinois: C. C. Thomas.

Banks, A. and Waller, T. (1988) *Drug misuse*. Oxford: Blackwell Scientific Publications.

Berridge, V. and Edwards, G. (1981) *Opium and the people*. Allen Lane/St. Martin's Press.

Brown, C. and Lawton, J. (1988) *Illicit drug use in Portsmouth and Havant*. Policy Studies Institute.

Dorn, N. and South, N. (1985) *Helping drug users*. Aldershot: Gower.

——(1987) *A land fit for heroin*. Basingstoke: Macmillan Educational.

Drug Abuse Council (1980) *The facts about 'drug abuse'*. New York: Free Press.

Earley, P. (1991) *The cocaine recovery book*. Sage Publications.

Edwards, G. and Arif, A. (1980) *Drug problems in the sociocultural context*. Geneva: WHO.

Fortson, R. (1988) *The Law on the misuse of drugs*. Sweet & Maxwell.

Freemantle, B. (1985) *The fix*. Michael Joseph.

Glatt, M. *et al.* (1967) *The drug scene in Great Britain*. Edward Arnold.

Glassner, B. and Loughlin, J. (1987) *Drugs in adolescent worlds*. Macmillan Press

Glatt, M. and Pittman, D. (1967) *The drug scene in Great Britain*. Edward Arnold.

Hanson, B., Beschner, B., Walters, J. and Bovelle, E. (1985) *Life with heroin*. Mass.: Lexington Books.

Heller, T., Gott, M. and Jeffrey, C. (1987) *Drug use and misuse*. John Wiley/Open University.

Julien, R. (1992) *A primer of drug action*. New York: W H Freeman.

Kalant, O. (1966) *The amphetamines*. Toronto: University of Toronto Press.

Larner, J. and Tefferteller. (1966) *The addict in the street*. Penguin.

Laurie, P. (1971) *Drugs*. Pelican Books.

O'Callaghan, S. (1970) *Drug addiction in Britain*. Robert Hale.

Pearson, G. and Gilman, M. (1987) *Young people and heroin*. Gower Publications and HEA.

Plant, M. (ed.) (1990) *AIDS, drugs and prostitution*. Tavistock/ Routledge.

Plant, M. (1992) *Risk-takers*. Tavistock/Routledge.

Sabbag, R. (1970) *Snow blind*. Picador.

Seymour, R. and Smith, D. (1987) *Guide to psychoactive drugs*. New York: Harrington Park Press.

Siegel, L. (1987) *AIDS and substance abuse*. New York: Harrington Park Press.

Snyder, S. (1986) *Drugs and the brain*. New York: Scientific American Library.

Spotts, J. and Schontz, F. (1980) *Cocaine Users*. New York: Free Press.

Spencer, C. and Navaratnam, V. (1981) *Drug abuse in East Asia*. Oxford: Oxford University Press.

Stewart, T. (1987) *The heroin users*. Pandora.

Stimson, G. and Oppenheimer, E. (1982) *Heroin Addiction*. Tavistock Pubs.

Strand, J. and Stimson, G. (eds) (1990) *AIDS and drug misuse*. Routledge.

Street, L. (1953) *I was a drug addict*. New York: Random House.

Tyler, A. (1988) *Street drugs*. New English Library.

Williams, T. (1990) *The cocaine kids*. Bloomsbury.

Wilson, C. (ed.) (1968) *Adolescent drug dependence*. Oxford: Pergamon Press.

COUNSELLING

Basch, M. (1988) *Understanding psychotherapy*. New York: Basic Books.

Brammer, L., Shostrom, L. and Abrego, P. (1989) *Therapeutic Psychology*. Englewood Cliffs, New Jersey: Prentice Hall.

Derlega, V., Metts, S., Petronio, S. and Margulis, S. (1993) *Self-disclosure*. Sage Publications.

Dryden, W. (1991) *W. Dryden on counselling*. vol. 1. Whurr Publications.

Egan, G. (1986) *The skilled helper*. Pacific Grove, CA.: Brooks Cole Pubs.

Haley, J. (1976) *Problem solving therapy*. New York: Harper Colophon Books.

Hill, C. (1989) *Therapist techniques and client outcomes*. Sage Publications.

Hobson, R. (1985) *Forms of feeling*. Tavistock Publications.

Jamieson, A., Glanz, A. and MacGregor S. (1984) *Dealing with drug misuse*. Tavistock Publications.

Kottler, J. (1992) *Compassionate therapy*. San Francisco: Jossey-Bass Publications.

—— (1993) *On being a therapist*. San Francisco: Jossey-Bass Publications.

Masson, J. (1990) *Against therapy*. Fontana Collins.

Mearns, D. and Thorne, B. (1988) *Person-centred counselling in action*. Sage Publications.

Nelson-Jones, R. (1988) *Practical counselling and helping skills*. Cassell.

Nunnally, E. and Moy, C. (1989) *Communication basics*. Sage Publications.

Oldfield, S. (1983) *The counselling relationship*. Routledge and Kegan Paul.

Rogers, C. (1967) *On becoming a person*. Constable.

Schiffman, M. (1971) *Gestalt self-therapy*. Menlo Park, CA.: Wingbow Press.

Stanton, M. and Todd, T. (1982) *The family therapy of drug abuse and addiction*. New York: Guilford Press.

Stevens, J. (ed) (1975) *Gestalt is*. Moab, Utah: Real People Press.

Velleman, R. (1992) *Counselling for alcohol problems*. Sage Publications.

Zinker, J. *Creative process in gestalt therapy*. New York: Vintage Books.

DEATH

Donnelly, K. (1982) *Recovering from the loss of a child*. Macmillan.

Furman, E. (1972) *A child's parent dies*. New Haven, Conn: Yale University Press.

Kubler-Ross, E. (1973) *On death and dying*. Tavistock Publications.

Pincus, L. (1981) *Death and the family*. Faber and Faber.

Nungessor, L. and Bullock, W. (1988) *Notes on living till we say goodbye*. New York: St. Martin's Press.

Qvarnstrom, U. (1978) *Patients' reactions to impending death*. Stockholm: Institute of International Education.

STRESS

Cooper, C. and Payne, R. (eds) (1988) *Causes, coping and consequences of stress at work.* New York: Wiley.
Fontana, D. (1989) *Managing stress.* British Psychological Society.
McMay, M. and Fanning, P. (1987) *Self-esteem.* Oakland, CA.: New Harbinger Publications.

JOURNALS – DRUGS

Anstie, F. (1868) The hypodermic injection of remedies. *Practitioner* vol. 1, p. 32.
——(1871) On the effects of the prolonged use of morphia by subcutaneous injection. *Practitioner* vol. 6, p. 148.
Arafa, A. (1932) Heroin addiction in Egypt. *Lancet* vol. 21, p. 922.
Bewley, T. and Ghodse, H. (1983) Unacceptable face of private practice: prescription of controlled drugs to addicts. *BMJ.*
Bick, R. and Anhalt, A. (1971) Malaria in drug addicts (letter). *JAMA,* 10 May.
Blackwell, J. (1983) Drifting, controlling and overcoming. *J. of Drug Issues* Spring.
Clark, J. *et al.* (1972) Marriage and methadone. *Marriage and the family* vol. 34, p. 496.
Howard-Jones, N. (1947) A critical study of the origins and early development of hypodermic medication. *J. Hist. Med.* vol. 1.
Hussey, H. and Keliher, T. (1944) Septicemia and bacterial endocarditis resulting from heroin addiction. *JAMA,* 28 October.
Jennings, W. (1901) On the physiological cure of the morphine habit. *Lancet* vol. 2, p. 360.
Kane, H. (1879) Hypodermic injection of morphia. *Lancet* vol. 2, p. 441.
Kreuger, D. (1981) Stressful life events and the return to heroin use. *Human Stress* vol. 7, p. 3.
Macht, D. (1916) The history of intravenous administration of drugs. *JAMA* vol. 66.
Mandel, L. *et al.* (1979) A feminist approach for the treatment of drug abusing women. *The Internat. J. of the Addictions* vol. 14, p. 589.
McLaughlin, H. and Haines, W. (1952) Chicago hypodermic drug use. *Illinois Medical Journal,* February.

Most, H. (1940) Falciparum malaria among drug addicts. *Am. J. of Public Health* vol. 4.

Obersteiner, H. (1880) Chronic morphinism. *Brain* vol. 2, p. 449.

Oliver, G. (1871) On the hypodermic injection of morphia. *Practitioner* vol. 6, p. 75.

Sonnedecker, G. (1963) Emergence of the concept of opiate addiction. *J. Mond. Pharm.* vol. 1.

Westermayer, J. and Bourne, P. (1977) A heroin epidemic in Asia. *Am. J. Drug and Alcohol Abuse* vol. 4.

Zinberg, N. (1972) Rehabilitation of heroin users in Vietnam. *Treatment and Prevention of Opiate Dependency.*

British Journal of Addiction

Abed, R. and Neira-Munoz, S. (1990) A survey of General Practitioners opinion and attitude to drug addicts and addiction. vol. 85, p. 131.

Bean, P. and Wilkinson, C. (1988) Drug taking, crime and the illicit supply system. vol. 83, p. 533.

Bell, J. (1992) Treatment dependence. vol. 87, p. 1049.

——, Digiusto, E. and Blyth, K. (1992) Who should receive methadone maintenance? vol. 87, p. 689.

Burr, A. (1983) The Piccadilly drug scene. vol. 78, p. 5.

—— (1984) The illicit non-pharmaceutical heroin market and drug scene in Kensington Market. vol. 79, p. 337.

Couss, P. and Bentall, R. (1989) Heroin users' careers and perceptions of drug use. vol. 84, p. 1467.

Dawe, S., Griffiths, P., Gossop, M. and Strang, J. (1991) Should opiate addicts be involved in controlling their own detoxification? vol. 86, p. 977.

Donoghoe, M., Dolan, K. and Stimson, G. (1992) Life-style factors and social circumstances of syringe sharing in injecting drug users. vol. 87, p. 993.

Friedman, S., *et al.*, (1992) Social intervention against AIDS among injecting drug users. vol. 87, p. 393.

Green, L. and Gossop, M. (1988) Effects of information on the opiate withdrawal syndrome. vol. 83, p. 305.

Greenwood, J. (1992) Persuading General Practitioners to prescribe: good husbandry or a recipe for chaos? vol. 87, p. 567.

Hammersley, R. and Morrison, V. (1987) Effects of polydrug use on the criminal activities of heroin users. vol. 82, p. 899.

Liappas, J., *et al.*, (1987) Thoughts on the Sheffield non-prescribing programme for narcotic users. vol. 82, p. 999.

Madden, J. (1987) The decline of longterm prescribing to opioid users in the United Kingdom. vol. 82, p. 457.

Marks, J. (1987) Treatment of drug addicts (letter). vol. 82, p. 815.

Marlatt, G. and George, W. (1984) Relapse prevention: Introduction and overview. vol. 79, p. 261.

McKeganey, N. and Barnard, M. (1992) Providing drug injectors with easier access to sterile injecting equipment. vol. 87, p. 987.

Murphy, P., Bentall, R. and Owens, R. (1989) The experience of opioid abstinence: the relevance of motivation and history. vol. 84, p. 673.

Oppenheimer, E., Sheehan, M. and Taylor, C. (1988) Letting the client speak: drug misusers and the process of help seeking. vol. 83, p. 635.

Robertson, J. (1989) Treatment of drug misuse in the General Practice setting. vol. 84, p. 377.

Ronald, P., Robertson, J. and Roberts, J. (1992) Risk-taking behaviour on the decline in intravenous drug users. vol. 87, p. 115.

Sheehan, M. and Oppemheimer, E. (1988) Who comes for treatment? Drug misusers at three London agencies. vol. 83, p. 311.

Strang, J., Johns, A. and Gossop, M. (1990) Social and drug-taking behaviour of 'maintained' opiate addicts. vol. 85, p. 771.

Taylor, J. and Mullin, P. (1986) Replacement of a prescribing service by an opiate-free drug programme in a Glasgow clinic. vol. 81, p. 559.

Telfer, I. and Clulow, C. (1990) Heroin misusers – what they think of their General Practitioners. vol. 85, p. 137.

Vaillant, G. (1988) What can the longterm follow-up teach us about relapse and relapse prevention in addiction? vol. 83, p. 1147.

JOURNALS – COUNSELLING

Atkinson, D. et al., (1978) Effects of counsellor race on Asian-American perceptions. J. of Counseling Psychology vol. 1.

Chiasa, B. (1992) A comparative study of psychotherapy referrals. British J. of Med. Psychology vol. 65, p. 5.

Clarke, J. (1983) Sexism, feminism and medicalism. Sociol. Health and Illness vol. 5, p. 1.

Cohen, G. et al., (1980) Treatment of heroin addicts: is the client therapist relationship important? The Intern. J. of the Add. vol. 15, p. 2.

Coleman, S. and Stanton, M. (1978) The role of death in the addict family. *J. of Marriage and Family Counselling* vol. 4, p. 79.

Demond, D. and Maddux, J. (1983) Optional versus mandatory psychotherapy in methadone maintenance. *The Intern. J. of the Adds.* vol. 18, p. 2.

Savicki, V. and Cooley, E. (1982) Implications of burnout research. *The Personnel and Guidance Journal* vol. 3.

Sue, S. and Zane, N. (1987) The role of culture and cultural techniques in psychotherapy. *Am. Psychologist*, January.

Ward, D. (1984) Termination of individual counseling. *J. Counseling and Develop.*, September.

Woody, G. (1983) Psychotherapy for opiate addicts. *Archives of General Psychiatry*, June.

Zahn, M. (1973) Incapacity, impotence and invisible impairment. *J. of Health and Social Behav.* vol. 6, p. 73.

INDEX

acceptance in counselling 136–40,
176, 205–6
addiction 4–5
  of babies 212–13, 218–19
  perceptions of 19, 46, 69, 74, 188
  to medication 90, 95–6
  to needles 74–6, 182, 183
adolescence, and starting drug use
22–7, 42–3
adulterants in drugs 3, 37, 179
age
  and acceptance of death 255
  and maturity 13, 82–3
  see also adolescence
aggression, of clients 275, 282
agreements, counselling 157–8,
272–3
AIDS
  care of family 249, 259–60, 261,
  262
  impact on relationships 256–8,
  261
  reactions of clients to 248–56
  reactions of others to 251, 252,
  258–9
  role of counselling 260–2
  see also HIV
alcohol
  as drug substitute 185, 238–9
  effect on unborn child 212
  legislation on 9–10
  in multiple-drug use 6, 183
  parental use of 27–8
  reasons for use 6, 14, 33, 44, 45
  tolerance to 4

ambivalence of user 207–8
  in coming off drugs 59–62, 64, 65
  in staying off drugs 86, 100, 104
amphetamines 6, 7, 212, 247
anaphylactic shock 244
Anstie, Dr 16
anxiety
  during withdrawal 70–1, 73–4
  of dying client 253–4, 261
  use of drugs to relieve 42–3, 44,
    45, 47–8, 168, 225
  of users child 232–3, 235
assessment in counselling 161
availability of drugs 22, 44, 102

babies see children; pregnancy
barbiturates 6, 7, 178–9, 187, 212,
  218, 248
behaviour
  drug use as rational 18–19, 30–2
  modelling in counselling 125
  normalisation 85–6, 111–12, 118
behavioural approach to drug use 35
benzodiazepines 7, 44, 69, 178–9,
  180, 187
boredom
  drugs as cause of 79
  drugs as relief from 42, 100–1,
    110, 169
  as threat to staying off drugs 193
buprenorphine 2, 442
burnout 264–7, 279, 280

cannabis 11, 12, 13, 33, 45
chasing the dragon 17, 182